RATOLOGY II

Who Gives a Rats?

Michael Wallace

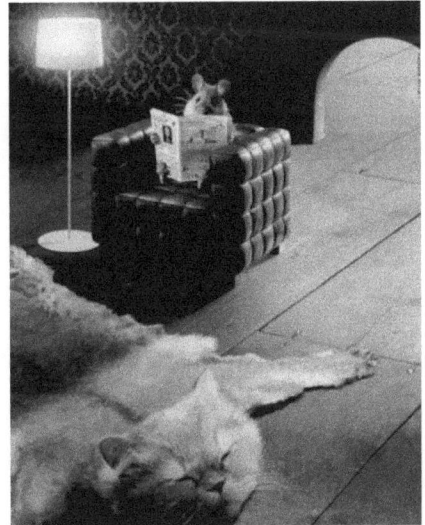

An Expose Into the Nature of Being Human

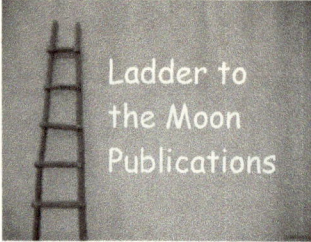

Other Books by this author:

The Book of Number Series

Jermimiah Versus the Grabblesnatch

The Divinity Dice Series

Ratology: Way of the Un-Dammed

Fragments of the Mirror

Water: More Precious than Gold

The Borringbar War

Fragments of the Mirror

Available on Amazon or at
www.laddertothemoon.com.au

My RAT is my saviour
Especially when I want
It is there with its clarity and simpleness
To waken me unto the obvious
That it is OK to be ordinary,
And whether I fail or succeed
My moment is still with me
Forever and ever
All the moments of my life

The Message is Freedom

The way to discover real freedom within is to see things clearly in the world about us, and understand the patterns inside that are driving our bus.

It's all about moving through and past our upbringing, and finding our OWN path, one not subject to the rules of 'should' and 'should not' that were instilled into us in childhood.

Be Warned! This book may offend those who do not like freedom.

RATOLOGY II: Who Gives A Rats COPYRIGHT 2016

This book is published under the Berne Convention. All copyright protected to the author. No prior use without permission except for excerpts for review or educational purposes. All enquiries via Email to: qrcaustralia@gmail.com
Published by Ladder to the Moon Publications.
ISBN: 978-0-9941798-1-4
Mailing: PO Box 1355 Kingscliff, NSW Australia 2487

CONTENTS

Illustrations courtesy of Michael Leunig

www.leunig.com.au

There is an argument going on inside us. There is the Baby Self, the original being, and the trained self. Our natural urges are usually at odds with our social programming. Our imagination often opposes our reality. We are a dichotomy of pieces cobbled together into what is, in truth, a fragile image of self.

RATOLOGY is a way to end this conflict, and this is done almost solely through seeing the obvious, and through this clarity, ending the reign of the should, and should not, in our mind. A clear mind does not obstruct the natural self, and in this way we come into agreement, rather than opposition, with our day to day moments.

Once More Into The Breach

S ome time ago, I ran a class on how to play the guitar in the public school system in New Zealand. Attendance was voluntary, and it was not a theoretical class, but one where you physically learned how to play.

With every group of new student, I started with pretty much the same mantra: *"First: I like you. Second: I am going to give you some of the best, clearest and most succinct techniques on how to play the guitar.*

If you focus, and practice, then at the end of this year you will amaze yourself. But if you do not do homework given, if you do not practice, I get paid, and I will still like you. You won't be able to play the guitar, however.

The same applies to Ratology. It is not a theory, it is a practise. Study it, use it, and you will "get" it at some point. Read it, breeze through, and you won't pull too much out of the depths.

This book (along with Book One) were written in one stream of thought in a two week period. Stream of consciousness is very intense, like a wild ride down the Colorado River. Every thought and feeling I had ever had on the nature of being human rose up to be addressed. Now, I cannot promise all this will be 100% true for you, as what is right for one person is not always right for the next, but I can promise this: *"If you read with an open heart and a focused mind, your life will change for the better."*

There are no great clouds of verbiage you have to struggle through. I try to keep it simple. Everything here is "plain speak" and based on observation of the obvious. My goal is to open doors and let in fresh air, not to clutter the head. This book is a simple, some have said a profound, voicing of how to resolve the human experience, and carve for yourself a little more freedom and choice in your world.

If you grasp what is said in these pages, there is nothing in your life that will look as it did prior to reading Ratology.

The term "Ratology" itself comes from me playing with some very serious religious and anti-religious people who were arguing on the early on-line newsgroups, in and around the mid 1990's. Discussion would get heated, and I would come in with a quip from "The Great Rat" to bring a little humour, and sanity, to bear on a situation.

People told me it was funny, and that I should write a book about it. Which is ironic, because I did, yet one of the greatest principles I outlined is that we should not "should" on each other.

Why Ratology? This is war here on Planet Earth: between others, inside ourselves, inside our own thoughts, there is an argument going on. This book will show you how to end the battle, and win the peace.

RATOLOGY II : *Who Gives a Rat's*

The Second Coming of the RAT

The core of this book was written inside two weeks along with Book One, "Way of the Un-Dammed". But it needed a lot of refining. When I first sat down to finish Ratology: Who Gives a Rats, it was 2010. The bank was holding the millions of dollars worth of what was once my property, and would soon sell it off for a pittance.

But the worst part, I had been forced to actually work for a living! No more trading and dealing my way through life. If I wanted to eat, I had to go out and earn dollars. It is almost unnatural for a Rat of my calibre to be subjected to such an insult.

And THIS was only the start of things. I was now subject to the whims and tastes of the person who employed me. This intrusion of other people's opinions even came down to the choice of fashion. I started at a place, quoting for blinds and window furnishing, and I arrive in my normal, fashionable attire. (I wore environmentally sensitive, good-label clothes from the Op Shops) To my horror, this simple act of fashion is regarded as a primary sin, and I am ordered to go get "Wash and Wear". I am required to purchase apparel suitable to the new workplace. In order to participate in quoting on blinds I must wear gaberdine! Clearly, they viewed their customer as one who, while decorating their home, would have absolutely no sense of modern décor or fashion what-so-ever.

Unfortunately, the "appropriate" apparel is synthetic. Fabrics like gaberdine are an abhorrence to most good designers. Why? For one, after 45 minutes in the heat, it skunks up. Can you imagine a Paris catwalk announcer proudly saying "And this world famous model is proudly wearing the latest in synthetic fabrics, gaberdine."

Why would anyone subject another person to such a thing? Because it is wash and wear and never needs ironing, therefore you will always look "smart". So why did I feel so stupid looking "smart"?

It got worse, much worse. The company shirt was (I chew my thumb as I write this) POLYESTER. Now if you want something that stinks of BO in 15 minutes, THIS is the puppy you need. However, it was provided, inclusive of company logo, and was to be worn at all times. Have these people never heard of cotton?

Working for thin-skinned, egoistic, greedy people was never my strong point, and inside a few months I came to a startling realisation. I really could not stand another day of this. I could no longer put up with the man who brags that his only goal in seeing clients was to extract money from them, and who publicly states that the extraction of as much cash as possible should be MY goal as well. There was now some money in kitty, and it was time to end this fashion debacle.

Given that I don't like the idea of a boss at the best of times, this should come as no surprise, but dealing with a guy who is a total furball was, for me, just impossible. I find it very hard to respect a person who struts about thinking himself important because he was able to sell blinds.

Worse than this, he had focussed on myself as the problem in the story of his life. He seems intent on making my time there a misery, and then the light bulb moment happens! All the while I have been thinking how I could not bear HIM, but the truth cuts both ways. He couldn't stand ME either! Well, it was a relief to get THAT sorted.

We were like two cats who didn't like each other, and it was never going to change. It made quitting a very easy matter, and as a result, I do. It seems my investment in the gaberdine pants has come to nought, and they are never to be worn again. I leave them in the cloths rack, though, as a reminder of just how low we can fall.

None of this alters the reality that the rebuilding process must continue. As at 2010 there is really too much to do to get Ratology Two underway. So I hit the pause button. I am in no position to offer advice or direction to anyone in this space. I am close to homeless, the Porsche has a blown motor that I can't afford to fix, and just making ends meet consumes most of my time and all of my energy. In other words, I am probably in a place a whole lot of people can understand.

Mind you, the process of being dispossessed has it's benefits. There is certainly no stress over finance, because there isn't any. There are no personal arguments, because there are no persons in my life. The health has taken a beating, largely due to the stress, yet at the same time there is no need to perform, so I can sleep in more than usual. It's not a happy place, but I chose to make it not a sad one.

Three years it takes to come out of bankruptcy, and five years to get back to zero, and be able to start again. So here we arrive at 2015 and at last I have come back to the place where I first began.

The millions in property, the lifestyle of the rich and famous, they are all gone, but I am left with one stark and simple reality: *Who Gives a Rat's!* It's like poker, I had a stack of chips to play with, now I had none. Onto the next game.

Moving forward to the present: November 2015

Really, who gives a Rat's? We live we die. We are born, we do stuff, we end. The only thing that really matters is that, in between these two poles of existence, we do something useful. Selling blinds for avaricious pricks is NOT doing anything useful. Get back to Ratology Two.

Gratitude in the little things is what changes everything. I am sent a link by a friend, and this pretty much sums up something we all need to know: **http://goo.gl/lCHVPV**

This article talks about the hard science of how the brain gets a high off guilt and shame, but that this is plugged into the same area that our sense of pride. To quote: *Despite their differences, pride, shame, and guilt all activate similar neural circuits, including the dorsomedial prefrontal cortex, amygdala, insula, and the nucleus accumbens.*

And the simple cure? Gratitude. Yes, it is hard to mock up gratitude when you have no money in the bank, no prospects for income, and you still feel like you have been taken out and flogged by a dozen bricks thrown by people who really dislike you, but it doesn't matter. You just have to be grateful for what you DO have.

I knew things were picking up when I sold the Porsche with the broken motor for $1000 less that I picked up one that was in good order and running. You feel you are getting your Rat back on when you can turn things like this. A fellow RAT helped me out with that one.

I also had another friend help out with a place to stay at a cheap rent, so now I have comfortable surroundings. It is time to refocus, reorient, and re-energise the not-very-ancient and but-yet-still venerable path of Ratology.

Too refresh the matter, we started in "Ratology: Way of the Un-Dammed" to talk about how we are ruled by invisible "Shoulds" and how social conventions have cornered most of us into behaviours that are not our natural self. Our "shoulds" are really our collected guilts and shames all rolled into a way we are supposed to act. Gratitude breaks this cycle, and being aware of the obvious completely terminates it's power over us. But this of itself is just the starting point.

In *Ratology Two: Who Gives a Rat's* we extend this and look at the actual mechanisms involved with the internal decision making process of our psyche. And not in a technical sense of intellectual study, but in the very real sense of what it means to be human and part of a society.

We are all human, we all have issues, and we all have to negotiate the battle inside ourselves, in relationships and in the work place.

An example: A drunken fool comes out of the bathroom at a party, staggering past the girls as he zigzags his alcohol-determined path. His wife, tired of the drunken behaviour, and conscious of the embarrassment he causes her, says, "I hope you put the toilet seat down!"

He sneers in her direction, his pride has been challenged in public and he must respond. To prove to all and sundry that he is not a downtrodden man stuck under the rule of the wifely thumb, he glares at her, saying in a uniquely Australian response, *"Who gives a Rat's Arse!"* It is not a question, it is an exclamation of freedom.

Of course, he will suffer because of it. Of course there will be war later on. And maybe, as they go through the pain, they come out the other side with a greater love, or a divorce. Either way, it is a freedom.

Freedom. Whole cultures have turned in it's pursuit. Plays have been written, movies have been made, songs have been sung, yet so few have achieved a true, intimate sense of freedom in their personal lives.

So, who gives a Rats? As I grasped the profound nature of this simple utterance, I went through the rabbit hole, and came out the other side with answers to almost every problem we have. Thus this off hand quip becomes both the subtitle and opening chapter for this book.

WHO GIVES a RATS!

This singular expression slices through the Gorgonian Knot of social expectation and gets right to the reality of things. Of course, for the fellow in our introduction, it will all end with endless pain and suffering from a nagging wife, bu at least it makes for an entertaining opener for our book. And right away, it brings us to the *First Principle of Social Truth.*

No one cares much about what you think or do, unless it intrudes on them. People only truly care about what affects themselves directly.

Let's face it: No one really worries about a toilet seat being left up. Yes, the practice of good Feng Shui says to leave it down, but given the generally inebriated state of the men at the barbecue, better the seat is left up, yes? The chances of it being pissed on by all the drunkards is therefore significantly less.

Now, the people at the party MAY find the fireworks of a domestic dispute interesting, but most understand that the argument between the drunk man and his controlling wife is not about the toilet seat, nor what they say to each other, it is about what the situation MEANS.

The REAL issue is SUBTEXT: What does the person MEAN? Rather than listen to what a person might say, we listen to what is behind the words. Clearly, anger, but what is driving the anger, the passion, the fury? Perhaps the woman is really saying, "I am sick of cleaning up after this man," yet what the drunken man hears is a challenge to his authority as the boss of the family, and his retort is really asking, "Who is in charge here?" Sadly, he will shortly learn that she is.

If you want a source cause for domestic violence, here it is. It is the core failure to grasp what another MEANS when they say something. When we fail to listen to, or grasp, what another means to say, it starts a cycle of frustration, anger and resentment with our partner. This is what perpetuates conflict.

Yet, when someone truly does NOT give a Rat's, it all changes. The number one change being that, up front, you just do not buy into the argument. The following is obvious, but let's state it anyway: *When you do not buy into the argument, you have a much better chance of hearing what another wants to say.*

I am not saying you do not care, I am saying you are free FROM care. By not giving a Rats and letting another be whatever they wish to be, you create a "freedom space". And in this space, you will be amazed at how much more information you can see and hear. Not giving a Rats really means not getting caught up in the whirlpool. If you are free to see the situation as it is, you have far more clarity, and a greater ability to hear what another MEANS. It is OBVIOUS! If we listen to what someone MEANS, we have a much better chance of understanding them. I will guarantee there is not one case of domestic violence that came about from two people respectfully listening to each other.

Listening requires freedom. It is a state of being free of the fear of what another thinks. It is self-evident you will be happier when you partner is happy and feels listened to. It defuses argument. When a tense person meets a relaxed person, they have to work hard to stay tense. All successful people are able to remain relaxed and focussed in times of stress, and there is a physiological reason to do so behind this.

Muscles are either on, or off. When you don't tense up in a situation, you are relaxed. A person that is relaxed is confident, and a confident person remains open to possibilities. In a tense situation, a relaxed person is automatically in charge. No one ever voted for a President or Prime Minister that panicked and looked stressed about everything. Churchill was a tower of confidence, Lincoln inspired people with his calm demeanour, yet underneath they were manic depressives, prone to severe mood swings. They controlled their inner world with an attitude of not really giving a Rats about anything other than the job in front of them.

In any relationship, the person who is most confident, most relaxed, is the one in charge. By not giving a Rats, you remain relaxed, therefore you remain in charge in any given situation. Take it a step further, and consider that if you genuinely CARE about a person, or a situation, you listen to what you are being told. The next logical step is that you look to understand what is MEANT, rather than what is SAID.

The net result is greater intimacy. Intimacy answers the most basic needs of the Baby Self, the pure state within, and by allowing intimacy we trigger in others a deep sense of trust. Thus, the war between people ends.

The US Civil War came to a close because General Grant understood what Lincoln said in what is now known as the "River Queen" doctrine. "Let them down easy." Lincoln said, and Grant took it upon himself to do just this in settling terms of peace with Robert E Lee. If he had NOT understood what Lincoln meant, the US would have fractured into guerrilla warfare, and not become the nation it is today.

In the extraordinary book "1865" by Jay Winik you see and feel the deep intimacy two opposing Generals who were once bitter enemies found at the Appomatox Courthouse. You get a personal insight into how powerful the words of Lincoln were, "Let them down easy". He meant, "Let go of the past. Don't look for revenge. It is better we all get on." But deeper than this, he meant "leave them with some pride."

Which brings us to the Second Principle of Social Truth!

The Mystic Rat Says: *What someone says is rarely what they mean.*

Lincon was an exceptional leader. In a world of flowery, verbose speakers, prone to embelishment, he spoke plainly, clearly, and said exactly what he meant to say. He liked Grant because this General was the same way, plain, simple, and essentially humble.

Most people are the opposite of this. What they say almost never involves logic or common sense, and their words are rarely directly connected to whatever the complaint or compliment might be. What most people actually SAY is INVARIABLY a subtext for what they MEAN. Only a person completely clear of fixed, internal patterns and emotional encumbrance speaks clearly, and says exactly what they mean.

I promise you, there are very few of these people around. How many Lincolns do you find in todays Prediential Race? So what we must do, if we are to have a sense of freedom in our society, is to start to listen to what people mean, not to what they say.

When we grasp the MEANING of what someone says, we respond differently. There is the alternative case to the drunken man at the start of this book. Another husband is heartily sick of being told to keep the toilet seat down. So he decides one night to leave it down while he pissed all over it. As he crawls back into bed he says to his wife, "You'll be happy to know, the toilet seat is most definitely down, dear!"

But he does this from a position of understanding her subtext. He understood she wanted to feel in charge of things around the house, and that she did most of the cleaning. Yet she needed to understand that he was the man, and that some respect needed to be shown. Yes, she would be furious in the morning, but he also knew that as she released the rage, he would finally be able to get a message across. You see, HE was listening, SHE was not. It cuts both ways.

One of my favourite real life Rats is Josiah the Monk. He is a fascinating being who walks through life immune to the social expectations of others. He also specialised in collecting back packers and young girls to his bed. One night, he picked up a Japanese girl, and she was extremely fussy. Too fussy, too picky, just too much of everything and he didn't like it, so he decided to piss her off, literally. In the middle of the night, he stood up, and urinated all over her.

She abused him, and screamed, and insulted him, but it was three in the morning and she had nowhere to go. She cleaned up and went back to bed. Josiah expected her to be long gone come the morning, but no! There she was, cooking him breakfast, and she had even cleaned the house to perfection. What is more, she BOWED to him as he came out, and apologised for her insolence during the night.

She explained that now she understood how she had been full of pride, and needed humiliation. And please, if he wished to piss on her, it was his right. Even Josiah was surprised by this turn-a-round. He just said, *"Giving permission to be pissed upon in an affront to God. If God tells me to piss on you, I do not need YOUR permission. Get out!"*

She then begged him to let her stay, and promised she would do anything to make him happy. So he let her stay for a while.

Now I can feel the hackles of the feminists rising about how this is demeaning, insulting and terrible. And it is! However, it also worked out sexually for them both, and cut through the complicated confusion that existed in the Japanese girls head.

Her SUBTEXT of why she was being incredibly fussy was not understood. Of course there are reasons why everyone is the way they are, but in this instance it was not needed to be understood. What really mattered was that Josiah didn't care what her concerns were, he was concerned about his boundaries being breached. His response (pissing on the girl in the middle of the night) was basically a way to get rid of her, yet it had a transforming effect on the entire situation.

What REALLY happened was emotional honesty. By cutting through the crap, by simply not caring about the crap, Josiah got to a higher level of emotional honesty with the girl. And back we come to a basic principle of Ratology: *Cutting through the crap.* If you want to be free, clear the desks of compromise, lies and self-deceit. Doing it properly is the secret.

We all know how Alexander the Great started his conquering of the world by taking his sword and "solving" the unsolvable Gorgonian knot. He simply sliced through it. Just like the great conqueror, Josiah didn't care to cater to the whims of social mores, the beliefs of others, or the existing social order. He is a real man! He just says, "Who gives a rats?" and acts as his inner direction tells him to.

The same goes to a lesser extent to the guy who tells his wife off for embarrassing him in public, by telling him to put down the toilet seat. But his "Who gives a Rat's!" did not come from a point of emotional honesty, it comes from a place of hurt pride.

I am sure in that moment he felt powerful. I am sure he felt confident stamping his testosterone based authority on his marriage, but let's face it, he's no Alexander. He'll regret it later. They will get home, and while he's still reeling from too much booze, the pain will start. His wife will go for him, "How dare you embarrass me in front of my friends!" etc. etc. He won't get sex for weeks, and he'll have to behave until it blows over.

Poor bastard. Like so many, he is living in a marriage that, in reality, is his personal Gorgonian Knot, but he has to carry on without so much as a sharp wit to cut his way free. He is doomed. Not because of his honest retort to his wife, but because his courage to be himself will fail. Why? It was fuelled by external sources (booze), and did not come from any inner recognition of self.

Josiah, on the other hand, acted in a way that was improvised, with full knowledge of the possible consequences. And come the morning, he was still happy to stand by what he did, without fear or favour.

This is verging on becoming highly esoteric. I apologise and will do my best to avoid this from now on. I must remember the words of the Mystic Rat, where he says: *Given the choice between complex and dumb, choose simple.*

Let me put it this way: Blunt Honesty pays dividends. But I am talking about honesty with our SELVES. You say "Who gives a Rat's" to YOURSELF, not to your wife. Inwardly you may feel this way, yet outwardly you know and recognise it is an issue for her, and say "Of course my dear." The point is that when you truly don't care either way, all argument ceases. And where there is no argument, harmony can exist. Where there is harmony, intimacy can evolve.

People say they want intimacy, openness and honesty in their relationships, but what they really want, mostly, is a lie. People want to feel comfortable in a relationship, and because they are secretly afraid of true intimacy and pure honesty, their sense of comfort in a relationship equates to agreements regarding boundaries, and compromise.

They want a partner who does not contradict them, or challenge them too much. Being comfortable, in other words, is more important than being free, open and honest. What most people truly want is irrelevant, because they don't even know what it is. What they SETTLE for is someone who will share their inner limitations and social constraints. In simple words: Most of us inwardly accept a position of compromise regarding our relationships. And in truth, this is better than continual argument and frustration.

The unwritten female rule is that during courtship it is OK for you to be the wild colonial boy, but when you get married, it's time to knuckle down and pay the bills.

The unwritten male rule is that during courtship the women is supposed to provide sex, and that after marriage the woman is still supposed to provide sex, but she is also expected to cook and clean the house.

We all know that neither model really works. Between the juxtaposition of these two polarities of invisible expectation (aren't they such big words?) the residual arguments, abrasions and conflicts of human relationships will arise. The easing grease between the natural states of these "Cat versus Dog" polarities are usually found in the little agreements we make: *You stick to your side of the gender fence, and I will stick to mine.* These types of agreements are our social niceties.

I must admit here, as a matter of open honesty, that I have a bias against social niceties. A social nicety is a false state. Break the term "niceties" in two and it reveals the truth: Nice Ties. They are the strings that hold everything in place, but these also tie you down, and in time, turn your life into your own, personal, Gorgonian Knot. This is your world of compromise, self-doubt and fear to express your true self.

I had a spiritual experience once, where I was out of the body, and observing all the "ties that bind". People saying something were really casting a line, fishing to catch something. Others were silently knitting webs to cast over the object of their desire. The world was full of fine wires, attachments that hold us in place.

Most of us feel somewhat confined by the need to cater to social norms. Most of us want to junk these unwritten rules, such as "seat must go down", and just go our way. Most of us carry a piece of the attitude that we really do not give a Rat's, yet the truth is we are afraid to BE this truth. We are largely afraid to truly let the crap go and let the dice fall where they may.

Not caring too much about the social mores is painted by those who DO believe in them as being the selfish desire of an immature soul. EG: How DARE the Greeks not want to pay back all those Billions of Euro! However, to some is is a way of saying you trust that life is bigger and better than the small frames of our social beliefs. Freedom is more important than social mores. One thing is certain, if you base your life on society, you won't have much of a life.

The Mystic Rat Says: *Society generally requires compromise. The True Rat will take a step back to get a better position, but they will not compromise. However it is good to smile, and acts as if you do.*

Josiah the Monk, our friend with the Japanese girl in his house, put it another way. He takes the view that life is a Garden of Eden, and the people he meets are like trees in the garden. Some have fruit he wants to eat, others don't. He doesn't care if another agrees or disagrees with him. That is the nature of their fruit. He just moves through the garden looking for the good stuff.

On the opposite side of the coin: I met a middle aged woman in the US, and when I mentioned I was from Australia, she said in a clearly disgusted voice, "Well, I met some of your fellow country men! At Aspen – swinging naked from the chandeliers in the hotel lobby!"

I am not sure what she expected me to say. Was I supposed to share her disgust, and apologise for my country? Was I somehow to blame for the ape-like tendencies of my brothers? Hearing the tick-tock of a little social mind whirring in her head like a clock, I decided to play with her. Looking quite serious, I asked, "How many men? was it a total of 13?" She seemed a little put off, but stammered that she thought it may have been something like that. But why was this important?

I explained, seeking to enlarge her blissful ignorance with layers of total fabrication, that this was most likely an Australian Football team coming to Aspen as a reward for winning a championship, because this is EXACTLY the sort of thing Australian Champion Football Players do.

I went into elaborate detail, that it was part of the primordial instincts, and described how the ape-like section of the brain reacts in this manner when the hormones associated with victory are released. As an example, I asked her, "Don't footballers in your country leap for joy in some way when they score points for their team? This hormone is particularly strong with Australian men, and forces them to celebrate any win in a very exaggerated fashion"

Now, she is nodding, taking all of this in as my RAT manufactures a story on the fly. The science angle was working, so after a few more layers of scientific reasoning were laid bare, I applied the coup de gras: "And, biologically speaking, as the Australian Male is susceptible to the effects of this hormone, we expect this sort of behaviour. We are well acquainted with it in our own country, and accept it as normal."

"Oh I see!" she exclaimed as the light of understanding dawned in her eyes. "So it's all OK! It is a CULTURAL thing! Why didn't anyone ever explain this to me before. I understand completely now. Thank you SO much for taking the time to explain it."

And so off she twaddled in her new comprehension of the universe, very pleased to have met me and have this piece of her life's puzzle sorted. Honest to God, who (apart from hotel owners) really gives a Rat's Arse about people swinging naked in hotel lobby's? The only interest "I" had in the matter was that is was a wonderful opportunity to pull the wool over someone's eyes.

I ask why do I do this sort of stuff, and I really don't know. It's the imp in me. You may as well ask why parents lie and tell children that Santa will bring them presents. For me it was simply play, and after all, I am a story teller. But let's look at it from HER side of the deck. It does not matter that she believes I was speaking truth or otherwise, what matters for HER is that she now has a new thing to tell her friends over drinks later that day. "It's a CULTURAL thing!" she can tell her people, as she describes how hormones drive Australian males to behave this way.

These weird cultural traditions of the Australian will give her fuel for chat for years. The real point is, she was clearly distressed by the bad behaviour of the chandelier swingers at the time, because it contradicted her social mores. When someone explained that the errant men were actually obeying a different set of social mores, she felt that the world was in order, and her personal Gorgonian Knot of compromise was safe from unravelling for another day.

Unfortunately, now that we have Google, much of my inventiveness can be compromised with a little research. The world is more complex, and to keep up my level of play, I now have to create false web pages, get them listed in Google, and do a whole lot of work I never used to have to.

On the UP side, however, it then becomes irrefutable proof because my stories appear as facts in Google.

Our first book. RATOLOGY: Way of the Un-Dammed, was about freeing ourselves from the prison of our social mores. I recommended the best way to do this was to found in learning to see the obvious. This required processing and clearing ourselves of the hand-me-down beliefs of our parents and culture. (Our Social Memes) We also expressed the concept that we are all Humpty Dumpty, Post Wall. We are all broken to some degree. We subsequently have bound ourselves to the Social Mores as a way to hold ourselves together.

This book is all about setting ourselves free from the strings that bind. And the core tenant of this is DETACHMENT.

This will raise an entirely new question, a potential area of tension. We must begin to ask ourselves: How detached do we become?

As a child, a very specific mood would occasionally come over me. I would feel what seemed like a powerful, almost electric, current running through me, and the world would recede into the distance. My family might walk into the room, but it was like they were complete strangers. Just people, and I have absolutely no connection to them. It is a state where you have no feelings, only thought.

Now, if this went on, clearly I would have become psychotic or pathological in my relationships with others. Fortunately, I had a mother and father who loved me, which pulled me back from this sense of dislocation, but the memory of being totally detached remained.

Pathological tendencies are really an immature form of detachment. A person feels remarkably free in their internal experience of being, but coming back to society feels like a prison. So, like a child throwing a tantrum because they do not want to go somewhere or do something, the pathological individual refuses to partake of society. Yet they are lonely, intensely so, and often bitterly alone.

This is the determining point between true detachment and pathological states. The detached person is alone, but not lonely. It is as simple as this. Now we can prove to ourselves that we can reach the detached state in a really simple way. In a group of people, if someone yawns, be aware of your response, and stop.

It is a social reflex to want to yawn, but if you feel the need to yawn when someone else does, suppress it. Do not yawn! Watch closely, watch your feelings as you stop yourself from yawning. This is an indicator of the detached state.

Detachment does not mean a lack of care. Being careless or too careful is not the issue. It is more a question of how much we are OWNED by the present situation versus how much we possess the moment.

The Mystic Rat Says: *DETACHMENT is the ability to be completely immersed in the situation, yet free from fear of the outcomes.*

How we achieve detachment is incredibly simple: *Let it go, let it flow, by inwardly not giving a Rat's.*

This does not mean we do not have external goals, or things we wish to achieve and drive for. It means we are not going to be tied to our fears of failure, social expectation, or our sense of not being good enough.

In the next few chapters we will seek to give you a brief overview of the core issues of Ratology. Here we will outline the basic choices we make that have cast us out of our personal Eden, the Baby State.

We go further, and discuss the "diseases" that have created a mutation in our psyche and cast us INTO the present shape in which we find ourselves.

Ratology Two is a book of short, to the point discussions on the human and social dynamics that go into building the persona, and has the goal of expanding on the principles outlined in Book One.

We discuss matters, such as being "Pinned", how we all live in a personal bubble, and go into depth on how faulty internal logic creates poor emotional outcomes in a topic we call "Spiritual Arithmetic". In particular, in the final section, we expand the "Rules of Rattyness" and give techniques for avoiding conflict and creating a more harmonious world for ourselves.

First, though, we look at the incredibly important subject of shaving.

A Close Shave

When I was 46 years of age my father pulled me aside, and decided that NOW was the time to give his son advice on how to shave. "The best way to shave is to wet the whiskers with hot water before applying the lather." he said as I visited one day. "OK," I thought to myself, "this is an interesting thing to bring up. I wonder WHY?"

You may consider it odd that a father would wait until their son reached middle age before advising them on how to shave. It was perfectly normal as far as I was concerned, as my father pretty much opposed everything to do with what we call the Law of Majority.

To explain: Something is "right" in any given society because the majority agree with it. If the majority disagree, it becomes "wrong". You may find it odd to see a person walking down the street wearing a bright green shirt. However, in a society where everyone wears bright green shirts, YOU become the one who is out of step.

Like the woman with the "swinging chandelier men" that we talked about in the previous chapter, if we convince a person that what is odd is perfectly normal, then everything very quickly shifts. Naked chandelier swinging no longer appears to be different. My father had mastered the art of making the odd seem normal.

Offering advice on shaving to a 46 year old man is not odd when you live in oddness, so from his viewpoint, all was in perfect order. But there was an "AH HA!" moment in this, waiting to be revealed. I am never one to let an opportunity pass by, and here was a perfect opening for my Inner Rat to come out to play!

This shaving business was pretty much sorted by myself at age 16. As I always shaved in the shower, hot water before lather was perfectly normal for me. However, and here's the twist in the tale, lather sticks and brushes cost money. I used plain soap.

I could have just nodded and ignored my fathers words. I could have said nothing, and just respected the good intention of my elder, but my Inner Rat goes, "No way!" and off I go. It's not my fault. My father had gone and opened a door, and for the sake of sheer adventure, I decided to walk through. In the process I offered some startling new revelations in and about the world of shaving.

At the risk of shocking his sensitivities I open my response with a powerful broadside volley. "Did you know I shave without a mirror?"

He was genuinely amazed, and didn't even know this impossible dream was achievable. "No mirror?" he questioned, shocked.

"No mirror." I confirm.

"How can you do that? How do you not miss bits, or cut yourself?" He asks, duly impressed by the incredible achievement by his progeny.

"I do it by feel, while having a shower. It took a lot of practice, father. Practice and sheer, unmitigated shaving skill."

He shakes his head in wonder, but I am not done yet. "And no shaving stick, no shaving brush either. I only use soap, and of course, the only way this CAN work is to wet the whiskers with warm water first."

These new revelations in the world of shaving certainly put him into a state of wonderment. He had no idea just how incredibly talented his son was in the manly arts, and he had to step back and allow this glorious new generation through.

The ensuing conversation pointed out the many advantages to this new way of doing thing; the primary one being that you didn't have to worry about cleaning up the wash basin. (Always an issue in relationships, but not for me!) You just let it all go down the drain in the shower. He was duly impressed, yet curiously, the subject of shaving has never been brought up again.

Do I hear you ask, "What has this to do with Ratology?" Well, quite a bit. We are dealing with the primary goal of the RAT:

    1. *Perceiving the obvious.*

    2. *Resolving matters to their simplest form.*

What can be more simple and obvious than the daily task of shaving oneself being made so much easier? The information I offered was CLEAR, USEFUL, PRACTICAL, and it CUT TO THE POINT.

Or, if not the point, specifically, at least it cut some facial hair.

ALSO PART OF THE EASTER STORY.

Last chance Jesus... Be a nice chap and convert to christianity. pleasant, sensible, polite christianity, and we might release you from detention...

NEVER!

Carrying a Double Standard

When a ruler erects the standard, or flag, of one king in battle, he is declaring he supports that man. But if it all goes badly, he might pull that one down and put up the standard of the opposing king. In other words, he carries a double standard. The ruler was prepared with either flag, to curry favour with whatever way the wind blew.

People do this all the time. They have an opinion to suit the circumstance, and change them like they change clothes. That is how people are. Two faced, double minded, and split into fragments of self. We all have these various standards ready to erect, yet the reason we do this is not always clear to ourselves. Why do we wish to curry favour with others? Usually it comes back to a fear. Often we are afraid of our internal fractures, or exposing our weakness, and finding external approval covers up these inner fault lines. We do whatever we can to appear whole.

Only when we understand that this inner duality exists inside us, and accept that this is just how it is, can we can start to see the obvious. Once we see clearly our own patterns, we can start to let go of the notion of how we 'should' behave and act. Why is this important? Every "should" inside us is like a false standard, a changing flag of allegiance, and this weakens our sense of being whole.

Revealing the fragmented self within was part of the goal of Socrates. He saw the double standards clearly, and through use of questions (Socratic reasoning) he got people to reveal themselves to themselves. He saw the obvious, and through a series of questions, by their own answers the individual questioned revealed the obvious to all.

Of course, this embarrassed many folk. The important people of Athens hated him for the "loss of face" he caused them, and they eventually forced him to take the hemlock. We went over this in Book One, and how the real reason he died was because he ignored his Inner Rat, and he allowed his principles to run the show.

Principles are very expensive. A rule of thumb: *If you are acting on principal, it will not only be more expensive, it will take more time, and produce fewer results.* High notions are fine to have, hold and cherish, but never employ a principle for survival. ALL principles, ALL ideals, are really just flags of allegiance borrowed from someone else's kingdom.

In our first Book on RATOLOGY we went over over the process by which our internalised lies become our personal truths. We dwelt at length on the concept of seeing the obvious and how this is just about the only thing that will separate the real you from your internalised lies.

Here we go a step further. Now we seek to become free. This means learning to live the Way of the Rat, and be utterly true and fearless within our being. Here we learn to BE a Rat by not giving a Rats!

We all know the new age drill: Find yourself, become aware of self, feel the inner power of self, etc. It is a step in the right direction, but finding you, and LIVING you, are entirely different animals. Yes: "Man Know thyself" is great, but "MAN, BE THYSELF" is better. Yet we can go one step further!

The Mystic Rat Says: *Man, GROW thyself!*

FINDING you is great, but to be genuinely happy, you need to LIVE as you. To LIVE as your true self means your true self grows and swallows up the double standards, the internal lies, and the false beliefs within us.

An example to consider: Most people would say that Oprah not only knew herself, and lived as herself, but that she grew and became more of herself with each passing year. She appears to be comfortable in her own skin, in other words. We all heard about Oprah shutting her show, and starting her own cable channel. So many people had regrets and felt a "loss", but really, the woman is obeying the First Law of Freedom: *Move on with your Groove on*.

As part of the closure process for the Oprah Show, she was looking at people from past episodes, and updating to see where they were now. I watched as this pastor (who got busted for Gay Sex, and lost his position) became "frank and open". Because of his humiliation, he now states about how it changed him for the better, and he spoke 'proudly' about how *honest* he is now with his wife. God has touched them, made them better, yadda yadda. I cringed when I heard him advertise truth and honesty as his prevailing wind, because he just looked SO damn deceitful.

And you know, possibly by instinct or good old street cunning, Oprah found the flaw in the facade. Oprah, in passing, makes a comment about how the wife's shirt perfectly matches the tulips in the background, and did she realise it?

Well of COURSE the woman knew. Everything there on the set they were sitting in was totally stage managed. Every little detail was set up. Yet this woman avoids answering a simple, direct question. Why?

You know what it is: They had a double standard. The pair wanted to appear open and honest, and down to earth, yet to admit everything was calculated revealed the more likely scenario. This is that they wanted to get back onto the milk cow that fed them with so much money. In my book, a person avoiding answering a simple question tells me a lie is happening somewhere. By not answering directly, you are telling the world you are covering something up.

And in their silence this hiding was, for me, horribly obvious. She and her husband had OBVIOUSLY tailored the "informal' setting as a completely staged set. I realised the husband also had a shirt that matched the couch on the set. It was all designed to perfectly coordinate with their clothes, skin type, and proportion. Why? We all know why.

It was a marketing ploy to relax the viewer and make the gay preacher and his money-hungry wife look good. You could see the womans face freeze for a moment, as she looked for a way to avoid the question from Oprah. Why do they avoid mentioning how they stage managed their entire presentation? This is a sin of omission, according to Catholic teaching. The irony of it all, and where the preacher couple completely missed the obvious, is that Oprah herself has this perfectly colour coordinated background.

She knew it. She designed it that way. What's more: She knew what THEY were doing, but let it pass. Oprah's question, and their response, was more than enough to light up the truth for those with the eyes to see.

Talk about double standards! This pair were blatantly lying while declaring their honesty. LIARS! Liars of the first water. But so what? It doesn't change my life. It's not my concern, nor is it my problem. Yet it raises the question: WHY do people behave this way? It comes down to what is driving the person's bus. In this case, the driver is one of those old favourites: Vanity, Attachment, Lust, Greed and/or Anger.

Vanity is why I suspect the Pastor and his wife lied. Vanity, mixed with other passions such as greed, etc. Of course they wanted to make a good impression. They are on international TV and it is perfectly normal to want to look good. So WHY would you want to hide it? They could have said, "Gosh Oprah, of course I realise the tulips match the outfit, and see how the tone of the couch matches my husbands shirt? We wanted to look our best for you." But the religious preachers didn't say this. If you catch a person in one lie, it's a fair bet they got more coming along.

They were trying to impress by tweaking every little thing with, I presume, the end goal of turning a profit rather than converting souls. They are simply hiding their callous, mercenary incentive for appearing on the Oprah show with little white lies of innocence. Well, who cares? After all, no one is innocent. We all tell lies.

It's not something crucial to the continuing existence of life as we know it. Now, I may not LIKE their double standards, but I accept them for what they are. There are far worse things in life that we will have to deal with.

As an example: On occasions it is myself. I look at my life, and I see the failures, the missed opportunities, the lost hours and days, and I feel a little disgusted with me. But is this disturbance vanity? I am fully aware that almost every single detestable aspect of myself is wrapped around some basic negative. It is really a case of getting over the small stuff. We all suffer a little vanity, and what's more it can be useful. For instance, I spend more time on this book because I want it to look good. It requires a little vanity. But when it goes too far, and all I do is edit, and edit, but never publish, then it is becomes a waste of time.

I have found that Vanity is pretty much the MOST expensive luxury we can indulge in. We all know the cliché of the guy who burns ten dollar notes to light his cigar. That is pure vanity. Well, a lot of us have done this with our life. We buy the flash car, the fancy house, the latest fashions, etc. And it burns money. It's all wrapped around our vanities. The best I can say to myself is: "Well, not any more".

I had a friend who sold his motor boat, and just happened to be out with a Jewish business associate who just happened to own the same sort of boat. "I just sold mine," said my friend, as a comment in passing. The Jewish man says, "This is for sale as well, $12,000 if you had any left over lookers."

They got to talking, and it turns out the Jewish man had bought the boat for $10,000 a year earlier. My friend asks, "So you bought the boat, used it for a year, and are selling it for MORE than it cost you?"

"Of course!" said the Jewish man, surprised at such a question. "Why would I want to lose money?" This is a perfect example of what happens when you refuse to let vanity, or any of your passions, drive your life. You choose to buy things that ADD to your value, not detract from it.

When all all your life is aiming towards a sense of completeness, you are removing the double standards as a matter of course. Even with something as simple as buying and selling a boat: Are we are living to have some fun, yet also increase our net worth? Or are we living with two faces, and just spending money to look good?

It all comes down to how well we own the moment. Carpe Diem, as the Romans would say.

Carpe Diem

Seize the Day, the Latin saying goes. But is a day something you can actually grasp? The original Latin interpretation is more to do with being fully involved with life and living, and means "pluck" the day. It is an opportunists proverb. Most people interpret this little saying to a notion of achievement: working hard, making every moment count, while enjoying life. The Romans saw it more as being aware of what's happening, and grabbing any opportunity that presents itself.

One day, some years ago, I was working on a project with a fellow in an upmarket suburb. I looked about, and what I saw was a whole lot of Rolls Royce, BMW's, Jaguars, and Mercedes Benz's. But I didn't see the cars, what I saw were items of vanity. Every one of these cars cost the owners money, a lot of it, and they were largely purchased for the purpose of looking good to others.

If we are doing anything for how we look, what others think, or for what we can get at the expense of another, we are being controlled by a passion. This means we are not located in our Omphalos, our central point of being. In this regard, we are not seizing the day, we are buying and selling it. There is nothing wrong with this, but it doesn't get us anywhere in terms of being our true self.

The real question is: Who or what is driving the bus? Are we seeking to expand and grow because it is FUN, or are we being driven by hidden passions and needs? There is nothing wrong with either, but one pays us off a whole lot better. It is fine to be passionate about our purpose, but when our purpose is driven by passion, it gets expensive.

Passions such as greed, vanity, anger or attachment work in a way that swallows our attention. They CONSUME the present moment, they eat up our moments like we might eat food. They steal you from your sense of being "here" and in doing so, place you "over there". You become disassociated from the NOW. Instead of seizing the day, your passions seize you. You become the mouse on the treadmill, running hard to stay in the same place.

And here I must point out, the same is true of our ideals. These ALSO place us outside of our personal NOW. Ideals will also force us to work hard to go nowhere.

Yet at the heart of NOWHERE is a greater truth, which is found by answering this question: *Are we going to be Now-Here or Nowhere?* If nothing else, if we find an answer to this question, it is the greatest thing we can learn from this book. Are we Now Here, or are we Nowhere?

When we truly get this notion, we realise that the CORE of the problem is neither our passions, nor our ideals. The REAL issue is simply that these things *distract us* so much that we do not realise when *we are no longer in the moment.*

I had a friend who was always very centred, very composed, and very much always HERE. Yet shortly after 911, I met up with him in the States. He was a New York resident, and experienced it all first hand. What surprised me was that he just looked elsewhere. I commented on this, and asked if he was OK. He looked at me oddly, then a flash of recognition entered his eyes, and he instantly once more became the self-centred, inwardly composed person I had always known.

"Thanks," he said. "I didn't even realise I had moved away from myself. I have been very caught up in the whole 911 thing. It affected me more than I realised." From that moment on, he was fine.

In *Ratology: Way of the Un-Dammed* we said it many times: *We are all Humpty Dumpty, Post Wall.* We are in pieces, with the various parts of our spirit shattered by our upbringings. Worse, we pick up a small shard of shatte3red self, and it seems to us that this is it, the whole self.

My friend from New York had moved from a state of being whole. The shock of 911 had broken into his consciousness, and his awareness had shifted into the pieces of thought within himself. As a result, he experienced fragmented thoughts, mixed emotions, etc. All he needed was a reminder to come back to the NOW, and he let go of whatever was pulling him away.

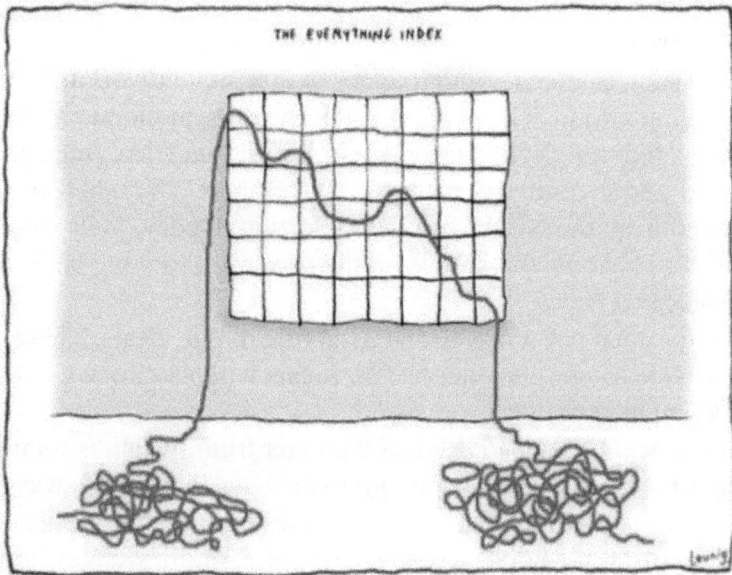

THE EVERYTHING INDEX

Choosing the NOW

This is all we are really doing here, choosing to be NOW. Let me voice this a different way: Folks, if you really want to "Seize the Day" it means you want to DO, you want to live life as a VERB. To DO anything effectively we need to BE HERE. To be, or to be, distracted, is the question. Being present is our focus, our omphalos, our belly button of truth. The search for "nirvana", "heaven" or "oneness", etc. is all wrapped around the quest for a SINGULAR reality: Being in the NOW.

Your Inner Rat will help you remain in the present. Why? Because it really doesn't care to be anywhere else, and you just won't find it in your future or your past. Neither does it care about appearance, social standing, right or wrong, and it is most specifically uncaring about personal greatness versus loss of face. Your Inner Rat only wants to remain in the present moment, because this is where it survives best!

So given this, why do we agree to all these social mores, double standards and the ties that bind that we have just discussed? Why can't we be cavemen dragging our woman by the hair? Why do we need to surround ourselves with restrictions? We can be happy and free without any of this, but there remains a magnet that holds us. There is something that draws us in to the Social Agreements.

I go into the physics of relationship, the causation of memes and the patterns of society in Part Two, but for now, we are what we are, and do what we do because in some way we accept this as normal. The problem is that living in the NOW is not considered the normal thing to do. What is "normal" is anxiety, stress, problems with creditors, and running hard on a wheel to get nowhere.

I have a New York Jewish friend, who comes from an upper middle class, well-heeled family. Yet he is always anxious, and tense. He was telling me one day that he had booked in to see a shrink, to see if he can find out what is wrong with him.

I know there is nothing wrong with my friend. So I ask him, "You are an upper middle class, New York Jew, yes?" He nods his agreement. "So tell me about your father, mother, brothers and sisters, as well as your aunts, uncles and cousins. Are they not ALL somewhat tense, anxious and worried about things all the time?" He nodded in the afirmative.

"So am I right in understanding that, therefore, it would be perfectly NORMAL for YOU to feel uptight, stressed and anxious?"

He looked up to the heavens, and said "Of COURSE! How could I be so stupid. I am perfectly FINE. I really don't know what I was worrying about. Thank you so much for clearing that up for me."

"And you are seeing the shrink when?" I asked.

"Shrink mink. Why would I be a schmuck and give him my good money. And what's he gonna tell me that I don't already know?"

Problem solved. All it took was a little perspective.

And this is true of all of us. We all have issues, and if we need a floaty ring to survive the pool of circumstance, that's fine. We survive this world in whatever way we can. The only thing we really need is a clear perspective on things. This is why we must develop our connection to the Inner Rat, to separate us from our anxiety and fear, and help us get a clearer look at what the obvious might be.

What I will say is this: when we begin to see the obvious, an extraordinary change comes about. There is a chemistry that happens that alters everything we do and say, and it is both irresistible and immovable all at the same time. We discover a space inside where we are free from tension, fear and concern. We discover that point where we really don't give a Rat's. When we truly find this attitude within us, we arrive at a space where we learn to become *invulnerably vulnerable*.

Being "Vulnerably Invulnerable" means we are in a state of personal intimacy with self, our present moment, and with those around us. It also means we are no longer distracted by our fears of inadequacy, or concerns about what others think.

We arrive, clearly, confidently, at the moment of HERE NOW.

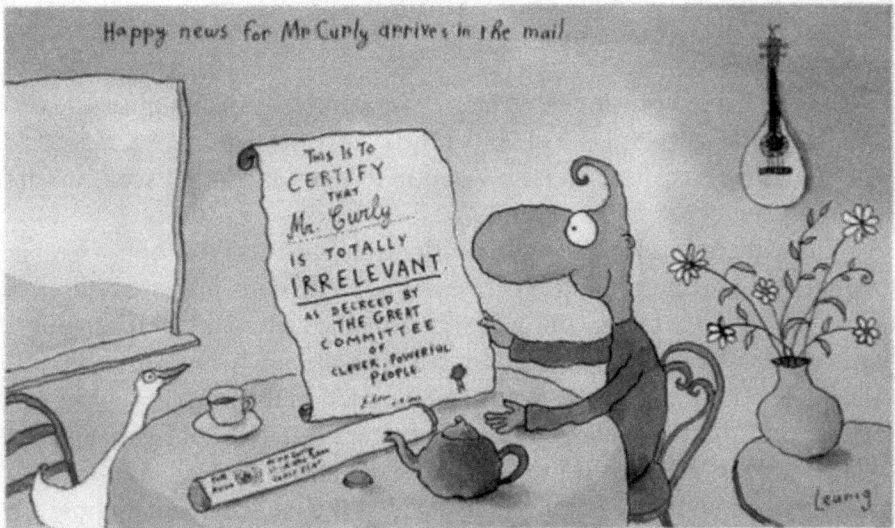

Invulnerably Vulnerable Versus Control Issues

Here is the real direction, the way of truth for all. *Invulnerably vulnerable*! This is the divine state of beingness coalescing with the natural state of humanity.

By accepting our humanity in equal measure as our inherent divinity, we find that the space between these two polarities begins to fill with a remarkable state of beingness. What is more, we find ourselves in a position of choice, moment to moment, and the choice is simple: Do we allow ourselves to be free, and live in the moment, or do we get owned and shaped by the inertia of our inheritance?

Wait a minute, I hear someone ask. Divinity? Where did this religious claptrap enter into the picture? And what the hell is divine about a Rat? In response, I will say a few simple words: When you fully experience the connectedness of self, you realise a state of knowing that is truly divine. You no longer have to THINK about something in front of you, you just KNOW. You realise that your inner senses, what we call your RAT, (Reality Awareness Trigger) is awake and seeing things.

When we are living in a state of emotional poverty and deprivation we feel the truth in the saying, "Beggars can't be choosers". However, when we start to live in the moment, discovering our vulnerable invulnerability, we realise the opposite is equally as true: "Choosers can't be Beggars".

But here is also where the first hiccup occurs. In trying to make choices, we hit an inner barrier to freedom. This barrier is the collected mire of shoulds that are our control issues. A SHOULD is a command that exists within that is not natural to our being. Whether we want to control, or are afraid of being in charge, or whatever variation exists between the two, our internal control issues rule us.

Why do control issue arise? We tend to like imagining a rosy future where all is aligned and in order, but we fear this isn't going to happen unless we take charge. Why? The inertia of existence shows us that things can and do go wrong. We know we are full of imperfections, passions and laziness, and because leopards rarely change their spots, we have to take charge and MAKE it happen.

OR we hide in the dark and hope it will all work out, handing over all control to the closest authority figure. Most people choose this option.

Logically, if the spots on the leopard are the issue we either need to change our spots, or cage the leopard, don't we? Either way, we need to control things.

In recent times we had the joy of witnessing Charlie Sheen hard at work attacking the fabric of society. How was he doing this? Apparently, just by being his weird and wonderful self. Didn't the media love those huge pronouncements about having tiger blood, being a Rock Star from Mars, and Winning!

Everyone laughed and called him drug addled, yet the reality is, he had more money, more sex, more good times than almost anyone else on the planet. That sounds like an advert FOR drugs, not a critique against using them. Recently we discovered this was around the time he was diagnosed with AIDS, so this is likely to be the catalyst for the explosive behaviour.

Yet WHY was he was so successful at the outset? I say he's a leopard that accepted his spots. His show was pretty much an extension of himself, and a demonstration of his ability to accept and live with his so-called "black marks". Society says "Drugs are bad", "Sleeping with hookers is bad", "Being inconsiderate of your fellows is bad", yet at the same time, society was rewarding Charlie Sheen with huge sums of money for doing exactly this. So where is the "bad" part?

Charlie Sheen lived a life that was "out of control", according to media. This was, apparently, also bad. Yet it happened to pay him off extremely well. Even when he was fired, he managed to get a HUGE payout. I think we can all start to guess that one of the core tenants of Charlie Sheen's persona is that he doesn't give a Rats about what external authorities class as right or wrong.

Remember this! If you want to be truly successful, which in context of being happy, really means living in the NOW, you must first accept yourself, and stop being concerned about what others think. So often we believe our natural spots are black marks, and seek to hide them. Forget that, and start accepting yourself.

In his book "Meetings with Remarkable Men" Nietzsche describe how he went up to the Sufi Masters and asked if practising breath control would lead him to discovering himself. They asked the obvious before answering, "Do you know yourself? Do you know who you are?"

"No," he answered, thinking that this was obvious, and the very reason WHY he was asking about breath control.

"Then how will you recognise 'you' when you find yourself?" If you use breath control to find yourself, but you do not know who you are, how will you know what you discover?

The reason we believe we need to CONTROL our own, or other people's, thoughts and actions is because at heart we fear them. The need we have to SEARCH to find ourselves and our place in the world is the essential proof that we do not believe we already possess it. On the other hand, when we are intimately involved with our environment (vulnerable) yet totally free of any restrictions, fears or threats within it (invulnerable) we no longer need to control or search for things. Why? Because we come to the place where things fall into their natural order.

Stop giving a Rat's and it will start to make sense.

This is one way of saying, "Step back from your inflated notions of importance." Stop pretending that we, the small business, are some big business. Stop pretending that our opinions are particularly important. Pull back from engaging the world in a way that seeks to dominate or control. Just stop, and smell the roses.

Once our attention withdraws from conflict, fear of what others might think, or any investment is seeking to "handle" external matters, then things start to line up naturally. We begin to see what IS. The present moment starts to come into focus.

When we touch the moment, and really feel it, we stop blowing bubbles up our proverbial. The truth is that we all live in a bubble of some sort, and what we need to grasp right now is what is manufacturing these inside us. When we get how we are creating a lens effect in our mind with opinions, passions and wants, then we can begin to shift our attention away from the inconsequential, and refocus on the things that matter. The first step in understanding self, without any doubt, requires us to stop investing time and energy into false beliefs, double standards, and erroneous thinking.

Just stop giving a Rats about it all, and this becomes so much easier to accomplish.

For now we take a look at "Bubble Creation"

As a child I used to get detergent, and a loop of wire, and create bubbles. I spent hours doing it, watching the amazing shapes wobble, float, and pop. We are still doing this. We take the tension of the moment, add a loop of thought/emotion, and by investing time and energy into this, we create bubbles of belief, bubbles of thought, and bubbles of bubbles.

Bubble Consciousness: What Is Wicked?

We are all living in a bubble, be it an opinion, a belief or just the physical bubble of skin that contains us. Looking out from our bubble, the external word conforms to the shape of our "lens", the bubble we look through.

"Something Wicked this Way Comes." This is an odd phrase we have all heard. What it means when it comes to Bubble Consciousness is very simple: We live INSIDE a cloistered environment of rights and wrongs, goods and bads, ups and downs, etc. Anything that does not fit the pre-set images within us, we tend to view as "wrong". It becomes what we call evil. We go into this attitude a lot more in the "Bubble Principle" but the core of this "evil" perception is that when we are INSIDE our bubble, all looks right. But when someone, or something, approaches our bubble, the very nature of the bubble is a lens, one that bends and alters any approaching reality. At a distance it is fine, but the closer it comes, the more distorted and terrifying this reality appears.

Yet with acceptance it all changes. To the Catholics, Protestants once looked evil. In the present day, however, the Christian tradition has become more homogeneous. Now that everyone is in the same bubble, so to speak, everyone looks normal. But when the Aliens come to visit, THEY will look distorted and terrible. And so it goes. Elvis was once the Devil incarnate, now he's a hero adored by millions.

All of this fades when you don't give a Rats about rights or wrongs, etc. When we release ourselves from fixed notions, then the paralysing fear that locks us into frozen beliefs and accepted institutions (all just bubbles of thought) does not take hold. The natural result of this is an increased sense of NOW, and we can start to enjoy the changing moments. The ever expanding face coming towards us is no longer "evil", just an expanding moment. Fear stops driving the bus, and we relax into the present.

When the genuinely "wicked things" turn up, as they do, you see it more clearly, and deal with it more efficiently. The external forces of life have less ability to manipulate you. In this way, regardless of outside circumstances, you become free.

More than this, what others see as wicked, you will learn to see as opportunity. Luck and opportunity, the true Sabine Gods of the Romans, are yours if you stop fearing change and start embracing the moment. "Seize the Day", in other words.

POST IT NOTES

A nother way to think of your fears, beliefs, passions and ideals are as "post it notes". We have been "tagged" by or upbringing and social situation. Society, or family, or circumstance has stuck everyone with a "post-it". But when you don't give a Rats, you release them. The post it notes of preconception, other people's notions, and social ideas just can't stick to your being when they hold no "glue" of fear, fascination or desire.

So many of the issues we have in life are really post it notes someone put on us. It may have been our parents, social conditions, or circumstance, but the universal truth of the Post-It Note is that its message is always invisible to us. Yet it is ALWAYS clear to those nearby. It's like the old "Kick Me" stuck on our back, yet something we remove easily when we know it is there.

These little notes generate activity in people around us. Many of the judgements and decisions people make behind out backs are largely based on their "reading" of these stick-it notes. In a sense, these are the truly wicked things in our life. But the real reason these tags stick to us is because of OUR attachment to the importance of what other's believe. In simple terms, because we DO give a Rats of what others think, then what they think affects us.

You could quite easily pull off someone's tags, but all that would happen is that they would re-manifest in situ soon after. Our attachment to our hidden beliefs magnetise them to us. Yet these signs, which are like neon lights to others, are invisible to ourselves.

Oh what gift the givee give us, to see ourselves as others see us.

And here's the thing: Yes, it IS true that other people's viewpoints can and do affect things like employment, relationships, and our external reality. When these "stick-it notes" extend out to official records, (bankruptcy, etc.) then they affect even the ability to raise capital to buy a house. But in all circumstances, the greatest effect we suffer from the "stick-its" is our attachment to them, but the "glue is always our concern regarding other people's notions and beliefs about ourselves. When we lose this, we lose the "stuff" that holds most of our issues in place.

When we are attached to other people's opinions, be it in social circles or financial circles or otherwise, the "Stick-its" become powerful forming energies that can, and do, affect us.

Think of it like a credit rating. Other people's gossip and nasty little whispers work their way into our internal self-esteem rating. These are black marks that emerge as spots on our external coat of many colours.

We don't actually see them, but we feel them every time we want to start a new social contract. These are your post-it notes.

As one example: The "I am a whimp" stain glows brightly to the pretty girl you are trying to impress, thus you fail to conquer her. The "I am not worthy" note stuck to your forehead is a bill board to a prospective employer, thus you get offered lower wages.

It is one reason I absolutely love the madness of Charlie Sheen and the "tiger blood". Everyone in the world sees the madness take hold, yet he doesn't give a rats! The media has beaten him up mercilessly, advertised his craziness, and tagged him with a million "post-it notes" but really, who really cared? They just didn't STICK to him. Sure, comedians got some mileage with a few jokes at his expense, but the fact is, we all know Charlie is what he is, and it's all a bit of a shrug. Why is he invulnerable to the snide and vicious remarks? You know why. A big part of it is that he doesn't give a rat's, so why should you? Why are we "shoulding" on him?

His hair is clean, I am sure he doesn't smell in public, and he knows how to hold an intelligent conversation. What more do you want?

By not accepting other people's "Shoulds" as anything but their viewpoint, and adhering sufficiently to basic principles of what is right for ourselves, we develop a thick skin of self-sustaining beingness. We move closer to the state of being Invulnerably Vulnerable. If you really want that legendary Tiger Blood, this is it.

How do most people deal with the whispers and shadows projected by others onto their life? It is a real concern. You may have your house in order, but gossips seem to want to break in an rearrange the furniture. It is something we must guard against, but HOW do most of us do this? Most seek to have a "good reputation". In other words, we polarise our external appearance to something deemed acceptable. It is not the best solution, but it works.

Rather than accepting our foibles, we tend to want to paint a pretty picture. We want to put correction fluid over the spots and act as if those nasty black marks just do not exist. This creates, like it or not, a state of polarisation. Because we choose to make one thing "bad", we elevate it's opposite number to being good. Our tags grow into black and white stripes of right and wrong as our external "shield". Further, as a consequence, we start to need to CONTROL the situation, to make things RIGHT.

This is when we paint over the cracked facade, put on false smiles, etc. and try to make the Humpty Dumpty Post-Wall Egg (HDPWE) look good. In the end none of this creates natural happiness, and this is the opposite of what is recommended in this book, but let's look at the process and decide for ourselves.

When we decide different aspects of ourselves are "bad" or "good" we create internal divisions within. These different areas that are our ideals, our causes, our sins, etc. In the short term these things appeal to the social consciousness, and can win you the support of a social group. But they are a King Canute to the reality of life. *We cannot stop the tides of humanity at work inside us.* Ideals and beliefs do NOT deal with the currents of change as they sweep in and out of our lives. The ability to appear upright and socially-minded may well attract groups of like-minded people, and get you a position in a company or organisation that will support you emotionally and financially, etc. But it doesn't pay at all in terms of self-acceptance, or natural growth, and we remain uncomfortable with our natural spots.

Know this simple truth: Society of and by itself is totally disinterested in what is right for the individual. It is only interested in order. Society wants to establish in the minds of it's citizens a social order. Once an entire culture takes on a set of ideals and embraces them, this society can withstand the shifting sands of circumstance for generations. As proof, in Western civilisation, the ideals of the Romans are still with us. Their culture still forms the bedrock of what we believe to be right, or wrong.

But our western ideals will one day fail. Soon enough we may all be speaking Chinese, or Russian, or whatever language they use in the Gamma system. Then we will have an entirely new experience of what is "right and wrong" in social terms.

As every earthquake proves, trying to control nature doesn't work. In the simplest terms, most social models are examples of dominance, not agreement. They work in abrasion with life, and require a continual application of force to keep functioning.

We saw how easily areas of Europe fell into the Dark Ages when the Roman influence receded. Fear of collapse, anarchy, with the subsequent break down of society is what keeps the social order, rather than a desire for the society itself.

Yet a new influence is rising. Things like I-Phones, the internet, all these changes instigate deep and lasting change into the social process. Just as the flower power movement of the 1960's instigated a core change in western values, so too will these inventions. Its a moveable feast, and nothing is set in stone.

On a personal level, when we can direct our nature to useful purposes, things work well. But when we try dominate it, and make our inner being into a one-sided ideal of perfection, then the "Safety Valves" are triggered. These valves are what we call the common neurosis. Paranoia, self-loathing and fear are whirlpools of negative focus, where we essentially spin inside ourselves. One of the reasons we create "bubbles" is to protect ourselves from this process. Yet let go of control thinking, and it all stops. Let go of the fear, and it all stops.

Your Rat has it's own safety release. If the ship is sinking, it gets out of there. If the house is burning your Rat doesn't stay inside to put it out: *It lets go, and gets gone.* Descartes said *"I think therefore I am"*. Your Inner Rat says *"I sink therefore I swim!"*

And what happens when you let go of fear? Freedom. Our freedom comes when we stop giving a Rats about unnecessary and extraneous matters. The hard part is knowing what these things are.

I was listening to the radio the other day, and a guy is talking about being a nudist. He and his wife became nudists in their late 50's. Why? The man went to a beach, took off his clothes, and felt incredibly threatened by every internal demon he had ever faced. He was literally forced to either stop, focus on the sun, the sand and the moment, or leave. Now, when he focussed on the moment, he discovered a remarkable thing: All his stress left. By doing his OWN thing, he became free.

His wife saw how happy he had become, and she joined with him.

But most of us cannot reach the rapid acceptance of what IS that easily. We stay in the thinking, feeling, worry zone. We want to MAKE things right, and we fight to do so. This internal argument creates the need for what I call our internal Counter Culture. A space inside where we embrace our difference with the world.

COUNTER CULTURE

Did you ever wonder about the term "Counter Culture"? Does it mean a culture growing on the counter of some sleazy restaurant? Does it mean we can iron out the top hat and tails and then count up the level of culture we have? Yes, we know it means a culture that runs counter to the prevailing wind, but I like the way the words play out. A good Rat develops their own "counter culture" in their life and this creates the external circumstances that allow them to move as they will. The true Counter Culture keeps us focussed on our OWN path, our OWN direction.

Freedom is an almost a reflex action for those who live outside the prevalent attitudes, and, when properly used, it is done without internal argument or conflict. It is more like a child playing in the sandpit, enjoying the sun. But when we are in ABRASION with life, when we carry about a fear derived from our society, the counter culture inside us becomes more tyrannical. And we see it every day in the barrage of conspiracy theorists, someone or something is out to get us.

If we haven't developed the ability to detach ourselves from other peoples concerns, (and in particular to remove any fear we have of failure, and/or of relating to the rules of society) then our internal point of difference becomes an issue. We develop a counter culture of dissent inside ourselves. We do this because we believe it helps us to survive, but it is somewhat of a paranoia. In some cases, where there is an oppressive regime for instance, the paranoia of not fitting in is justified. Mostly it is just a fear that drives the bus. Either way, we get POLARISED.

A perfect example is Che Guevara. He stood against an authoritative regime, but rather than just argue with a greater force, he developed a sense of faith and belief in his people. He educated the local people in the notions of being free. He grew a counter culture with a purpose of freedom from oppression, and he brought an entire nation to this purpose. His personal belief magnetised an entire country.

But these self-same ideals and beliefs can just as easily blind us.

Just like wearing polarised glasses, our ideals and beliefs polarise what we see, and certain bandwidths of light are filtered out. We simply stop seeing aspects of the world around us. It's like listening to Fox News: Totally one sided and biased information that defies natural logic seems now perfectly acceptable.

The OTHER effect of this follows the the Law of Polarity, which in essence means that as you erect any one thing, an equal and opposite thing will come into being.

All of civilisation has come about because someone set in motion a pattern of belief that others could follow. Any counter culture is just another new, emerging pattern, one that alters both the perception and reality of those within it. If they "catch on", these can become fads or trends that run for many years.

A good example is old fashioned "Positive Mental Attitude". In the 1950's and 60's this was used to energise sales people, and get them to achieve bigger and better targets. "What the mind of man can conceive and believe, the mind of man can achieve!" was the catch cry.

P.M.A. is a perfect example of what society says works, but which creates more issues than it solves. Firstly, the "Mind of Man" isn't really a dumb robot you program as the PMA people (and all the others who favour mind control as a technique) will have us believe. When you have to make a "positive" statement as a conscious effort, the inner part of the mind automatically questions the input. Your mind goes "Oh, and so why are we saying this?"

Logically: The fact that you have to make a postulate to GET means that the inner part of the mind believes it doesn't HAVE, or it holds fears of a LOSS. Think about this obvious example: A teenager doesn't say to him/herself that they want to be young, do they? A child does not have to say "I will be more child-like".

If you say "I have wealth health and happiness" as a positive statement, the inner mind goes looking in those boxes inside the brain, and guess what it finds there? Usually, it discovers fears of poverty, poor health and misery. It's obvious, isn't it? You are saying the positive statement BECAUSE you suffer the opposite.

The mind of man is a series of opposites. Mind Control - be it positive mental thinking, praying for health, or whatever it is you use the mind for to control external environments - is essentially a way to POLARISE the mind. It seeks to weigh the scales to a benefit without regard to the equal and opposite reactions that occur.

Our personal "counter culture" is not too dissimilar. We have a fear of something, so on one level we try not to see it, and on another level we generally go out of our way to try and defeat the fear in some way. Seen in this light, Positive Mental Attitude is just a technique people use to defeat their fears.

In this sense, using PMA is really you being run by secret fear. If you are fighting it, it is because you are not in charge of it. Fear once more is the bogey man. Keep in mind, all fear is, by it's very nature, something we do not understand. So the REAL answer to all this is in this simple adage: *If we understand a fear, we no longer fear it.*

Social structures fear counter cultures. Society wants things to run as they always have, and disruptive influence are generally not welcome. The great point I am trying to make here is that when you reduce the fear, and thus the need to control things in your life, you begin to develop a **harmonious** counter culture within.

You learn to walk a comfortable mile in your OWN moccasins, and, don't laugh too much at the next terrible pun. The sad fact is we are "cobbled" with other peoples views and beliefs, and the shoes we wear are anything but what is natural for us.

The truth is that there is NO normal, and nothing is average. There is nothing about any of us that is exactly the same, but for people to progress in society, they need to set aside their natural differences and agree to a common course of action. We all want to want to believe our present course could be improved, but rarely do we have the ability, tenacity and courage to change it. It is easier to follow instructions, and bow to the guy who says he has the best plan. There is nothing wrong with this, only that as we wake up in consciousness, the inner RAT says otherwise. It says "Chart your own course!".

This is where you discover your true counter culture, the life you were born to live. However, we avoid this, and we will specifically avoid this by involving ourselves in an argument about ideals versus hedonism. This is the social argument that remains the source of our greatest friction, and fiction.

... ANOTHER LOSER HAS-BEEN FADES INTO OBSCURITY...

IDEALISM Versus HEDONISM

This was the great argument of the Ancient Greeks and is still with us today: the Idealist versus the Hedonist. What is the better path? The Greeks generally agreed that the arts soothed the argument, and that MUSIC was the greatest of the arts because both the hedonist and the idealist could sit together in harmony during a performance. Yet the Ancient Greeks never found a clear argument to say which one was better than the other. They both had their good points, and bad points.

What we can say for certain is that finding inner harmony is better than constant argument. The question is more how we find harmony inside our own head when it is milling around with all these fuzzy and non-directed beliefs and wishes. Harmony indicates order and alignment, not a discordant random jumble of bits and bobs.

In the past most of us protected ourselves from our internal problems by using Ideals as a guide out of the quandary, OR we became hedonists and sought to just enjoy life, ignoring the complication. The Greeks never really solved the question of which was the better path. They didn't have RATOLOGY to help them.

For the most part, Western Civilisation has followed the Roman path (via the Roman Catholic Church) and opposed individual passions (and other supposed negatives) with the tools of mind control and ideals.

The accepted counter to our Passions were mainly IDEALS. These were the heroes we employed to defeat the monsters of our depression and depravity. They work for a while, but our ideals can be an avoidance of self, a protection from fears (remember the movie "Forbidden Planet"?) and they will eventually fail.

When I was free lancing for Playgirl magazine in Sydney during the 1980's I found myself reporting on prostitutes, and often got invited to their parties, etc. This was an eye opener, because here was a collective group of people who ignored the so-called ethos of upright behaviour, and sold their bodies for sex. But the reality is, these girls all had their own set of rules, designed to help them deal with their unique circumstances. They had their own ideals, agendas and arrangements to protect themselves from their internal demons, as do we all.

Let's take a moment and inspect the process we all tend to go through in trying to establish some firm ground for ourselves to stand upon.

The Three "C's"

In any given societal group or class of people, there are always the three "C's" which are the basis for all social contracts. Please pay close attention to these, because it is a pattern you will find repeating inside your own mind. These constants are:

1. *Comparison to find Norms*
2. *Categorization to find Position*
3. *Castigation/Congratulation to keep things in allotted places*

We do the same with ALL external experiences and situations. We want to categorise them into specific areas, or boxes. For Example: Country and Western in that box, Rock and Roll in this one, etc. Yes, it's all music, but what TYPE of music is it? We then like to argue that one type is better than the other, and when two groups oppose each other, they then fight for the right to be right. This finding of social, financial or other accepted norms and positions is done via comparison, categorization and castigation. Obviously, this opposes internal unity, but it DOES create group consensus. It also gives us a sort of collective yardstick by which we can measure our life and experience.

Sounds great, except we usually use that yardstick and go beat everyone who does not fit the "norm" over the head with it. And this is everyone. Why? Because we always paint our societal norms with ideals or perfection, and no one can live up to them. Everything we subsequently measure comes up showing us a shortfall. Have you noticed how ideals are always set on a backdrop of perfection, one that no one can ever realistically attain? Perfect Example: *The Garden of Eden*. There we were, perfect, then Eve goes and spoils it all.

But really, it was inevitable. Curiosity is the driving force in man, and since when did someone wanting to take fruit from the tree of knowledge become a crime? Of Course Eve was going to bite that apple! It was a GIVEN, but it gets painted as evil.

Our IDEALS are designed as sure-fire failures, impossible goals that we cannot attain. The rainbow of our great and noble intentions invariably becomes a stainbow of grief and mayhem, and even if we do manage to find the pot of gold at the end, by that time it will have turned into the remnants of a spittoon.

YET, it need not be so! We can avoid both the polarising effects of ideals versus passions and the indulgence of hedonism in one easy state of awareness. I just need to keep my RAT to the fore. *My RAT, my Reality Awareness Trigger, is my saviour.*

Here is the Rat Psalm for you:

My RAT is my saviour
Especially when I want
It is there with its clarity and simpleness
To waken me unto the obvious
That it is OK to be ordinary,
And whether I fail or succeed
My moment is still with me
Forever and ever
All the moments of my life

You know what I find? When I am sharp, awake and in tune with my Inner Rat, all is well. When I am not, the wicked sense of "should" rears its ugly head and ruins my day. I have learned from my Inner Rat to not seek perfection, or be concerned if things are considered either good or bad. What I seek is just awake-ness and IS-ness in this moment. My Inner Rat gives me respite from the inner slave driver of ideals that insists I am not good enough, or paints the "been there done that" in large red letters when I go chasing stupid dreams. But more importantly, in that space between high expectations and an acceptance of what is, my RAT shows me where there is freedom. And always, freedom lies inside the borders of the Fun Zone.

A wicked sense of fun increases our existence in the moment, and our vision of the obvious moves us through the aspects of doubt, distrust and anarchy. We become alive and increasingly get to the state of not giving a Rat's.

Of course, as taught in Book One, we will always reject the "should". The "should" is a reflection of the herd opinions of social order. That's the first step, but it is when we no longer give a Rat's what people think, and we live life according to OUR notions of right and wrong, then the Inner Rat wakes up and gives us something that no moral code, noble intention, or wise thing can offer. Good old Fun.

Your Rat makes life FUN. If you ask yourself every day: Why am I here? The answer is: *To have a little fun.* Yes, there must also be some purpose to things that fulfils us, but if you are not having any fun, what's the point?

And as the wise Guru Adrian graffiti'd all over the walls of Inner City Sydney during the 1980's: *Half the Fun is having Fun.* It was an inspiring message that I read every day, and in part, it is one of the important core elements that went into the creation of Ratology.

So, after all this preamble, let's get to the tin tacks of what erodes our sense of FUN. This is the "should" or restriction zone. There are three main areas that are the main creators of fear and anxiety that we will deal with in this book.

- *Pinning*
- *Bubble Consciousness*
- *Faulty Reasoning*

The first area of constriction, the Pining, occurs in the transition zone between the child becoming the pubescent adult. In this period, we can get "pinned" by our emotional responses to our emerging sexuality and the awakening sense of becoming an adult. It can also occur earlier through sexual interference (whether consensual or otherwise) and/or physical abuse of a child.

I knew one girl who actively sought sexual encounters with adult males at the age of eight. She did this because it gave her a sense of control. Even now, in her late 50's she is still seeking to control everything around her. This is her PIN.

The second main area of congestion is the "Bubble" we develop to protect out current circumstances. This is also part of the belief zone we fall into, such beliefs often being created by the osmosis of social patterns around us. We all live in a belief bubble of some sort, and these effectively control our perception of the world.

The third major area is simply faulty internal logic. We just do not add things up correctly. This is the most obvious area, and yet one of the hardest to deal with. This is where our internal arithmetic causes us to add up experiences that life presents to us in ways that are just plain wrong. These are called the logical fallacies. It is where we construct faulty conclusions based on erroneous perception: being one-eyed, not seeing eye to eye, living the biblical eye for an eye, etc.

SUMMARY: Part One

We started with the simple saying "Who gives a Rat's?" and moved on to the notion of SUBTEXT, or understanding what people MEAN, rather than what they say. Then we rolled into the notion of social niceties being Nice Ties.

We discussed double standards, and how people are not strong enough within themselves to just BE themselves. This often comes about because many people have two opposing streams inside them: Their natural desires, and the internal rules they employ to combat these.

We spoke about Seizing the Day, and moved this to the principle of being in the Now. The conversation then moved to the notion of Invulnerable Vulnerability, and how people's need to control external affairs was an avoidance of this state.

Then we had a brief discussion on what is "wicked" and how what we experience is more a state of HOW we see things, than what is actually there. This is important for it leads to a major section in this book on the Bubble Principle.

We gave the example of Charlie Sheen as a way to look into how someone breaks up control issue mentality. We give the concept of leopards wanting to change their spots versus the acceptance of spots.

We talked about how people place "post it" notes of beliefs and expectations on others, and how the only real cure for this in society is detachment. We give a concise definition for Detachment.

We then moved onto the Law of Polarity and how we set up a sort of "counter culture" within ourselves. Here we looked at Mind Control and ideals as a technique we use to control base desires, and how this is pervasive in society.

We then gave a summary of the Three "C's" that set up social orders.

Finally we got to the real point, which is that by finding our Inner Rat we get an antidote for all of the above. Essentially it's all about awareness, and a good deal of THIS is to be found when we find good old FUN in each moment.

Let's get right on to one of the "big" subjects, the reason most of us never move towards any sense of real maturity or attainment in this life.

PART TWO: Inner Realities Meet Outer Conflict

In this section we look at the specific inner dynamics at work that shape our outer consciousness. The three main areas are as follows:

PINNING

Here we discuss at how the individual get "pinned" by some some strong emotion or event in their formative years. Everything a person does, all their choices, even the people they marry, the places they work, and the friends they have, are connected to these "Pins" inside us.

BUBBLE CONSCIOUSNESS

Everyone lives in a bubble of some sort. The "Bubble" is in effect the inflated options, cherished beliefs, and fixed realities that people will hold to be truth. We talk of the various types of Bubble Thinking, and why we associate with those who have similar views

SPIRITUAL ARITHMETIC

Whatever we do, it is not merely happenstance. Our actions, thoughts and emotions are really a gestalt of many aspects of our being. In this section we begin to identify the core elements that form the building blocks of self. By learning how to recognise the blocks, we are then in a position to rearrange them, and maybe build a bridge where once we had a wall.

PINNING

We are all very malleable during childhood, but at some point we start to "lock up". This is usually somewhere in puberty, where pretty much everyone experiences powerful emotions or feelings that "pins" them to a belief about themselves. It is something that often becomes our internal pivot point. At some point along the line, we all got our tail pinned to something that we believe is absolute truth for us.

I need to add here, the molestation of children, either sexual, physical, mental or emotional, causes that child to "invert" and get "pinned" to the fears and emotions surrounding these circumstances. Even if the child is consensual, it still creates PINS inside that control that child all their life.

Almost all our personal issues in communication and relationship evolve from, and revolve around, these "Pins". And what is more, the Pins can transfer from parent to child. I know for myself, the intense guilt I once felt about sex seemed to have no basis, until I realised my mother had been sexually molested as a child. My MOTHER's Pin became a point of disassociation for myself in my personal relationships. However, secondary "inherited" Pins are not as powerful as those generated within us, from our own intense emotions and experience.

The mysterious area we never quite grasp of how we "miss" with the opposite sex, and most of the confused relationships between people, so much of this comes from the early point where we got "pinned" in an emotional and mental state.

The PIN is an internalised "should". In Book One we went over how all children are born innocent, in the "Baby State" but it doesn't mean they grow up that way. Why? Because they get absorbed and controlled by the Should's around them. The SHOULD has become the most insidious and life draining mechanism in our society.

The SHOULD is your true Satan.

But having a bag full of clothes and carrying them about does not mean you need to wear them. We are surrounded by "shoulds", but they need not affect us, However, when we are PINNED, we have no choice. The PIN is the place where you WEAR the should, and make it part of your being. The PIN is where your personal "Shoulds" dress up as your psyche.

There are a million little social rules and, yes, they confine us to a greater or lesser degree, but only the ones we are "pinned" to will do us any lasting harm.

In our first book on Ratology we took up the basic premise that we have been soaked in a world of "should". We have been raised with social myths and fabricated truths, and we have subsequently lost our child-like ability to see the obvious. Instead, we tend to live life according to the patterns laid down for us, and run along the track of convention. In other words, the opposite of the road less travelled.

When I was in India, I understood the term "The Teeming Millions". Wherever you went, thousands upon thousands of people were just walking. I presume they were walking somewhere, but as a collective, it just seemed so utterly random and pointless. In a similar sense, most of us DO believe we are going somewhere, but when you ask people exactly WHERE this is, very few truly know.

The truth is, our lives are spent walking down well worn tracks, some might call them ruts, set by the influences around us. These are created according to the Memes and Themes of our society and upbringing. What does this mean to you? It means you have very little choice. You think you do, and you could if you DID have a choice, but you don't. Like Eve in the Garden of Eden, all roads lead to the forbidden fruit and we will call this predestination an inevitability, not a real choice.

People, Eve had no choice in the matter. Think about it for a minute. It was a set up! There she is, put in a lesser position (made from a RIB can you believe?) and forced to serve a guy she only just met. She wonders "Why?" "Who am I?" What's this all for?" and along comes a talking snake to explain to her that all her questions will be answered if she just eats this fruit from the tree of knowledge.

It would make sense to me. I want to understand what it is all about, and logically, there is a tree of knowledge in the garden.

She doesn't know if the fruit has passed quarantine, and she has NO clue about nutrition. Eve's a dumb thing made from a rib, and she is hearing this fuddy duddy old man making threats about staying away from a stupid tree that HE planted in HER garden. Clearly Adam is a bit of an idiot, just wandering about wanting sex whenever he fancies. She wants a second opinion, so she finds the only other intelligent creature to talk to, the talking snake.

Mr Snake simply speaks the truth to her. *"Why have the damn thing there if you can't use it?"* It's like those useless rich men with garages full of Ferrari's. Let's face it, if they leave the keys in the ignition, and leave the door open, they OBVIOUSLY want you to take it for a drive.

Seriously people, at least with stealing a Ferrari you could worry about whether you have a driving license, but we are talking a piece of fruit that was supposed to make you smart. Der! Of course she took a bite.

There was no other realistic option: Either God lacked common sense and an understanding about dumb blondes, or he intended it this way.

You want to know something curious? In the original Babylonian Myth, Lillith was the first woman, and she was the EQUAL of man. In the later Judaic Myth that was copied from this, Lillith morphed and became the snake. Now Eve was promoted to First Woman, but she has become the subordinate to man. So our "Satan" is really a pissed off woman saying to the dumb floozy that supplanted her, "Don't be an idiot. Get smart, eat this apple, and get (the hell) out of this fool's paradise".

And dammit, we know what happened then. Eve was PINNED as a result! How many bucket loads of guilt and shame could you dump on a single person? Every night Adam comes home, hot and tired from hunting mammoth, and says "Damn, it was SO much easier in that Garden". Her own kids argue, and kill each other, and then Caine says, as his excuse, "Hey, this wouldn't have happened in that Garden you lot talk about. It's not MY fault we are stuck out here!"

She tries to say "But, you know, it was there! What could I do?" but everyone sneers her down, saying she is a miserable bit of useless rib made flesh, so shut up and go wash these skins, woman.

Let's look at the overview: Authority Figure (God) hands out a "should" in the form of "Must Not". Secondary authority figure (Adam) goes "Yessir!". Third actor in the play has no authority, no position, and is effectively a child being bullied by forces they don't understand.

Forth actor enters, says "Hey, this is a set up. Who plants nice fruit in a garden you can't eat? It's God we are talking about here, he can put that damn tree anywhere he wants! Obviously what he REALLY wants is for you to eat that fruit, yes? I mean, he even put me here to encourage you." Come on people, the silly girl never went to school and has no idea of a pass or fail marks on a test. She doesn't even know what a test is. EVERYONE knows what she will choose, and it is just a matter of time.

It's human nature. What is the opposing argument? That God really wanted the people that he created, the people with human nature, to go against their very God-given human nature? Eve was being true to herself, and her natural self said "eat the damn apple". Yet she is punished for this, but worse, as a result the entire human race suffers. It sound pretty absurd, and it is, but this is EXACTLY how a PIN works.

Dumping all of man's issues onto the shoulders of an uneducated girl who had no idea about anything is like saying Suzy from Grade School failed a test, and now everyone in the country must suffer as a result.

There is a very simple principle we can extrapolate from this origin myth, and herein lies the real value of the Adam and Eve story.

This is as follows: *When our NATURE runs contrary to our SHOULDS, at some point we will breach the walls of should. The subsequent emotional reaction is what often creates our PIN.*

Humpty Dumpty WILL fall down. Humpty WILL get fractured. The effort of trying to put it back together in order to look good means we need to create a central point to base things on. Just like we find a core group of pieces that fit in a jigsaw, we say, "This seems to be the spot". This is where we set up a PIN, a pivot point that seems to give us control of the fractured past, but which in time controls us.

...And on the third day, Humpty Dumpty was all back together again.

The Choosing Paradox

Let's look briefly at the loop involved in the Paradox of Choice:
1. You cannot choose how your parents will indoctrinate you.
2. You cannot choose the rights and wrongs of your society.
3. What you CAN choose is how you deal with these.
4. But only when you know HOW to choose.
5. This creates the Paradox of Choice. How do we choose when we do not know what, or how, to choose?

Choice, above all things, is a major goal for the growing child. This is what "Grown up" is supposed to mean: You get to choose what you want. But normally, when we DO get "all growed up", we don't choose anything other than the pre-set plan given us in our upbringing. Why? What is it that stops us leaping from the pre-cast beliefs of the past and into a free world of choosing?

Somewhere along the line we got PINNED by powerful emotional or mental charges, which tied us to a set of circumstances. Our attachment to this "pin" means we rotate around this as a central pivot. (This is possibly a reason why "Pin the Tail on the Donkey" is such a popular children's game; a part of our inner psyche is calling out for recognition.)

As an eight year old child, an engineering friend of mine, Johnno, decided that moving the large lawn on the country plot his family owned could be done better. He had a self propelled lawnmower, the old fashion type with the rotary blade up front, and he did a little math. Working out the necessary diameter for a central hub, he tied a rope to this, and pegged it into the middle of the yard. He tied the rope via a split hitch to the front and rear of the lawnmower, and set it off.

Perfect? Round and round it went till it reached the centre, where he came out to see a clear, clean circle of cut grass. Unfortunately, there was also a line of chopped clothing that had blown into the yard, and so his mother put a stop to that inventive nonsense. But Johnno was not through yet. The first automatic lawn mower may have been shut down, but all that meant was he had to invent the ride-on mower.

He tied his billy cart to the mower, and by means of simple ropes, controlled the thing and, for quite some time, this was how the lawn got mowed. Any wonder he became an engineer?

The power of invention, harnessed to freedom of choice, is a very powerful thing. This is the real solution to the effect of conditioning. Invention and choice open doorways to new options, but for most, like Eve in the Garden of Eden, they really only see two choices. Do I eat the apple, or not? She really had a hundred options, but she felt she was pinned down to just two. She could have left Adam. Grown vegies, built a house, gone out with an ape. She was not even aware the options existed. Here is a secret: A lack of options means that you have been PINNED.

Most Pinning happens during the years of 12 to 17. People usually get caught up on a set point around which their beliefs of self and society will revolve. Due to some event that occurs within or before the puberty cycle, a strong emotional signal is sent that "freezes" a section of the mind. But adolescence means we want to explore the boundaries, to break the taboos. This is like Eve starting to explore the garden. She has been under the minor authority figure (Adam as Parent/Partner) and is stepping into the world of the major authority figure (God as Society).

There are all these rules, and we KNOW what adolescents like to do with rules. They break em, and when they get caught, or not caught and get away with it, the emotional buzz can create the fixed PIN that holds them in that space. A classic example is the stereotypical girl, Miss Attractive, who could do no wrong. She was SUCH a good girl, did all the right things, and her parents loved her.

But puberty hits, and she wants to escape this suffocating coyness. She finds her first boy friend at age 14. He gives her a drink, and a little smoke, and she's as high as a kite. Soon the first great barrier to growing up is broken, she loses her virginity. She ate the apple, and she liked it. But this is not the issue.

That rush of freedom is now associated with booze and drugs, and it breaks the parental orders of "Thou Shalt Not". So the internal arithmetic goes "Freedom = Sex + Booze + Drugs". Because this is now part of her belief, every sexual experience becomes associated with drugs and booze, which reinforces the pattern. In simple terms, because she never breaks this pattern, she never has sexual encounters outside the circle of booze and drugs, and the wheel of becoming is complete.

The FLIP side is the reverse of the pin. Even when she meets the man who wants to marry her, have kids and settle down, all she wants is the cave man to drag out the party girl, and have a wild time. The net effect is that at age 29 the girl is still living with and inside the emotional responses of a 14 year old. Her first highly charged emotional experience OWNS her life. This is a Pin.

Some 7 years after I left my private boarding school, (Left, you question? Well, let's say I was asked to move on. The unkind would say expelled.) at any rate, 7 years after I had left the prestigious private school an old friend invited me around to visit some former classmates. We chatted for a bit, and naturally we all mentioned what we were doing.

These former classmates were, as was to be expected, all freshly minted solicitors, doctors and dentists. This is what the school said was expected of us, to become professionals, and my friends accordingly fulfilled the wishes of their society.

Whereas, I was the black sheep, a wandering character that had travelled all over Australia. I was regaling them with some of the adventures I have been on, and at age 24 they were many and varied, when I realised they were all looking at me with an odd look. This is where I first saw, in clear, stark detail, the effect of the PIN.

I thought they were the ones who had been successful, but surprisingly, they were envious of ME! What's more, every one of these former classmates that I barely knew (apart from the fact we shared a classroom for some years) were apparently of the opinion that they EXPECTED that I would be the one out there having all the fun. I asked them why, and they said they KNEW I would be the one to not get caught up in the trap. I was completely amazed. Firstly because I had NO idea that anyone noticed me at all during those years, secondly, because they seemed envious and, thirdly, because they all seemed to realise they were in a trap.

I said to them, "Well," I said "There is no big secret here. You can travel anywhere you want. You all have cars, and you have keys to those cars. All you have to do is get in your car and go!"

They all agreed that, while it sounded so simple, they could not possibly do that. They all wanted to, but there were jobs to keep, women to get married to, and responsibilities to obey. When they put it in these terms, I reasoned that, indeed, they really could not just up and leave. They were PINNED. The tail had been firmly pinned to its donkey.

They were, each one of them, fixed to a set routine and obeyed the psychic profile dictated to them by their social network. Like wrestlers who gave up the fight, they were pinned to the mat by an opponent they could not see, and who held them down with rules that did not exist anywhere but in their own minds.

In our first book RATOLOGY: Way of the Un-Dammed, you were urged to look at young children as a model of naturalness, and seek to compare your often inhibited actions against those of a three year old. The majority of us live life according to beliefs and presumed truths that are both self-generated and handed down by family. Many of these beliefs arise from seeds planted in the Socialisation and Sexualisation stages of our growth, and these beliefs, combined with whatever other influences, are really what create the choices we make.

Just like Eve in Eden, external forces corral our dreams and wishes to a set level of expectation, which create for us a narrow band of options.

They look like choices, but they are really just variations to fate.

Really, we are all just Adam or Eve, wanting to hang out in paradise, and having no clue about anything. Can you imagine a world where going to a University (Tree of Knowledge) is an offence punishable with ostracism from society? It really is a little unbelievable, isn't it? The first chapter in the Bible, a foundation book for all Western Society, is apparently an anti-establishment document!

But go PRIOR to Socialisation and Sexualisation and we see a different picture. Fact is, a three year finds it easy to choose what they want. Why? They are not bound up by the good versus evil world of SHOULD. To quote a cliché "You can't pin em down!" Kids choose to do what is fun, not what is right and proper, and they are happier because of this.

We looked at the "should" in Book One. Overall, we came to view that the state of "Should" inside our heads was held in place by the glass ceiling under which lived. The Should is a part of the belief factory within us that pumps out stories to convince ourselves that we are OK.

Now we take this further. We look at the tin tacks, the substratum of this belief factory, and in this chapter we look at the PIN that holds in place our personal and not very benevolent "Dictator Consciousness".

To re-hash briefly, I came to the understanding that no one was the best or worst, fattest or slimmest, smartest or dumbest. There is no "end point" to reality, and nothing that is the highest or lowest. At this point it also occurred to me that if we DO have a sense of "higher than/ lower than", it is a never ending circle to nowhere.

Yet when we look closely, we all tend to have a comparison addiction in our heads, to a greater or lesser degree. (Number One of the 3 "C's")

It is also clear that young children do not suffer this comparison addiction. So, if are we to become as little children, it seemed to me that getting off the wheel of comparing ourselves to others is a good place to start.

One of the core pressures that puts the PIN into place in our Psyche, and holds it there, is the pressure of comparison. You tell me, can you toss everything aside? Can you just throw away all the beliefs you are trapped within, all the expectations of others, of society, and of our peers? You can when you drop the comparison habit. These are all held in place by an internal comparison mechanism.

Consider for a moment that you no longer give a Rat's about all the above, or have any concern as to whether you are right or wrong, or worry at all about what other people think. Let me stop and capitalise this to emphasise: CONSIDER FOR A MOMENT THAT YOU NO LONGER GIVE A RAT'S ABOUT WHAT OTHER PEOPLE THINK !

How long a moment do you need? Just imagine you really give no thought of concern about other people's thoughts or feeling, or anything. So tell me: Have you suddenly become a homicidal maniac? Did your world view shift to that of a murderer and unworthy person, totally unfit for society? No, it didn't. It doesn't, it won't and it never will be the case that disinterest in society equals a threat to society.

What really happens is that you RELAX. You drop your tensions, and when you drop the tension you suddenly realise you are basking in the moment of being here and now. You instantly become FREE.

When you get this, you start to see life differently.

BREAKING with the FEARS the DRIVE US

I met first-hand the remarkable change in persona that happens when we drop the fears that control us. This occured when I took my father to see his brother (my uncle) some years ago. Both men were elderly, and I knew they may never see each other again. (The video is up on YouTube as: *Geoff Meets Reg. https://goo.gl/oKk2va*)

Here I discovered a totally different Uncle Reg to the one I knew growing up. He used to be incredibly surly, arrogant, short tempered and just plain rude, but now he was happy, laughing and carefree. I was very pleased to see the different side to him, obviously. As we were leaving Reg just happened to ask if I remember Uncle Colin.

Uncle Colin was quite mad, but great fun. Of course I remembered him, and then Reg says "I thought Colin was an idiot, you know. He did not give a crap about what anyone thought, and I thought him a fool. But you know something, he was RIGHT. We was RIGHT not to care about what others thought!"

It went "bing". All the surly rude behaviour was a shield. Reg was worried about what others thought, and so he erected this shield to protect himself. When he STOPPED being concerned about what others thought, he relaxed, and the naturally happy, cheerful soul came shining through. This is what happens when we break with the fears that drive us. We drop the pins that hold our false behaviours in place.

In the 1980's I went to see an acupuncturist called Dr David Ty. He was a proper Chinese Doctor, not someone who took a course for a few weeks, and stuck in the needles wherever. He stuck me like a pin cushion, but that's not the point. (pun intended) He came to check, and when he saw a number of the pins had fallen out, he smiled. Apparently this meant the job they were meant to do had been done. That's nuts, isn't it? A pin stuck into flesh that seems to know when it needs to fall out? It happened again and again, so I know it wasn't chance or a one-off thing.

The Pin inside us is like an acupuncture needle that has not finished it's job. When we get the message, it just falls out. And the message is ALWAYS wrapped around Comparison, Categorisation, and Castigation.

The Three "C's" are part of the evil world of Should. Sounds simple enough. We can just toss it to the side now we have got the message, can't we? Well, yes and no. If I wanted to pick up a girl at a party, I could just say "hi there, you want sex?". Well, I knew a plumber that did do this. He got his face slapped a lot. To have greater success we would have to play her comparison and categorisation game.

The girl wants to get the best guy at the party (comparison and categorisation), just as most men are chasing the prettiest girl. Yes, it's stupid, but that's how things are. Who knows what it will be that a person will use to measure good or bad in another, but one thing I do know is that, when given the choice between a Rolls Royce and a broken down Toyota, most will go for the Roller. Who wants to buy an old beat up car? We all tend to prefer the newest and best, and accordingly most relationships start out as relation-shops.

In the end, of course, we end up with an old beat up car, because no matter how new things start, they all grow old. But who is thinking about this in the teenage years? We just want sex, and someone who looks good to have it with. Which brings us to the principles of attraction. But what are we attracting? If we are filled with fears, and shoulds, and problems, we will attract those who will either capitalise on our poor self image, or those who suffer the same effect.

It is this very power of attraction that is the core PIN for everything that follows.

You have to be attracted to something before you want to buy it, yes? The same truth applies to our feelings, thoughts, and externally to such things as partners and occupations. Here is where the Memes and Themes of our society get in and work to control our actions. If I want I catch the fish, I have to bait it with something the fish wants to eat. If I want to impress a girl, I have to align myself to what SHE thinks is the business. If I want to attract a job I want, I have to align myself to some degree to the standards an employer believe to be important. We shape shift to suit conditions.

But our first shape shifting happens in puberty, and usually for sex. Let's say I bend over backwards to impress this girl, and it works, she says YES, and I have my first sexual experience, then one of the PINS that will rule my actions from that day forward will be, "Bending myself out of shape to please another is good!"

Get it? Do I need to shout it out to you? *Whatever PAYS us, PINS us.*

If I am a miserable sod, moping about singing Leonard Cohen songs, and a girl happens to like me because I am a cynical, depressed poet, then being cynical and depressed becomes GOOD. It makes me miserable, and I am glad for it! WHY? Because it gets me sex!

The VERY FIRST emotional signals we sent out that connected to another, which in some way encouraged them to say "Yes" to sex are some of the most powerful pins we can experience. This is why child molestation by any authority figure (church, etc.) is so destructive to the individual, and in due course, to society.

If a comedian wants to get a laugh, they have to connect with the audience. So often, the first words they utter set the tone for the whole performance. I recall a guy on an amateur night who used the same routine, night after night. Every sixth performance, people found to be incredibly funny. But the rest, using the same material, fell completely flat. Why? He generally didn't connect.

Likewise, in all societies, move ahead you must present, perform and parade your goods in a fashion that is acceptable and desirable to others. The jeweller sets up the shop front with all the good stuff laid out on velvet in order to get people to stop and get interested. So, accordingly, we hide our the crap. We hide the lack of confidence, the weird thoughts, the strange feelings, and present a false image, a smiling person willing to connect, in order to get laid.

I did this for a bit. I had routines to create impressions, clever tricks I employed to get attention, but at the same time I was hiding what I thought was the "real" me. It worked for me for a while. At one point I had women throwing themselves at me, but it all just seemed empty. That was the curious sort of PIN that got me. I knew it was fake, I knew it was a routine developed to cover my fear of rejection. This created a pin in my relationships that became wrapped around performing, but not receiving. For myself it was like I was driving a fancy car, but when people stopped to admire it, I "knew" they were not interested in the driver.

Of course, the girls WERE interested in seeing more, but my own fears of unworthiness, derived from guilt and shame from earlier Catholic Pinning, stopped me seeing this.

At the same time, while I was using society to get what I wanted, it struck me how mechanical it was. I just had to create an image that people want to buy! This got me girls, money, whatever I wanted. This is not a bad thing. If I succeed in creating a positive perception of myself, it means I am to some degree in charge of the situation. It's good to be in charge.

But the truth was, I wasn't in charge. Like a photographer, I was good at taking pictures people wanted to see, and presenting them in a nice light. But the internal process was still being driven by social patterns and pinned by a deep sense of unworthiness. I was able to love, but could not stop and allow myself to BE loved.

There are many pins that hold us to the walls inside. A classical example: The Catholic Church mastered the use of guilt, shame and unworthiness to Pin people to a false set of morals. The U.S. uses patriotism to Pin people to ideals that cause them to want to send young men off to die in useless wars. These are generic pins, or pivot points, used to control people internally.

We all have a Pin of some sort. What we want to uncover is the EXPERIENCE that caused us to get Pinned. This is not so easy to find, but when we do we start to understand it, it's power no longer controls us. One small example: My son got in contact with his childhood sweetheart, a girl he always fancied in school, but never really connected with. She was with the "in" crowd, and very cool, always at the best parties. But now, out of the blue, there was an invite to come visit, so he drove 600 miles to go see her.

It seemed wonderful, the total realisation of a dream. They connected, hit it off, and had a great time. Yet a week later as he is driving back she calls him up, and basically drops him on the phone. He was really hurt, but came back, looked at me, and said "She got pinned to Age 14 by drugs".

That simple passing comment is the core of this chapter and one of the motivations for RATOLOGY: Book Two. It really struck me how right he was. People DO get pinned. In this girls case, it was the party world of the 14 Year old, and the effect magnified by the drugs, that created a fixed point, a reference spot that the rest of her life would be used against for comparison and categorization.

She wanted life to be a party, and settling down meant that was going to end. So she needed to reject anything that would unsettle the pin that held her life in place. Did it matter that it hurt another? No. What mattered is that the unconscious decision, her personal dictator, was obeyed. She killed off love, and kept her addiction to an unconscious, driven state.

Everything in relationships, every little thing we think, dream and imagine, always starts with the *Law of Attraction*. This Law draws to us the circumstances of our hopes, fears, wishes, and expectations, but it also draws us towards or negatives: the fears, compromises, and anxieties within us. But what creates this attraction? So often what magnetises us to things is the static electricity created by us running round and round our pins inside.

Because our mental energy is circulating some fixed point within, it builds up a charge. This becomes either positive or negative, and attracts or repels energy in affinity with it. This is one reason why women and men so often stay with abusive partners, their mutual fears magnetise each to the situation.

ANGER BREEDS ANGER

Soon after my sons meeting with the old school friend, a fellow came to stay with us who was extremely angry. He didn't show it overtly, but at all times there was this simmering anger underneath. I noticed my son also started to get angry. It began with sharp comments and critical observation, and I could see it was all going into negative vibes. This continued until I pulled him aside, and suggested that this anger was not really "his", but something he had caught, like a cold.

"Bing"! A light went on. He found a PIN inside. "That's right. I am normally pretty happy, but when I visit my mother I get angry, and when that guy is here, I get angry. THEY are the angry ones, not me. But here I am becoming a part of THEIR process!"

At age 14 my oldest son had witnessed his mother locking up. She became totally paralysed and was hospitalised, all as a result of sheer, unmitigated anger. As a result, it was a turning point for the mother, who started to undertake university study and better her life, but it also meant an isolated single child became even more isolated.

He realised he had grown up in a world of anger. He had joined the Army as an angry young man, and was still, to this day, perpetuating the myth of "anger as a right". Why? At age 14, anger and frustration was a core emotion at the turning point of his maternal relationship.

The light dawned. His only serious relationship had been with an angry, ambitious girl. All his associations in this life had been connected with anger, and his then excessive drinking was a symptom of anger.

Long story short, the constant drinking stopped, the sense of balance and harmony started to come back, and soon enough after this he found himself a trade and an entirely new life. When the PIN is no longer needed, it drops out! You cannot give it up, but when you understand it, it gives YOU up.

We talk about habituation, and people who get addicted to substances and emotions. Well, most alcoholics are where they are because of an Anger Pin. Most compulsive ecstasy users are there because of a Lust Pin. Most compulsive narcotic users are there because of a Vanity Pin. Most marijuana addicts have an Attachment Pin. Most addicted gamblers are there because of a Greed Pin. They are just extremes of a process that is ALREADY happening in them before they get addicted. Remove the Pin, and you remove the addiction.

Do you grasp how powerful this simple statement is? In one stroke you can cut through the entire Gorgonian Knot of addiction. If you remove the

Pin holding things in place, you loosen the addiction connected to it.

If some young girl has an addiction to being a victim, you may track the source of this back to her pretending to be sick to get out of school. After faking it enough, a small part of her mind believes she is unwell, while another areas recognises the reward for being ill. What it adds to is that, when required to do something she doesn't want to, she plays an excuse card. She feigns illness.

Now add this to her meeting a handsome young man. She wants his attention, so she fakes a sort of weakness. It is the old fashioned "feint" to get him to come and hold you. She plays the victim to get what she wants.

But the PIN is that her behaviour helps her to control her world. The smart man will give her something she IS in control of. A baby, a role in a company, something where she feels genuinely in charge. The victim self will soon drop away.

So, where are the Pins in yourself? Easy. Look for any area of your life where you have little to no control, and you will find them. Maybe you are a control freak, and will say all of your life is in order. Well, there's the Pin, the need to control. ("Need to Control" is often related to the Unworthiness Pin.)

Mea Culpa. Mea Culpa, mea maximus culpa. Can you imagined how PINNED Eve and Adam felt when they got booted from the Garden of Eden, with God frowningly pointing them out the door?

Yes it IS all our fault, but what can we DO about it? That, my friends, is the question. Well, typically modern psychologists will say we need to understand the process before we can be released from the pattern of inertia. Well, yes: To a degree, grasping the process helps with unleashing ourselves from a mindless slavery to our internalised past. But really, it is just a matter of moving on. There's only so much room for understanding, and eventually we just have to just call things in the past that gave us problems a loss, and move on.

When we are truly DONE with a situation, an attitude, a fear, or whatever it may be that is holding us back, then the Pin that held in place falls out. In simple terms, it is just physics. Your tension is a monkey grip on the situation, and you can't let it go. Let it go, and it lets YOU go.

Just move on, and when we do, the anger evaporates. The Pin falls out. The sense of regret evaporates. We go "meh" to ourselves, and move on, leaving the past where it needs to be, in the past.

This is called the almighty Power of the Shrug: Call it a loss, and go forwards to a better place. This is the easy way to move past the past.

So, NOW you ask, "How do I move on?" How DO we remove the pins that hold us in place?

Negotiating Your PIN

Life, of itself, does not care how an individual feels, or thinks. It is like a river that flows, and if you get dammed, it will apply pressure until you break. Obviously, if we can get to a state of free flow without too much suffering, it is better. A "pin" is like an eddy in that river, where we get caught going round and round rather than moving on. So what is pinning us to our habits and issues? Simple hunger, for the most part.

We want to eat something, be it food, love, emotion or could be despair, loneliness and pathos. It is all "energy food". But starving yourself is not the answer. The notion of the ascetic monk is pretty much opposed to the nature of the Rat,

The real question is whether you want to be helpless, or active. It is a little like the difference between the carnivore and the herbivore: Do we live in fear of being eaten by the hungry others, or stand true and proud, and unafraid? The Rat is omnivorous. It eats whatever is on the menu, then it goes and does what it does. You are not owned by your hunger, in other words.

Now I would imagine that, to a rabbit, being eaten by a fox would feel somewhat unfair. But really, this is just what foxes do. You don't blame the fox for wanting to survive. Likewise, to be pinned to a pattern, or karma, due to some event that usually occurred as happen-stance in puberty may not seem fair, yet what is happening is that we are eating ourselves. We are the fox and the rabbit, the victor and the victim. It is part of our puzzle box to solve. Everyone gets pinned by something, and whether you consider it fair or not doesn't really count. Solving it is all that matters.

When we stop feeding that inner hunger for more, when we are able to stop and be in the moment, we are free from the argument. This is perfect, if you live in a cave and have no bills. The hard part is finding this space INSIDE the process of hunger. Yes, we all hunger for something, and it is fine to eat whatever, but the pin forces us to keep going over the same ground. *"I can't get no satisfaction"*, is a Pin effect.

There are three basic alternatives you can employ when you wish to move past some issue that has pinned you inwardly.

1. *Snipping: Kill It*
2. *Substitution: Replace it with something else*
3. *Reversal: Move from being Pinned to being someone who Pins*

Apart from the three basic techniques I have mentioned, the overall desire to "de-pin" must first come from an awareness that something is pinning you. This is the real issue, people are entirely unaware of this inner control point that is running, some would say ruining, their lives.

The awareness of a "pin" came to myself at age 17 when I had a curious inner experience. This was as real as any day-to-day event in our lives, and on this occasion I was sitting beside a black lake that had flames burning in patches all over it. I knew this was symbolic of something, but I had no idea what. Then a jolly, fat monk approached, called me by name, and asked if I was ready to leave.

I looked to where he indicated, and only then did I realise I was in a dark cave. In the distance there was a doorway that opened to a beautiful meadow, with blue skies in the distance. Freedom! This was what I wanted, this was my hearts desire. I really wanted to leave, but something held me back.

I said, to my vast surprise at the time, "I can't go. I still have too much religion in me." The monk just nodded and trotted off, quite happy with his band of followers. This was when I awoke in my bed, sitting bolt upright, saying "No, this cannot be! I rejected the Catholic Religion at Age Four!"

And indeed, at Age Four I had been travelling on a train, and seen what looked like nude swimmer in a waterhole by the tracks. When my natural curiosity went to look further, my head was PHYSICALLY turned to look away. It was like there was a hand on the top of my head, turning it, yet no one was there. I turned back, and as I did, I realised Mother and all her Catholic guilt and shame was somehow responsible for this. I rejected the Catholic control mechanism at that point, and said emphatically that this was not right for me.

Then it sunk in. Despite this, I realised how deeply Catholic I had become. I was not by nature a Catholic, but stuck in the pickling jar of a Catholic upbringing, I had become this. I now carried guilt, shame and all manner of inhibitions, and believed it to be normal. Even though I could see these things inside me, and knew it was wrong, I felt helpless to do anything about it. I was well and truly pinned.

So often, as people wake up to the fact they have been pinned to the wall of circumstance, they face a basic choice. They want off the treadmill, but how? Do they cold turkey the habit, or substitute, or forget it all and just play the victim card? It sounds a lot like dealing with a Heroin addiction, and it is.

Cold Turkey would be like the girl my son went out with simply choosing to say NO to the party animal inside her. This is the mind control approach. With a lot of will power you succeed, but the reality is, it is a moveable feast. When you try to pluck this the pin that trapped one aspect of your being, it simply slips off into some other dark corner. It takes repeated and continuous tracking down of the pattern in order to finally quash it.

The alternative to this is simply to substitute. This is the easy way. Instead of being a party animal doing drugs, a person might get motivated to become a born again Christian, as one example. Lo and Behold, it works, and what's more the person is forever converted, because they believe Jesus has saved them. In a sense, he has, or at least the image and faith in the figure has worked. We like to think we allowed life (or call it Jesus, or the flying spaghetti monster if you will) to come in and heal, but many times, we simply substituted a negative energy for a positive one.

The Third path is one where you reverse the energy itself. Many times this means you become the PINNER. You take on the role of taking the pins out of your psyche, and sticking them like you would a voodoo doll into another. A classic example of this occurred in the Inquisitions. A severe and repressed cleric would conduct interrogations over a helpless inmate, and very often it would bring about what seemed a remarkable reversal. The "saved" person converted, the cleric felt he had served God, and all was well with the world. Marvellous what a little torture can do.

What has really happened is the psychic pressure has shifted the pin, and this release from being held in place gives the individual a powerful spiritual experience. All your energy now revolves around the new experience, and the pin is forgotten. Most often this person becomes so fervent with their new faith, that they become an evangelist, the one who installs the pins of their new belief into others.

But here is where there is a FORTH option that presents itself. Just get excited about something better. This shifts the energy around to a place where a pin affects us less and less, and this is really a combination of all three previous options.

I would love to advise you to just shrug the shoulders, and don't give a Rats. But this is a little difficult to do when strapped to a rack.

People under torture would often have a "release" in the form of a powerful revelation, many times leaving the physical body and experiencing what we call a Spiritual Experience. With the Inquisitions, they naturally associated this with Christianity, and thus converted willingly to the fold. People fell in love with their captor, in other words. What really happened was that the "pin" or dammed energy in the inquisitor released itself psychically into the being of the prisoner, and pinned itself to them. But the effect on the people was often quite uplifting, because it released them from their OWN pins.

The salient point is that our PIN is a moveable beast. It can shift about.

If you pray fervently, practice austere fasting, or do anything that polarises the mind and emotions, you will shift the pins around inside you. Whatever we put our devotion, faith and belief into will become the place to where our inner pin shifts.

And this can be anything. We might become totally dedicated to fishing, gold prospecting, or even selling things on EBAY. If we think about it, like religions, these things all have a huge following of dedicated people. ANYTHING that captures your mind and emotions can cause your inner pins to shift. In simple terms, your dedication to a new goal will open up your life to a different room. This is why we are so often happy with a hobby, and why it is so important to have new interests in our lives.

Now, here's the real secret. *When your heart opens to a brighter place, you enter a larger room.* In a sense, the size of your pin remains the same, but inside you become "larger". The effect is that the past looks less important, and loses a degree of control over you. Alternatively, if your new interest spirals you down into neurosis and inhibition, you enter a smaller room, and the pin appears to get bigger.

The worst possible de-pinning practice comes through manipulation. This is where you go from being a Pinnee, to the Pinner. You use the power of the Pin is such a way to control others by pinning them. Yes, the person who converted under torture may well be set free, but the person who instigated it generally suffers the opposite over time. A classic case is the controlling husband who totally dominates his wife. He appears to be free from his Pin (usually insecurity) because he has found someone willing to wear it for him. But over time, as his heart grows smaller, the pin regains it's power over him once more. In old age, she becomes the one running him.

Many people who seek positions of authority and power in our society are manipulators, and they are always identified by the use of SPIN. Spin is really a pin with the slippery person attached to it, one who is often trying to escape their own concerns, but who ends up going round in circles, and spiralling into them.

Another example is the high pressure salesman, the one trying to get you to decide to buy NOW. He will look for any perceived weakness in his target, and try to use it to twist the person into a buying decision. An example: Trying to sell encyclopaedia, and saying "Don't you care about your children?" when the person hesitates. That is using a Guilt Pin to force you to move in a certain direction.

Governments love to use slogans such as "Speed Kills" to control people's driving habits. This is a PIN. It is also a lie. Speed, of itself, doesn't kill. If it did all the racing drivers in the world would be dead.

Driving at speeds beyond your personal capability as a driver, or beyond the limits of safety in the prevailing weather condition will cause accidents, but speed itself is only the majority factor in two percent of all vehicular deaths. Yet speeding is a huge focus in our social order in the West. Take the smallest step outside the narrow margins imposed by government, and you will get PINNED with a fine.

One statistic I find fascinating is when the Northern Territory of Australia finally bowed to pressure from the central government and introduced speed limits on its national highways. *Death rates by car accident went up forty percent in the following year.* If death rates had increased with a LOWERING of speed limits, there would have been an enormous hue and cry. Yet not a whisper did we hear.

Media is a good example of external pressure used to control a society, whereas guilt and shame are internal pressures we use to control ourselves. Yet for the self-directed person, the one who follows their own interests, the external world or the internal turmoil has little traction.

THE PLODDER

You'll get left behind!   HOW WONDERFUL.

You'll miss out!   HOW LOVELY.

You won't achieve your personal best!   HOW ENJOYABLE.

You won't be influential!   HOW TRUE.

You won't be attractive! You won't be clever!   HOW DIVINE.

You won't know what's happening!   HOW PEACEFUL.

etc.

leunig

INTERNAL and EXTERNAL PINS

When we bring external authorities into the picture, we start seeing that are two levels of PINS. One is INTERNAL, the other is EXTERNAL. The effect is much the same, and many times the two are mixed in together, but here we give some example you might recognise.

Clearly, traffic fines and such from government are an external way of controlling the individual. But there is also the Pin installed into you using the external weight of authority. Guilt, fear, and shame are all the classic concepts used by the powers-that-be to control the masses. This is the source of the SHOULD/SHOULD NOT mentality. It is when we accept it as real that it shifts to become an inner Pin that holds us in place.

We dealt with the "should" in RATOLOGY: Way of the Un-Dammed, and looked at a number of external forces that control us. Now we are more looking at the INTERNAL aspects: Pins, Bubbles along with the mental and emotional "Arithmetic" that control us.

What I want us to focus on right now are the internal self-created Pins, as well as taking a brief look at the external ones, those generated by peer pressure, and any of the other controllers that exist in our immediate environment.

There are a myriad of these, more than we can cover in a single book. For now, it is enough to understand they exist, and affect our behaviour.

We offer here a small example of the types of Pins we deal with every day. You see these in people in the workplace, at the hairdresser, at social gatherings, everywhere. And what is most remarkable is that when you start to SEE it, you will start to grasp how little people understand about themselves. Blissful ignorance is the common denominator.

All of the following are fairly easy to fix once you see them in yourself. But this is the hard part. When you DO "get it" it takes a little time for the habit to wear off. The trick is in not fighting, or arguing with yourself, but just dropping the problem and moving to greener pastures.

Self-Depreciating Passive Pin: *A person that is never quite happy. Their smile is a half smile, and they always hold themselves separate from others. They love to see the good in others, but compliment them, and the clam shell shuts.*

God is Watching Pin: *These folk live in constant fear that someone or something is watching their every move. As a result, they can never act in a spontaneous and natural manner. They are always looking and adding up their surroundings.*

Unworthy Me Pin: *This person suffers with an abject sense of stress and tension over the "fact" they are less than everyone else. Yet, they also have this curious arrogance that no one is as good as them. An inability to accept love is a keynote, and a terrible fragility of the heart follows this.*

No One Love Me Pin: *The paradox of this pin is that the person suffering it wants to fall in love, desperately. They will marry the first person who says "yes", and when they realise the error they made, they will just suffer along, passive and yielding on the outside, depressed and angry on the inside.*

Beggar Pin: *This is a very common, but sometimes hard to pick Pin. Often, very wealthy people suffer its effects, and you see it in miserly attitudes, and a sense that there will never be enough. It is seated in a fear of loss, loss of face, loss of finance, loss of control. Beggars cannot be choosers, yet equally, choosers cannot be beggars.*

There are as many Pins as they are archetypes of human nature. Time and practice will reveal these to you, but I do want to touch on a peculiar one, the Religious Pin.

The Religious Pin: *This rarely is connected to a religion. It is a calm, apparently "at peace" state where the person feels noble and secure in their beingness, but it is what we called the quiescent state. Many who gain great understanding of the mind reach this, and feel they have "arrived". You have, to a passive heaven. Smug mediocrity is the real result of this, not any ground breaking new revelations in human endeavour. You see this in many "New Age" advocates.*

The simple answer and solution to all of the above is to wake us. Stop sleep walking through life, and start to see the details and moments for what they are. SEEING things is the start point, and the next section focusses on this.

The Zen of Being, the Tao of Journey, the Creation of the Awake-Self out of the slumber pattern! There are so many ways people describe waking up. What I say here is that, as we move past the PINS inside us, our natural self shakes off the weight of ages, and takes over with a sort of internal revolution.

Literally, a turning of a leaf inside allows us a new way to look at everything. We gain an intimate and unique PERCEPTION that will allow us to walk through the minefield of the trapped self into the higher places of our being. It also allows us to see how the "post it" notes we wear are PINNED to us by our own inner Pins.

This next section is looking at what is looking. Here we will understand that WHAT we see is not as important as HOW we see.

PERCEPTION: Touchani

The Tao says: *Why does the King of the Ocean Rule? Because he rules from below!* The Great Rat says: *Learn to see the obvious.*

The two comments might not at first seem to be connected, but if we are going to be in charge of our lives, we have to be in charge at a very deep level within ourselves. To get to this point, we need to see, and accept, the obvious about ourselves. To be in charge, we need to SEE what is inside us, and specifically, observe those implants (or pins) that are secretly stealing our sense of personal authority.

Everything in life is about perception. We are going to be talking a lot about perception of truth as it IS, not as it suits us, in this book. We discuss how SEEING rightly, leads to ACTING rightly, which in due course, allows us to osmose from our artificial social-self into the natural state of being. This is all a lot to swallow, so bear with me while I nibble away at the pieces of this huge cheese of truth.

Perception is everything. What we see is critical in making clear decisions, but HOW we are seen is also important. In mating, finding a good job, getting a higher paid position, HOW we are seen is crucial.

This is where we learn to incorporate the SALESMAN inside us. Believe it or not, the SALESMAN is something that grows from your Inner RAT. The salesman inside is a driving force. It puts you in the driving seat of your life. More importantly, it supplants the passive bystander (watching from his seat at the back of the bus heading to nowhere in particular, other than towards the cliffs of oblivion) and installs an "action figure". This is the salesman in you, and it is a VERB! It is a active energy that bridges and connects the facts and dreams of your life, turning them into a reality.

If I succeed in creating an external perception that makes me attractive to others, then I have obtained a quite powerful talent.

A salesman's job is essentially based around adjusting the perception of a product by a prospective client. You have to refocus the client, in a way, that this new car is not just "A" car, it is "THE" car for them. Or this house is the right one for their family. Or buying this tool will mean you do your job better. It is the talent for offering an object outside of a person and encouraging them to bring it inside their life

And this cuts two ways. Consider: If I can change another's perception of external reality, this means that I can change MY perception of my internal reality. Seeing myself with fresh eyes means I can gain a new insight into my patterns. Once I can see the patterns, and the PINS that hold them, then I am in a position to remove them. Being unpinned means I move more freely. Surely this is obvious?

Here, then, is the secret core of this book: Perception. In Ratology One we learned that by seeing the obvious we can break up the patterns of habit and lies within us, and set us free from our state of "Should". When we get to seeing what our PINS are, and where they are located, we can slowly unfold our life experience outside of their influence.

For myself, it took many years to get past the "Pin" of the Catholic upbringing. Even when you know exactly what the problem is, it doesn't mean you grasp WHERE it is inside you, or HOW we can best deal with it. It takes time, and perception of our own nature. Eventually I came to see the pattern and resolve the issues. Only then was I able to finally leave the cave of my religious prison and walk free.

And I did this by not giving a Rat's any more.

I look back, and it all seems like some weird drug addiction. I kept trying to break free of the guilt habit, but I always went crawling back to it, helpless as a baby. But when the pin was removed, there was no guilt. There never was, I just imagined things to be that way. I walked from the cave of sorrows into the light of the day, and now that I see clearly, the shadow of the past can no longer haunt me.

In this book we look closer at the actual state of perceiving, and the "meccano set" of mind, emotions and expectations that we work with in order to create our individual platform of existence. Ideally, we create a place where we can sit and enjoy a higher view. But of course, we can also create a guillotine.

Our perception will determine what path we take towards our reality.

In the meantime, we must work though many invisible barriers, the internal shoulds, and the other various impediments to get back to the natural state of what the Hindu calls Retumbarra, or Wisdom of the Heart.

More on perception later in this book. For now we are going to look at the thought bubbles that get in the way of clear seeing.

The BOY in the BUBBLE

L et's talk bubbles. The Boy in the Bubble. It's more than a cliché you have heard, it is an absolute reality. For example: Your SKIN is really the surface of your physical bubble, it is your personal containment field. Every single cell in your body is a BUBBLE. Every piece of you is held by a containment "bubble" in some way.

We all live in an Emotional and Mental Bubble. We live inside groups of people, which form a "bubble of agreement" on how we 'should' behave, etc. What's more each "bubble" has a designated ruler of some sort, someone or something that makes decisions regarding the bubble.

We think that we are all thinking our own thoughts: But in truth, we do not. We believe we have our own emotions, but again, we do not. Every thought and feeling we have can be tracked back to ancestry and conditioning. Every single thought you believe, and emotion you feel, is simply a belief. And a BELIEF is nothing more than an opinion inflated into a reality. It's a bubble that can, and will, be burst at some point.

Does it make it wrong? No. Does it make it right? No. What it makes is a state of seperation from our natural self.

What exactly is a Bubble? It is a skin of separation, a line of differentiation between an inner and an outer reality. The Catholic Church defines "Sin" as the thing that causes separation between ourselves and God, and this is not so wrong as we might think. Most of us are living in a bubble that leaves us separate from an intimate connection with our own life. Our social beliefs, personal expectation, our fears, our world of imagination, these are all "bubbles of consciousness" that we live inside. They protect us, yet create a barrier between us and our natural state.

We are all here to burst some bubbles. It is called GROWING. Growth is living. If you still believe exactly in what you believed in 5 years ago, you are dnot growing. Genuine growth demands the bursting of bubbles.

There is a simple truth to remember here: *No ones reality is static!* No one is able to withstand the powerful finger of fate as it writes its way through our personal universe. Life is a sword that will either destroy or liberate us. And here we find the TRUE reality: *That which we choose is that which we become.*

The Mystic Rat Says: *In order to CHOOSE we must first learn how to leave the past. To leave our past, we need to learn how to burst our bubbles.* (And guess who the main agent of Bubble Bursting agent in your life will be? Your Inner RAT.) Let's look at how tese bubbles affects us.

The BUBBLE LENS

Imagine you are living inside a large Bubble. There are people in there with you, and they all seem pretty normal. These are all the people in agreement with your social norms. But what happens when you get a visitor? Anyone who approaches you from OUTSIDE your bubble will suffer a "lens effect" and by refraction of light will look distorted.

This is all part of what we call the "Bubble Consciousness". If you are in a white person bubble, the black man approaching will look like a demon. It's an optical illusion, but to the person inside, the very shape of your personal bubble will change the appearance of all who approach. Yet when someone approaches who SHARES your Bubble Beliefs, there is no distortion. All looks right and normal.

It is the red glasses versus green glasses experiment. Put people in a room wearing red and green sunglasses, and in short order all the people wearing green glasses will be with those wearing green, and likewise the red will associate with red. Why? Because when you have green glasses and look at a person wearing the same, you can see their eyes. If they are wearing red, all you see is black. The two colours oppose each other.

You literally cannot see "eye to eye" with the opposing colour glasses. Every single opinion we hold is like a piece of coloured glass we put before our eyes. When we meet people with similar opinions, we feel comfortable and in agreement. When different, we do not.

Remember how people saw the Hippie Movement in the 1960's? These long haired freaks who smoked drugs were all degenerate misfits who had no place in a decent society. How DARE they contradict the government and suggest that Vietnam was not a good place. What's more, how DARE they and those other civil rights creatures suggest that African Americans should have equal rights in White America.

And yet today, THAT view seems distorted and out of place.

This is because of the Minority/Majority Rule. Whatever the majority believes becomes the conforming norm. Regardless of common sense or reality saying otherwise, the belief of the majority is one huge bubble of thought that holds sway over the minority view.

Gay Men were once evil, but now YOU are if you say this. Rock and Roll was Devil Music, but NOW it is in the Music Hall of fame. Elvis Presley was once Satan Incarnate and once the only good civil activist was a dead one. etc. etc. etc.

The USA was once the epitome of a racist society. It was one of the last places in the Western World that condoned slavery, for one. Yet by the late 1970's leaders in the US were saying how evil South Africa was for apartheid. This, in effect, was a policy the US itself had only recently discarded in law, yet which it still practised in many and varied ways. It is not being two-faced so much as multi-faceted!

ALL our social mores rotate around the views of the majority. Being upright, going to church every Sunday, saying your prayers, and listening to the radio were once the central standards that all good Americans were expected to uphold. Now you look kind of weird if you do this.

Now flip forward to the present day, and those incredibly stiff and unhappy people are struggling to uphold the view, saying the young are foolish, and voting Republican. The majority see all those who still practice the prevailing conservative beliefs of the 1960's as Dinosaurs who have lived well past their use by date.

Now the Bubble did not burst. It just deflated because the majority moved elsewhere. But it is still there, and waiting for the cycle to turn. What happened was that a whole lot of people MIGRATED out of that consciousness and left it in the minority. Society and the people in it have simply hitch-hiked to a new bubble. There is only one guarantee in all of this, and this is that in 40 years what people believe NOW will seem archaic and foolish. This requires no degree of prophecy. It's just the way things are. Whatever belief you hold today will change tomorrow.

When the prevailing wind of opinion changes, when people put on different coloured sunglasses, all perception alters, and we live and breath in a different bubble.

Let's spend a moment and look at the many and varied types of stereotypical "bubbles" of consciousness that are out there.

Types Of Bubble Consciousness

There are many types of Bubbles, far too many to do justice to in a single chapter of a book. However, let's look at a few. You may well realise there are one or more of these at work inside yourself.

1. ***Self-Inflator:*** *This is the Bubble that inflates itself, based on the considered "truths" that are established in your stereotypes. This is generally based on the Logical Fallacy that you are the centre of the Universe. No matter how you disprove a belief held by a Self-Inflator, they will ALWAYS reply with words to the effect of, "Yes, but WE believe"*

2. ***Replicator:*** *This is the Bubble that reproduces itself in any form that seems to fit the circumstances. This is the People Pleaser who morphs into the shape of the current faith or belief that surrounds them. When proved wrong, the Replicator will just say "I was just thinking that myself" The desire is to be UNIFIED with a greater cause, but the result is simply a loss or self-respect and self-worth. Zelig, the movie, is a study in this consciousness.*

3. ***Impersonator:*** *This is the Manipulator's Bubble. Your OWN Bubble is mimicked to a degree that you feel you share the same space with the Impersonator. You trust them, let them in the door, and then they will rearrange the furniture, telling you that it looks so much better this way.*

4. ***The Impressionator:*** *This is where the Bubble you live in is used as a stamp. You "approve" persons of interest, and in effect act totally superior to all around you. You have a narcissistic tendency where you see yourself in those you approve, while in reality you are "swamping" other people and surrounding them with YOUR beliefs. You intend to make a lasting impression through affirmation. Paradoxically the Impressionator will invariably act BELOW you, and almost grovel at your feet singing your praises. They do this in order to control you, and for no other reason. It is how they stake territory and gain your trust. Your trust is the doorway to what they really want.*

5. ***The Attacker:*** *This is the blunt aggression projection. It is the Bubble maker who simply seeks to burst your beliefs in order to force upon you their own belief in their own particular faith. Most evangelical groups fall into this category. These people are all sweetness and kindness, but when you appear to break ranks, they show their fangs. Just try to leave them, and they will turn and seek to extinguish your resistance utterly in whatever way they can.*

6. ***The Blobber:*** *This person is the "Zelig" type that simply conform to whatever wind is blowing that moment. It is similar to the Replicator, only far more lazy. The Blobber will not change themselves to suit a situation: They allow the situation to do it to them. They practice a peculiar version of the Law of Non-Resistance, where they do not resist anything.*
   Yet at the same time they will hold to a stubborn belief in their own right to exist as a Blob. Curiously, this type is often highly creative and inventive, but too lazy to do much about it. If the Remote is out of reach, they will keep watching a TV program, even when they don't like it. Why? Meh, it will do.

7. ***The Conjurer:*** *This is a fascinating Bubble formation. It takes the reflected glory of other bubbles, and reshapes them like Balloon Animals. You have seen the people in fairs who do this? It is like a Bubble within a Bubble within a Bubble, and the practice is such that it catches your attention, and thus the person OWNS you. Conjurers only exist to OWN other bubbles by catching the attention and fascination of other bubble owners.*

8. ***The Stiff Resistor:*** *This Bubble is a controller, pure and simple. The person will often speak of Love, and Kindness, and how we must all get on peacefully, but in truth they will want to organise everything, control everyone and make sure their piece of the pie is the largest. Because most bubbles are malleable, the Stiff Resister has worked out that all they need to be is inflexible, and other people will conform to the shape of things as they project it.*

9. ***The Vibrancy:*** *These seem like wonderful pieces of sunlight that shine with a light unto themselves. They seek to enlighten all who they touch, but really they have an electric charge running through them and it NEEDS another's bubble to light up and switch on in order to feel alive. They are the ones spiking the punch and getting the girls naked in the pool during the party.*

10. ***The Tattler:*** *Nasty and frequently back stabbing, this is a Gossip Bubble that absorbs the negatives in their environment like most people absorb food. Unfortunately, they then regurgitate the piece\s of information they find all over other people's bubbles. This is a way of creating a binding identification, or a "tribe" where the person does not feel so isolated. The gossip is really a person who feels powerless, and they use the negatives they find to bind others to their cause. This makes them feel strong.*

11. ***The Hermit:*** *These are rare, the ones who are locked away deep inside, and unable to speak their truth. Their inner light has become drawn into the gravity of their own beliefs, and like a collapsing Black Hole, they drag others into their personal nothingness. This is the type who wants you to believe their conspiracy, and the sense of paranoia is strong in their conversations.*

12. ***The Priest:*** *One of the many archetypes that have taken on Biblical Bubble Proportions. This is the Bubble where you fear that "God is Watching" and so ALL your actions are on the basis that you might be getting judged by others who are watching you. You must always appear "good", and secretly you are judging all around you.*

13. ***The Fencer:*** *These are people who really believe they are Bubble Bursters. They see that they are doing you a favour by pointing out the weakness in your argument. These people are really arbitrary confiners who want to fence you into to THEIR view point.*

They can be fun to tease and play with, yet oddly, they find themselves getting very irate when they feel their own logic being hemmed in with reasoned argument. By "fencing" with you, using the cut and thrust of argument, these people are really trying to fence you in to THEIR beliefs.

Therefore their critique is not about improving YOU as they would suggest, but more about YOU "approving" THEM. Argument is their way to get approval. But life is more than a game of chess, and the secure person generally loses interest in these game players soon after meeting them.

14. ***The Enveloper:*** *This Bubble Personality seeks to swamp and swallow all around it. This is really a greed habit that disguises itself as a helper. The Enveloper will want to love you to your grave, service you to death, and generally encase you in a claustrophobic cocoon. Like an oyster envelops a grain of sand, the ideal is that by 'swallowing' someone, somehow life's grainy experiences will all turn into Pearls.*

    The problem is, the enveloper wants to OWN what it imagines it creates through its actions. This includes YOU, and people tend to rebel against this form of ownership. The Enveloper will often be heard saying how they have been "betrayed" by those it cared for and trusted. Walking away from them is seen as a betrayal.

15. ***The Dancer:*** *This Bubble type loves to experience the momentum of its own imagining. They imagine you are something great, someone to be worshipped, and will wrap themselves around this ideal or dream. Eventually you either become it, or reject the Dancer completely. The ideal is to "Become One with Everything" but the reality is that the Dancer wants YOU to become what IT imagines you are.*

Your Inner RAT sees through each and every bubble you generate, and through those that others generate and try to project upon you. Your RAT has a baseline knowledge of the REAL you, not the inflated version, or the "Bubble Self" that is cow-towing to social mores. The above list a small brace of the INDIVIDUAL Bubble types. It's just a short survey, but it covers the main varieties. However, there are many more.

The ones that matter in any given society are the Combined Bubbles. This is where individual Bubbles are merged into a greater force of nature, the GROUP. The obvious Bubble Groups are the religions, political parties, and general groups who share specific and particular beliefs such as the National Rifle Association, etc.

In each Bubble Group, there needs to be a GLUE, or more to the point, a detergent of sorts that forms the skin that creates the bubble. As an example: The Catholics talk about "Love Thy Neighbour", but the REAL skin that keeps the Catholic Bubble happening is guilt and shame. You can control any good Catholic with guilt and shame, and the structure of this Bubble is such that, without these elements, the religion as we know it would collapse and no longer exist.

This may seem an extreme statement to some people, but the basis of the Catholic Faith is a shared belief in Original Sin. In other words, you are BORN wrong. There is little in that church that is based on what Jesus said or did, and the fact is, Jesus was not part of the Christian Teaching.

This all came LATER, and Bubbles were created around the myth of the individual in order to construct the Mother Church. The external religion is really just a machine created for the express purpose of organising the group belief, and it does this most effectively by generating the guilt and shame that is the hallmark of the Catholic Bubble.

Think of each religion as a Bubble, and you are closer to the truth. They are very fragile, insubstantial belief structures that in many ways make little sense. Take the hatchet of common sense to most religions and you discover they are very fragile, and readily transparent to logic and reasoning.

Why would anyone want to worship a person DYING and SUFFERING on a CROSS? This makes no sense at all. But when you say he is dying for your sins (You know, that nasty Original Sin thing that the kind and loving God put on your shoulders because of Eve?) then it starts to seem reasonable. And why did we get this SIN stuff to begin with? Because of Eve! Go on, blame her and make her feel guilty. You know you want to.

So someone you never knew, who isn't even in the family photo album, and who you only read about in a book, has decided your fate. All because of a decision she made, which an all-knowing, all-loving God knew she would make, thus sending everyone to hell and damnation UNTIL he sends his son to die for these sins, the sins he knew would be created when he put that DAMN TREE in the garden. Does anyone really believes this? It just doesn't make any sense. However, when you go to church, and feel the very real love that people have, and feel the closeness between neighbours, you just don't see the need for logic.

Here is the truth. Logic and argument are good for breaking things into pieces, feeling and emotion are good for bringing people together. It really does not matter that the Garden of Eden in a myth, in fact, it works BECAUSE it is a fairy tale. It strikes the emotion and reaches into the heart, and thus many choose to still believe in the church, and accept the bubble in which they live, despite the fact that sin and guilt are the cost.

Logic prints the T-shirt as: "The Catholic Church: You too can go to Hell if you don't sign on to the Catholic Bubble, and accept the guilt of some hungry chick who ate an apple."

Emotion prints the T-shirt as: "God loves me so much that despite all my unworthiness, he will let me into heaven, but only if I go to church and pray. And here I will meet a lot of people who will become my new tribe, therefore I am SAFE here."

Sell the sizzle. The church marketing is fairly simple, and appeals to the group dynamic. Join and take our your insurance policy against the afterlife, as opposed to standing on your own reasoning, and hoping for the best. The Heisenberg Principle, the principle of uncertainty, drives people towards the group.

And it is in our DNA. We inwardly know that as a tribe we survive. We have friends, we have a sense of belonging. As the individual lone wolf, we were always at risk. We can not be awake all the time, and in sleep we are vulnerable. We need the group to survive. Same story, in death we are vulnerable if we are not members of the afterlife club.

I loved Steve Jobs humour, creating a logo directly challenging the Garden of Eden myth. Go on, bite (byte) that apple. Yet there are some who say that the current Apple Corporation is a denizen of the devil because of the knowledge to be plucked from the fruit of their electronics.

Getting the idea? This bubble of belief is based on EMOTON not common sense. It makes no sense, but it is believed regardless. To assert that one man and woman started the SIN thing is just an absurdist comedy. Don't forget they also started the entire human race and all the various shades and colours that come from it as well, which genetics say is impossible.

Logic says: An all-knowing all-wise God stuffs people into a garden where a Devil would tempt them with fruit that the all-knowing all-wise God KNEW they would eat. The only conclusion is that, because this plucking from the tree of knowledge was a given, God effectively condemned his only-begotten Son to death on a Cross: Dying for sins he knew would be created before he created Adam and Eve. This sort of logical fallacy would make a tree frog scratch his head and go "Huh?"

But it does not stop people from believing in their bubble.

However, when a person's inner Rat starts to wake up, it starts to pop bubbles. Why? It is just what it likes to do. But here is the thing to remember: You cannot collapse a bubble from the outside using logic and reasoning. It will only collapse from the INSIDE.

So how does your Rat collapse bubbles? It has FUN. It loves to play and enjoy life. When you start having more fun outside your bubble, you start to ask questions about why it is there. Then the logic of common sense, seeing the obvious, and acting in a way that makes your life better starts to take hold.

Then, "Pop!" goes the bubble.

Columbus Bursts the Bubble

One of the great bubble bursters of all time is Columbus. He burst through the fear of sailing off the edge of the earth, he burst through the binding that held himself to the old world, and literally discovered a new one. And when he got there, he realised what an absolute keg of dynamite he was sitting on.

How so? Well, apart from religious thinking spending 73 years or so discussing how many angels could dance on the head of a pin, in the West Indies he discovered an entirely new race. Now, current religious thought had everything sorted. After the flood, there was Noah, and his sons. They were the new Adam and Eve, and the starting point for the entire human race. The Negro, the Chinese, the European, all derived from the three sons of Noah. Simple, done and dusted.

But if he turned up mentioning a FORTH race he found, well, he was no fool. He knew that this sort of talk would be called blasphemy, and he, along with his entire crew, would most likely be put to death, rather than cause a huge argument to rage across Europe. People ask why on earth he took natives back with him to Europe? Tthe fact was, this was an act of self-preservation.

If he presented actual natives, a totally different race in the flesh to the European court, this could not be argued with. Columbus understood the nature of people and religion. He knew he had to present clear, unmitigated evidence that this forth race existed, or he would face the chopping block. This act, by the way, almost split the church, and indeed it DID burst their bubble.

The argument over this forth race went for decades. Finally the problem was SOLVED when it was officially decreed (by an Infallible Pope) that this FORTH Race were the ones punished by God in Sodom and Gomorrah. What happened is that God did this to the red skinned people to make sure they REALLY suffered. God plucked the worst of those sodomite offenders and threw them to the far end of the universe, where they had to live in the JUNGLE as SAVAGES. Surely this represented a fate worse than death.

VOILA! Problem solved! The Bubble is kept in tact, and that also meant you could do what you liked with those evil sodomite bastards.

No barrier to entry: raping, killing and pillaging to get whatever gold or slaves you wanted was perfectly fine. After all, God had already rejected them and sent them to the hell of South America. You were just finishing his work.

The Pope then turned his attention back to the far more important issues, such as how many Angels really could dance on the head of a pin. I wonder about this. As I write this, I think of Douglas Adams, and the discovery of the number that contained the meaning of life, the universe, and everything. I think the church came to 72 as the number of angels on the head of a pin.

I do hope you haven't missed the pun, on the subject of false beliefs and Pins?

Pins burst bubbles, or they would in an ideal world. Unfortunately, our inner pins are the ANCHOR point for bubbles to build themselves around. The inner Pin, such as guilt or shame, or the impresed outer Pins of "should" and "should not" become the focal point around which we wrap or fear-filled beliefs.

Even when presented with irrefutable evidence that the three race theory and Noah's sons was wrong, the bubble of belief reasserted itself with a concocted story that allowed the prevailing winds to keep blowing.

The point is that, regardless how well you collapse a bubble, it will seek to re-inflate itself. This is what the MIND does when you go to burst a Bubble. It concocts ANY SCENARIO that allows it to stay in shape. It is called Re-Inflation. Why? It is a habitual survival reflex. This is what your mind will do. It does not NEED a reason, despite our belief that the mind IS reason, it just needs a motivation. And resisting change is a good enough motivation for your mind to do what it will.

But no one believes the three sons of Noah theory today, do they? What collapsed the bubble was the Age of Reason. Science, common sense and practical observation, over time, reduces belief and shrinks the bubble. And here we come to the third major aspect of this book, the disciple of Spiritual Arithmetic.

SPIRITUAL ARITHMETIC:

Here we have a subject that is something you just do not see written about in any book, or talked about in any religion. It is based on the fact that we are an addition of elements, at work creating a whole.

I first saw this concept in my early 20's. I was very much at death's door from starvation and poor health. For various reasons, my body had turned against me, and every day could have been my last. In a fever I fell into a place which was a mechanical "chess world". Here every possible move you made had a mechanical series of combinations that created it, and very specific set of consequences as a result.

Now I see that is was no coincidence that RATOLOGY was started after I fell into another 6 day fever, some 30 years later, and lived the whole time back in this "Chess World". When I came to, I saw clearly the lies and distortions presented as truths in our society. I saw the inner working of how things "added up".

Spiritual Arithmetic was the term that came to me in my youth. It was an understanding of how the inner pieces add up, then form into a composite image. This is what becomes our reality. Life is not a random collection of atoms, it is a process of choice, attraction and acceptance that creates the form we know as self. We, as an individual, are BUILT: by belief, by circumstance, by society, and by parents.

We are CONSTRUCTS. Logically, when we understand the process of construction, we can remodel, rebuild, and alter every single aspect of our lives. But we have to be able to SEE IT first.

The Mystic Rat Says: *Seeing Truth, and Seeing Ourselves, these are the same things when you see them clearly.*

The first step in this process of "true seeing" (or VIDYA as the Vedantists call it) is something akin to learning your basic "three R's" in school. When learning our Spiritual Arithmetic we also have three R's:

1. *Reading the Situation,*
2. *Responding* to the Circumstances, and
3. *Rejecting the BS.*

All this is a process of learning our forth "R", our Spiritual *'Rithmetic*. Every school starts out with the basics, and in RATOLOGY one of these core principles is grasping the somewhat mechanics nature of how we humans act and interact. It is fairly easily grasped and, when you get the hang of it, it will surprise you how transparent people seem to be.

In Poker, it is a very important tool. When you master this unique way to add things up, you appear to get very lucky to other players. What really happens is that you develop a sensitivity for when people are faking it, hoping to make it, and when they have got it. It is all to do with assembling the information we are given.

In my early 20's I started to see the bits and pieces of attitude, emotion and mind that people would cobble together in order to form a persona that would make them "look good" to others. To really grasp this notion, we need to see that we, as the social animal, are essentially a "Meccano Set" of bits and pieces that are put together with various screws and bolts to make things work.

This "bits and pieces" consciousness is because of a basic separation within us, which generally occurred in the transformation between the child and the adult. We have a child and an adult inside us. These tend to be in conflict rather than any sense of harmony. When we learn to "add up" ourselves correctly, this conflict fades away.

The duality in our lives generally comes from a chasm between the adult state of social consciousness and our childlike experience. The naturalness of the child and the social consciousness are not easy creatures to get into the same corral. In a sense it is the question: How do we marry the natural self (child) to the trained (adult)?

It is a matter of just accepting this duality. *We are pieces and we are whole, all at the same time.* Our task is to get the pure Inner Being (The Child, for want of a better word) to work hand in hand with the Socialised Self (The Adult). We aim to make the Child wise to the world, and get the Adult to become free of its Shoulds.

Spiritual Arithmetic is a study that comes from an understanding that we, as the social being, are an assemblage of three different elements: pieces of truth, part truth and non-truth. These all surround a central point of true-self, the inner child where "True Seeing" or VIDYA lives. The premise is that when we grasp the mechanics we can learn to rearrange these disparate bits of our being into a jigsaw that makes sense.

First, we start to see life as a jigsaw, and second, we work towards creating a complete picture. Why bother? *If we can rearrange and restructure our internal position, we will be then able to alter and reform our external reality.*

In the beginning of this book we spoke about detachment. The only way to truly "get" our self is through DETACHMENT: Letting go of the external and internal influences that hold our attention and beliefs to fixed viewpoints. In other words, we need to learn to not give a Rat's about anything but our true, core issues.

Ratology: Who Gives a Rat's is offering a toolkit to collect, rearrange, and assemble your own fragmented self into a better version of you.

Imagine our true nature as a lake, high in the mountains. It's full of beauty, but life draws us out into the "real world" and parts of us flow into a river of experience. Yes, we are looking for a deeper connection to the sea, but the process of getting there is full of logjams and debris. This stops the inner beauty flowing to its natural destiny, the ocean. As we clear the blockages and allow the flow to occur, everything starts to work for us. It's just that simple.

The blockages are essentially whatever we think, feel and believe. These beliefs are PINNED in place by the experiences we have had, and this in turn creates the turmoil in our lives. The free flow we seek comes only when we know true needs, recognise our genuine emotions, and develop a two-way connection with life.

Opposed to this is our normal experience of life, which can be summed up as a sense of bump and grind: an abrasion with the outside world.

The falling water is a driving force, and it creates a charge, an energy. As we lump into things, rub shoulders with who-ever, we pick up a sort of static electricity. Just like electric current wound around steel creates a magnet, the charged bits of self in our aura create a "pull". This starts what we now generally call the Law of Attraction.

In a study conducted in England, many hundreds of people, equally divided between male and female, were put into plain sack-like clothing with all make-up, and identifying marks between social strata removed. People were told to walk up to another person, at random, and just "pick" someone they were attracted to. When you did, both person's left the room, and the experiment was over.

What happened, people from lower class picked lower class, people from broken families picked someone from a broken family. People with an alcoholic parent picked someone with an alcoholic parent. Without ANY external information, people still "matched up"

This is Spiritual Arithmetic at work. This is the little adding up machine inside us collecting invisible data, and making connections. What we are about in this section is starting a process where you become consciously aware of the internal abacus.

A primary thing to remember during this discussion: *Everything we experience, every opinion we hold, every belief we share, is all an "add on" to the natural child-like state.*

Opposing, and in general conflicting with, our natural state are the negatives processes of society and civilisation. These are the conforming forces, the things shape the raw child into a vessel that works in with and promotes the principles of the society it lives within.

This is how civilisation survives, by squashing the very mould-able child-self into the shapes that serves societies purpose.

Yes, it is negative, but the alternative of free, wild children running amok behind the wheel of a car is not something I want to meet in oncoming traffic. So it is necessary.

We have been conformed, and now we need to start re-forming. We need to see the elements that made us, break them down, and re-add them into a new person. But how do we resist the negative tide of society?

To start with, we need to erode our negative beliefs with a constant pouring of the water of clarity, mixed with an understanding of the moment, over our concerns. This separates us from our circumstances, and polarises our world into a state of possibility. We learn to expect the unexpected, and start looking for the surprise in life.

Please remember this concept: *We are seeking to move into a state of possibility. We are looking to live in anticipation of change.*

Expectancy, added to clarity and an appreciation of the moment adds to a new being, one that looks forward to every new challenge. In this state of mind, the past no longer owns us, the Pins no longer hold us, and the Bubbles no longer contain us.

Now, here we take a curious side road that may seem out of character with this book. When we do all of the above with basic kindness, it all works much better. Our entire existence is based on someone loving us. Does it not make sense that we would seek a loving connection with life?

Or would you prefer all the freedom in the world, yet be a dry rock sitting on a mountain, enjoying a great view, but having no sense of intimate connection with another? We are Mammals, we need other people, and we need to love and be loved.

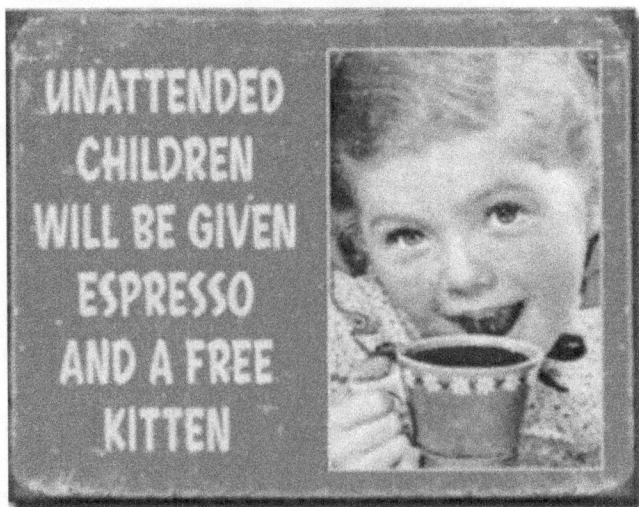

UNATTENDED CHILDREN WILL BE GIVEN ESPRESSO AND A FREE KITTEN

FIND the CORE STATE

O h HO!" you say. "What's this? The Rat is talking about LOVE! What nonsense is this! All we heard in the first book was learning to see clearly by seeing the obvious. Now we get to woolly concepts of kindness to all souls? What is this crock we are being fed?"

Well, remember that whatever you believe is probably wrong. There is one certainty: At our core we are mammals, and the one thing that differentiates mammals from dinosaurs is that we care for our young. This is LOVE. I know this sounds almost in opposition to the last book where I am talking about waking up your Inner Rat, but I have to take things one certain step at a time. Have patience and all will be revealed.

Stop and think about the obvious. We are MAMMALS. The Love of the Mother is what brings us from infancy to adulthood, and protects us from the wild. The most basic truth of our being is found in the blank canvas of a baby. You were loved then, and it is why you are alive. You were trusting, and dependant on life to support you. You didn't question your right to live, the natural state of being loved, nor your desire for needs. There was no complication, no socialisation, and no hurdles to jump internally. LOVE is what we were then, and this is our true centre.

You are still this simple Love. You just have all these little bits of "stuff" tagged onto you that prevents you from seeing and experiencing the Child State. When you wish to draw down the water of your life from the lake of your being, it is this same raw, natural state of pure emotion that you will draw on.

Everything about Spiritual Arithmetic is wrapped around the truth that we are Love, or at the very least, a being that responds most agreeably to the frequency of loving. Every aspect of understanding we gain from this study will come back again and again to this reality. More to the point, the things that attach themselves to this reality, the issues and tissues we deal with as humans, can be resolved by going back to, and removing the "pins" that attach the problems to our natural state. All of our concerns, all our attachments, are tagged onto us like the "Pin the Tail on the Donkey" game. We are here to learn to take off the blindfold .

Let's take a little look at the "hooks" that cause our natural Love State to become affected by human conditions. A classic example is Jealousy. Jealousy is simply LOVE (Natural pure emotion) tied up with the fear of LOSS. You get jealous because you think he/she is tripping off with someone else, and you imagine that you have a LOSS. So the equation runs: *Natural Love/Self + Fear of LOSS = Jealousy.*

Get it? Jealousy is the sum of two things inside us. The problem is now one of addition. Jealousy creates a sort of madness where all sorts of imagined scenarios get added to the mix. The Fear of Loss creates a new reality, and as our jealousy bounces around inside our relationship, it sets up anger, frustration and resentment. This reality becomes an absolute truth for the person. You become utterly deaf to anything but what the whispers your fear-drenched passions are saying to you.

You can discuss anything with a jealous person, EXCEPT the object of their jealousy. It's the red flag to the bull. They will charge at you, and confront you, and abuse you if you dare to suggest they are wrong in their jealous belief. All they will see is that their very existence is at stake. Any rationality that reveals the pattern of fears that drive their concerns will be absolutely invisible to them.

Please note: There will also be a Pin in place in the background, and the mixture of the fear, the need and the Pin creates pretty much every aberation of human behaviour that exists.

Yet if they could see the fear that was driving them, they could then pull back and think clearly. If we take away the fear of loss from a jealous person, the jealousy instantly departs. The Jealousy and the Pin that holds it in place just drops off. Get it? In almost every situation, the negative conditions we suffer are held in place by the magnetism of fear.

The Natural Self, the inner baby, has only two concerns: Not being loved, and not being fed. The UN-Natural Self is filled with many other concerns, all of which are ATTACHMENTS to the real and true state of being. By not giving a Rat's we learn to free ourselves from false states of being, and come closer to our natural self.

And there are layers within layers here. As an example: Jealousy is not ownership, yet ownership issues often get mixed up with the jealous conditioning. But someone who wants to OWN another is not jealous, they just want to control and confine the object of their desire, their pet. It is the fear of anarchy, not jealousy, that drives these types of human relationships. But ownership gets mixed up in the issue. The classic case here is the mother who will interfere in a newly married son's life. The mother isn't necessarily jealous of the wife of her son, but she wants to make sure the woman knows who owns him. The wife, however, may well be jealous of the mother.

In Book One I describe how I fell into a pattern of jealousy, and how it completely distorted my world view. When I moved out of the attachment, I never thought about the former object of my addiction again. I no longer needed to be jealous, because I no longer had a fear of loss controlling me.

When you raise yourself above the fear of loss and recognise that all things pass, then you discover the adage "plenty of fish in the sea". Now, when the fear is set aside, if things go wrong with love, (or whatever) rather than curse the one that got away, you get out the fishing rod and start angling for new adventures. However, if you remain inside the fear, it grows. You gain greater fear, more angst, and increased bitterness. This in turn attracts greater loss, which equals greater jealousy, which generates greater fear, which diminishes the natural ability to love. And the circle goes spiralling on downwards until you say, "Who gives a Rat's anyway!".

We all know the fisherman who continually thinks about the one that got away. A classic example came to me when a good friend of mine, Jim, went fishing with one of these "what got away" guys. My friend was taken to this old codgers favourite fishing hole, and though no great fisherman, Jim wants to keep the old guy amused so casts a line.

Now we need to understand the view from the old guys side of the picture. My friend has not spent years perfecting his cast, nor did he have any technique for making the bait look more alive. He had zero finesse or skill as a fisherman, yet he just throws a line in the general direction of the ocean, and hooks something!

But it is not just any sort of something! What he pulls out is a fish that looks plain weird. He was going to throw it back, but thought to ask the experienced fisherman what it was first. Well, the old guys eyes literally bulge, because Jim has just landed the most prized and rare fish a man could find in those waters: A Star Gazer. Now you would imagine the old guys would express surprise, delight, or perhaps joy? But no. Jim gets an almost opposite reaction.

The old guy is SO pissed off that he shouts, "An F…ing Star Gazer! All these years I try, and this useless prick gets one on his first cast. You have GOT to be joking!" He gets into a HUGE humph, and storms off down the beach, muttering how unfair and ridiculous it all is. How dare this whipper snapper come along, knowing absolutely nothing, and score the prize of a lifetime!

The old man's perception altered his reality. His self-loathing morphed into jealousy, his jealousy side stepped into anger, and his first hand experience of his highest positive became a negative.

My friend, Jimbo, called me up, and needed a lift home. It worked out well for me because the fish went straight into my oven for our mutual pleasure. I have to say, it tasted fabulous. But the question remains: Why the old guy see things the way he did?

Short answer: He had many options, but instead he chose jealousy. And here is the paradox: *The net result of his choice was that he missed out on tasting of the very prize he had always longed for.*

I mean, really, isn't the idea of catching a fish all about eating it? Who cares whose hook it lands on? Not so for the old guy. He had bound his identity up with his ability to fish, and when some whipper-snipper comes along and catches what he couldn't, it became a challenge to his sense of self, and with a lack of self worth running the show, he just exploded internally with the contradiction.

He added things up wrong, as a result. It is a simple equation: Fish + fisherman = supper. But his equation ran: Fish + Myself + Star Gazer = Important Person. What he got was: Fish + Jimbo + Star Gazer = "I am worthless". This then added to: Insecurity + Failure = Depression.

The Star Gazer was the Holy Grail of fish to land in that area, and its flavour was described as utterly unique and unlike any other fish. THIS was the point of catching one, but the old man got so caught up that the pursuit meant some sort of "proof" of himself as a better person. Thus he forgot the very reason WHY he wanted to catch a Star Gazer. He completely forgot that the idea was to be able to EAT it. And you know something? He died a bitter man, without ever eating a Star Gazer.

It could have so easily added up differently for him. If the man had simply been able to reconnect with the child-self, and delight in the moment of play with a friend, then everyone would have shared the love. But his fear ruled the day. I have to say, the reputation of the Star Gazer is exceedingly well deserved.

The Mystic Rat Says: *Our perception determines the way we deal with our reality, which in turn modifies our perception, which then alters our reality.*

When we are caught in a negative spiral, the first thing to do is stop, let go, and take a deep breath. Remember the child, remember the trust, and start again.

A Vicious Circle

*O*ne of the ultimate negative spirals seen in recent times has been the *Financial Crisis of 2008.* I predicted this in 2006 when I wrote the first draft of RATOLOGY, but there was no great psychic power required to do so, it was simple arithmetic. The numbers no longer added up to anything but disaster. Where and when were the only questions left unanswered

Spiritual Arithmetic is a curious beast. It has many equations, many possibilities and variations. Yet every time, each set of factors adds up or down to a very specific reality. This is the whole point: The elements at work within you add up to very specific realities. You are CREATING your next reality as you read this. Can you imagine that right now you are a Reality Creating Machine!

Your RAT is your Reality Attention Trigger. It wakes you up to what IS. It is the little bird that whispers in your ear. Your RAT is also what helps you understand the bits inside you that drive your bus. Your RAT is what awakens you to your POSSIBILITIES, and helps you rise above your Preconceptions.

Oddly enough, the RAT inside the financial machine was doing just this prior to the crash. All these people and firms were altering their preconceptions of how financial instruments could work, and expanding into the world or derivatives. Loans were no longer loans, but bundles of possibility all put together and packaged as a single instrument. But greed took over, and good ideas became vicious circles

This, dear people, is the Financial Crisis in a nutshell. Putting the 2008 crash into clear perspective, it was a simple case of gambling fever. I had a chat to one fellow who got out before the bubble burst. He had sold ONE of those sub prime mortgage roll-overs, and said it was a simple "package selling" expedition. ONE Hundred Million Dollar package of lousy mortgages got you 2.5%, or 2.5 Million Dollars. It was one weeks work. Of COURSE everyone was out there pushing this crap.

At the time, electronic money was everywhere. It littered the halls of commerce and had to get stuffed into whatever nooks and crannies it would fit into. If you managed to stuff some into some deal somewhere, you got paid a commission. I raised 1.3 million dollars from the banks for property development without ever showing them ONE earnings slip, or income statement.

But at least my loans were against actual property, stuff that had value. What the banks were investing Trillions of dollars into in was pure

PAPER. Honest to God, the dealings that these bankers got up to make Bernie Madoff look like a SAINT!

Raw, naked greed got dressed up in a three piece pin stripe suit, and talked about all sorts of rationales for its existence. It was all about astute marketing, leveraging dead weight, uploading financial instruments to a more liquid purpose, etc. And when it became obvious the losses were starting to happen, did any one pull back? Not a bit! The fever hit. Banks started going "All In" and bet the family jewels on ridiculous notions that were never going to hold up. Capitalism had caught its Star Gazer, and didn't know how to eat it.

It all started with the perception of what was possible, but in the financial world this possibility, via leverage, became a world of pain. Like the fisherman who never got to eat what he caught, because he was too busy trying to sell it, the banks eventually starved themselves on riches. These large conglomerates lived on the preconception that Trillion figure digits in the digital universe actually meant something in the physical.

Paper fortunes has the same value as paper currency that is not backed by a government. The world of Derivatives fell over, all the "money" vanished, and who paid? Not the bankers. The banking cartels are a viscous circle that feeds itself, and which ultimately feeds on you. But he who is without sin must cast the first stone. We all do this to some degree, we allow our passions control us, and remove our sanity. We need to break these patterns in order to see clearly.

Let's have a look at the Spiritual Arithmetic of this process, and see what ways we can find to break out of our own vicious circles of circumstance.

Circle of Anger

Dale Carnegie once asked a man how he was doing. *The man replies, "Oh, OK, under the circumstances."* Without missing a beat, he popped back with, *"Gee, what are you doing underneath those?"* People get caught in circles of despair, conflict, and any number of emotional and mental conditions. What is to stop you dropping them and walking away?

There are a number of things that keep us locked in place. Let's look at the "Circle of Anger", which creates a state of powerlessness. For brevity sake, here we will only look at the most basic emotions and principles that cause us to act in certain and particular ways. The point is that, no matter how negative the emotion, or how refined the sensibility might be, they all "add up" in one specific way or another. We are here to learn how to do this "adding up" via Spiritual Arithmetic, and we are learning this in order to gain the power reform any given aspect of our personal reality.

Have you noticed that people in charge of a situation rarely get angry? People in charge have the power to control events, and because of this, the perceived need for anger simply does not exist. The equation for anger is:

1. *LOVE + NEED + FEAR − POWER = ANGER. (Powerless, fearful people suffer Anger. This makes them more powerless, which makes them angrier.)*

Let me explain this, Anger is condition that comes about when we have a need but feel powerless to get it. It's like wanting a beautiful woman you know is not interested in you. It's frustrating. It weakens you and "adds up" in your head to a conclusion. Generally it convinces you that you're not good enough in some way.

Some years ago on the islands of Greece I was wandering about with this little German guy. He was good to travel with, but suddenly everything changed. His world was rocked by love! When we stopped at a hostel on Naxos he fell instantly in love with this beautiful creature. And she was stunning. I suggested he go up and hello, but he said she was a Princess, and would have no interest in a peasant like him.

I said again that he really should talk to her, because from where I sat it was obvious that she looked lonely. But he refused. Anyway, I chatted to her without any real problem, and we got on fine, to his dismay. But we were leaving that day and as I went out the door, I waved goodbye to the princess and thought no more about it.

Yet as fate would have it, two weeks later I am in the Athens museum with my German friend, and there she is again. I remembered her name, so went up and said hello.

She was astonished, "How did you remember my name?" she asked.

"Well, I would be completely stupid to forget the name of a beautiful woman, wouldn't I?" I sometimes forget my old fashioned habit of charm, and didn't even think about that response! She laughs, and I mean, really laughs. Clearly something is being released. Once more, my German friend is watching my apparent ease with chatting to his Goddess, and I feel him wishing it were himself.

At any rate, I ask how she went with her holiday, and THEN to my surprise she bursts into tears. It seems that she had fallen in love with a Greek man, and did not know what to do, as she had another boyfriend back home. I double checked, a Greek guy? The ones that say the utterly terrible chat up lines like, "You are a Godess who has stolen my heart."?

Yep, it had been one of those, and yep, she fell head over heels in love with him. Why? Because he oozed emotion all over her, and all she got in Germany was reason and practicality.

All the while my German friend stood there, jaw agape, finally realising what he had missed out on. That was when something snapped. When she left, he got very angry, and said "How can you do that? How can you so casually talk to her like that?"

This surprised me, because he was usually so well natured. I looked, and saw the circle of anger. He wasn't really angry with me, but himself. Yet he was in no mood for my clinical explanation of what his problem was. He knew, though, that fear had taken control of him. He really did like the girl, I am sure, and I am equally sure he needed affection, but his fear rationalised everything and prevented him from acting clearly. He made himself powerless to act because of his fear. As a result he got incredibly angry with himself. Of course, he blamed me for it.

Anger, like all passions and virtues, works in cycles. One thing leads to the next, and here is one of the Causation Chains that are part of the Circle of Anger: The Anger example I offer here is not isolated. Like all the spiritual equations, they do not exist in a vacuum or out there on their own, but are part of a causation series.

A good deal of Anger is based around a feeling of helplessness, but it breeds and mutates into other forms when other emotions are added to the mix. As an example: When fed by a sense of authority, natural Anger can breed to become Righteous Anger. When married to self-loathing, anger can turn into disgust. There are many children of Anger, and they are all part of a vicious circle.

Have you ever noticed that Angry people almost always try and control events? Angry people are seeking power, and have to dominate to get it. This creates a circle of Anger, and the series of additions goes like this:

2. *LOVE + (NEED + FEAR) – POWER = ANGER. (Powerless, needy people suffer Anger. This makes them more powerless, which makes them angrier.)*

3. *POWER + GREED = CONTROL MENTALITY. (Power conscious people who want MORE invariably look for control as a way to achieve this)*

4. *ANGER + CONTROL MENTALITY = RIGHTEOUS ANGER*

5. *RIGHTEOUS ANGER + SOCIAL INTERACTION = ISOLATION*

Does this make sense to you? It is hard to grasp at first, but it is pure logic and common sense when you do. The CIRCLE of Anger draws itself into other negative fears, and promulgates itself into an entirely new emotion. Thus the isolation you feel is really sourced in anger, yet no Psychiatrist one ever suspects this as being the cause of your depression, and gives you a pill to cure it.

Think about this: Let's say you saw the President of the US get angry on camera, stamping his feet about the Mexicans, for instance. You would say "He's lost it!" And he has. He has lost his grip on Power. What's more, he would have ruined his image and the voters would not put him back in next election. He indeed would become powerless. (please note: written 2006, well before Trump's bid for the Presidency)

And what happens if he doesn't learn, and correct his inner position? He writes a bitter memoir, believing himself truly correct in his anger, and it would further isolate him more from his peers.

So let's insert ACCEPTANCE into this mix, and see how it modifies the equation.

LOVE + (NEED + FEAR) + (NO POWER + ACCEPTANCE) = ANNOYANCE.

You may well find yourself UTTERLY ANNOYED by a situation you have no power over, but you are no longer emotionally weakened by it. This series of connecting dots doesn't paralyse you. You are just annoyed. Does this make sense?

Things like powerlessness, frustration, insecurity and unworthiness really add up to an equation that has no ACCEPTANCE in it. Typically, this is all part and parcel of the non-acceptance of your natural self as being good enough. Here's the secret: True power and confidence have little to do with what you hold, and everything to do with how you accept the flow of life around you. When you allow life to flow, you rarely get caught in negative passions.

Eric Clapton sang, "Let it Flow". It is an anthem to peace and harmony in our life. *Let it run, let it flow, let it blossom, let it grow.* This is the antithesis to the power consciousness, and yet there is enormous power in this way of being. Until you get this notion, most of what I am writing here will not make much sense to you.

The Paradox of Power is that it comes to those who do not need it. So many of our human relations are a power struggle: Yet can you tell me what the struggle is for? In Ratology: Way of the Un-Dammed we looked at the Romans, and how they used power and control to dominate the masses and create an empire. However the 'real' success in this area was Caesar, who despised the open use of power. He worked very hard to create consensus. Why? He knew State authority had to be accepted, willingly, by the people if in the government was to stand. He saw the need to Romanise Gaul, and Germany. Why? He knew bringing barbarians into the Roman sphere of influence was necessary for the long term well-being of Rome, but they needed to be civilised. Civilisation comes with agreement, rather than domination.

Julius Caesar had studied the Etruscan techniques for conquering an area, which was to provide such benefits to the people so that they WANTED to be led by them. The Etruscans would find useless land, and with their superior engineering skills they would drain swamps and make them useful. These unowned lands became their own, but someone had to farm them them. So they promised the local peasants free land to farm, as long as they handed 30% of the crop to the government. The government, in turn, provided military protection and safety from invasion.

This is how the North of Italy was founded and became prosperous, and in due course the Etruscans also created the City of Rome. This is part of the vision Caesar had, and he worked hard for negotiated settlements with the local Celt leaders. Of course, he also had a large army, and if you broke your agreement with him, or opposed him, your city would be burned to the ground and every citizen sold into slavery. So he had, and did use, power, but Caesar preferred agreements as the way to settle things.

In simple historical fact, Caesar was forced to come back to Rome in order to conquer the place, and become the dictator. If he did not, he would have been pilloried by the ruling establishment, who both feared and hated him. Yet the man who was so ruthless in battle was known for his clemency towards opponents, and respected for his incredible organisational skills.

But more than this, the people were with him. He was also loved by the "headcount", as the Roman lower classes were called, for his books and his amazing feats, such as turning the Coliseum into a lake when he was Tribune of the Plebs.

Caesar was a man who had innate spiritual power. He was known for his ability to plan, control and dominate, yet at the same time he could let things go without a second thought when needs be. He is an almost perfect image of the true ruler, a man who allowed power to run through him like water, dispensing it where necessary.

Opposing this are politicians we see today. Lying, greedy, self-interested: These are the terms that come to mind when most people think of their local members. As this is being written, Bernie Sanders is vying for the Presidency of the US, on a platform of inequity and promoting how government votes are being bought by business. I agree with him, and wish him well, but one man struggling to defeat the monstrous machine of avarice driving the US electoral system: It's a big ask.

So where does Spiritual Arithmetic come into all of this? The above describes standard patterns we all know and recognise. Too much greed, hatred and/or anger with too little love, and it adds up to an unpleasant ending for the most part.

Here is where it gets into Spiritual Algebra. In this example we need to take it as a given that an Angry person is always coming from a point of belief in personal powerlessness. When someone feels a sense of their worth and a genuine feeling of a power running through them, they are slow to anger. This is the real reason for containing our temper, it is a way of focussing and retaining our personal power. Imagine you have complete and total power in a situation; imagine you are always in a position to change things according to your will. You have no reason to feel angry, do you? You are a King who enjoys the fruits of power!

Like the King of the Ocean, you rule from below.

But all the personal power in the world will not change luck. In Poker, chips equate to power, yet no matter how much power you have, in the end the cards determine your fate. You cannot control the cards, you can only control yourself. Imagine if you got angry every time the cards dealt someone else a better hand? Bad Poker players invariably do this, good ones do not.

Every time you get angry because someone seems to have gotten a better deal, or you bought something that broke, or when the queue beside you is moving quicker than your own, you weaken your connection to the Child-Self. Over time, the cards will fall your way, we call it luck, but really it is patience.

When you get angry, it means you are demanding life provide, and life just doesn't work that way. You have to trust to luck. If you force life, it works for a bit, but eventually the tide turns and you get swamped. So, do you get really angry? If we "lose it" we lose our connection with our divine flow. We break the link with the child within, and we invariably do stupid things.

However, if we can remember our Spiritual Arithmetic, we can start to get a hold on the passions that want to control us. If we can observe our passions rise when the times of stress hit, we can get in charge of them. *No Rat survives if it cannot control its desire for Cheese.* Somewhere, someone will have laid out a rat trap, and if we do not control the desire to grab what we want, we will suffer.

Take someone who is angry and out of control. They have become disconnected from their source, and as a result cannot handle life's natural change. They live on the self-generated fury, which is a battery that lasts for but a limited time. What's more, the anger that flares in them is a wedge between people.

Subsequently, no one will respect them or give them acceptance (which is a form of power) so they want to just try to take it. We feel the only way to get power, yet retain all the negatives of our anger, is to push harder and harder until something breaks. This is a form of Greed being added to the mix, and the effect is to extinguish the LOVE aspect of the equation. (as follows)

POWER + ANGER + GREED (– LOVE) = ABSOLUTE CONTROL.

This equation describes the Nazi's, where the natural order is perverted, and control becomes the rule. True power is a natural flow but anger and arrogance stops this flow, and as a consequence we steal it from the world around us. Remember how, in Star Wars, the Sith Lord tells the acolyte to USE Anger to bring in the power? Well, it does. Anger steals energy from people and is a form of energy theft. If you are beside an incredibly angry person, you feel drained. Why? Because your energy has been stolen!

When you accept that Anger is a condition of powerlessness, you will see that natural power absolutely opposes it. So a powerless person, in order to gain power, draws in things to counteract the lack of power: Greed, or Vanity, etc.

Here is the thing: In order to effectively combine the negative energies, the quality of Love must be reduced, or removed. Anger, and specifically, righteous anger (the most destructive type of all) cannot coexist with a kind and charitable heart. If the negatives are successful, the person desires Absolute Control. In small things at first, like control over a dog, and then onto children, wives, etc. When a person gets a taste for it, the desire to control is worse far worse addiction than heroin.

These are the people that become the mini-Dictators. There are some people who, if they wrote a personals ad, would say: Miserable control freak seeking to dominate. No love to offer. Intimidation and sarcasm only. People with no self-esteem are encouraged to apply.

Any time you meet a person who is willing to hurt another to get what they want, then you can be assured that they have dislocated their consciousness away from the Baby Self and put their awareness (or lack of it) into their Passionate State. We ALL do it to some degree. Most have experienced a relationship where someone hurt someone they purportedly were in love with, in order to get what they want.

The cure is simple. If you want to be happy, you just need to bring the LOVE part back into the equation. And a very easy way to do this is to ask the three question: Is what you are saying, intending or doing A: Necessary: B: True and C: Kind.

The Bible puts it as: *Do unto others as you would have them do unto you.* Sounds good, but if you are a control freak, you read those words as: "Control others before they get control over you."

Spiritual Arithmetic approaches things logically and sensibly. It follows certain and specific paths that describes the bones of every situation perfectly. Let's look at a few examples of how Spiritual Arithmetic adds up:

- *CONTROL MOTIVATION + GREED = POWER HUNGER.*
- *NEED (– POWER) + ANGER = LOVE HUNGER*
- *LOVE + FEAR of LOSS = JEALOUSY*
- *LOVE + VANITY = ATTACHEMENT*

That last one often surprises people, and this is the real message behind the Myth of Narcissus. Essentially we have very basic elements at work. We have Love and we have Fear as the base lines. Then we have five basic Passions and five corresponding Virtues. That's just 12 elements all up. Lets take a look at them.

Obviously, Love and Fear are self-evident. We are either moving forward with love, or retreating into fear. The essential Passions are as follows:

1. *Anger*
2. *Lust*
3. *Vanity*
4. *Greed*
5. *Attachment*

The essential Virtues that counter these are:

1. *Acceptance*
2. *Compassion*
3. *Humility*
4. *Service*
5. *Surrender*

When you have a genuine acceptance of Life, it is impossible to get angry. If you have a deep compassion for others, it is impossible to suffer Lust. When your sense of Humility overrides your need to impress, vanity departs. When your desire for Service is greater than your personal needs, there is no room for Greed in your heart. And when Surrender is a natural choice for you, you are then willing and able to let go of the past, thus your Attachment to objects, beliefs and notions dissolves.

The two main driving forces in the Human Psyche are Hunger and Sex. Sex is obvious, it is the desire to connect and be accepted by another. But Hunger takes on many forms and shades, and even the ascetic who starves himself every day will suffer from it. The hunger for perfection, the hunger for the impossible dream, etc.

The HUNGER aspect is the real driving force of most of our passions and virtues. It will drive you to find completion of the elements of desire that are inside you. Now the Buddha said desire is the source of pain, and the only cure is the removal of desire. He is probably right, but I just can't get past the simple fact that if you have a desire to not suffer pain, this is still a desire. How can you desire not to have desire?

Ratology, on the other hand, states that we need to train our desires, and then use them to target what we want to do in order to achieve something useful.

The Beatles sang: *All you need is Love*. True, but we also need the other aspects of ourself, otherwise we would be sitting just another a fat pumpkin baby waiting for mummy to feed you. Getting in touch with your Baby State is good, but the point in growing up is being able to DO things.

Anger is an expression of a loss of power, but there are lots of other passions and needs and wants and beliefs that create patterns of activity within us. For example: What exactly is Greed?

Well, the textbook explanation is simply that if you want something too much it becomes greed. The reason you want something is an aspect of LOVE, but when we want things "too much", this brings up a Fear of Loss. Your imagination starts looking at what it would be like without the object of desire. This creates a NEED to get that thing, but once you got it, then you find a new desire, the need to PROTECT. These are all primitive, basic emotional responses, but when the desire to Protect is threatened, we find a new choice. Let go, or get more? Most people are now attached, so they want more. Thus GREED is created. If you want to protect, but do not have the power to do so, the energy ends up as ANGER. So:

1. LOVE + NEED + Fear of LOSS = GREED. Whereas:
2. LOVE + NEED – POWER = ANGER.

We can read "LOVE" as the true and natural Baby State, or in other words the real YOU. Looking further at these equations, aspects such as Protection, Attainment and Achievement are all aspects of POWER. They are the YANG or Masculine qualities. The LOVE aspect is the Drawing, attracting, welcoming energy, and is the Feminine or YIN energy. Looked at in this way, what we are really painting is a vast and complex "Yin-Yang" symbol inside ourselves.

However, consider this! There is a striking area of Spiritual Arithmetic that has NO downside. As an example: Take the GREED away from LOVE and it still equals LOVE. In fact, it means MORE love in a sense. Love and Fear are the fixed points, and as such, Love and Fear are pure expressions of being.

Spiritual Arithmetic has an innately positive aspect in that it only ever adds up from a base point of LOVE. The State of the Baby, the Love State is the Numero Uno. This is the Number One pivot point in all of this.

It is a curious thing that so many spiritual leaders come from an orphan background. The fact the maternal love was NOT there seems to be an even greater magnet to finding a state of true love.

Love incorporates a state of being that is very powerful. It is what everyone wants. In the purest sense, Love and Power are the same thing in as much as they both emerge as aspect of divinity. Yet, just as we have the Yin-Yang balance, (in that both of the positive/negative elements occur in greater or lesser degrees in each individual) we have a Love/Fear balance. And to tip this balance we need power.

You might imagine your RAT would be quite unconcerned with notions of Love, and far more interested in the Power side of things. In a sense it IS. Yet we are not talking about a Love OF something. We are talking about the Immanent State of BEING. This is a Core Energy, the real LOVE VIBE that drives everything. The paradox is that it is ALSO the Power within us.

Spiritual Arithmetic is a book unto itself, and for most, it is a fairly confusing thing at first. To really 'get it" you need to understand the base motivations that drive others, and yourself, but in the meantime, just accept that your anger, or frustration, or whatever, is really just an addition of a variety of aspects within yourself. Acceptance short circuits just about every negative, and allows you to find a balance.

Most people have their connection to the "Love-Power" matrix inside them. For the most part, our natural Yin-Yang balance is disturbed by the lies and distortions in the fabric of our personal reality. So let's look at the "add ons" in a way that is a little easier to spot, the tags we collected during our upbringing.

The TAGS that CONTROL US

Let's look at the "Add Ons": The Tags that are the cause, the doorway, for the external influences that flow into our lives. These are areas that are like open portals on a ship, and they flood our being with external energy every time a storm hits us.

The "Tags" are our Passions. Anger, Vanity, Greed, Lust and Attachment are the main ones, but there are many more that get birthed from the interaction of these "Parent Passions" with our inner nature.

Anger is possibly THE overriding negative emotion in the Western World. Anger comes from a sense of being powerless to get what you want. Take the WANT out of any object of desire subject, and the Anger of not having it goes. It is just that simple, because without the WANT you don't need the Power to get it. You can ALLOW it to occur rather than seeking make it happen, in other words.

If you are shooting hoops and you no longer WANT the ball to go into the hoop, you are not angry when you miss it. You can still WISH for it to go into the hoop, and the WISH will cause you to practice until you succeed, but you will no longer suffer frustration when you miss it. Western Culture calls it wishful thinking!

Which begs the question, can we have ambition without pain? Can we want things WITHOUT stirring up Anger? Of course we can. We simply need to understand that GREED is really LOVE plus a NEED that gets twisted up with a Fear of LOSS. (This Fear of Loss masks itself as many things, but an overtly competitive nature twists it up, and often it is sourced in a fear of competition) So we can approach things two ways. We can GIVE more, which reverses the Fear of Loss, or we can learn to compete without competing. Either can be practised, or both. The result is we will have less Greed, and therefore less Anger.

A fascinating example we have all seen play out in recent times is the Armstrong doping scandal. Here is a man who clearly was one of the greatest cyclists the world has ever seen, yet he was afraid of fair competition. His driving need to win was the excuse he gave himself, but really, he was scared of losing. His racing career famously emerged from his fight for life and the defeat of the cancer that was eating him. This of course gave him the oxygen boosting drugs that enhanced his riding ability, and gave him the message that drugs were the secret to success.

But if drugs are so bad for you, why do the people use them? What is "bad" is the unfair advantage,. The fact that Armstrong so clearly embraced this shows you how much he had shut down as a human being.

He thought he was in charge, in control, directing the show. Yet in truth, his fear of competition drove him to excesses, the like of which the world has rarely seen. It made him incredibly greedy, and utterly blinded him to the obvious, which is that one day it would be discovered. And even when discovered, he denied it.

Here's a few more curious equations in the Armstrong scenario:

Love + (Need + Fear of Competition) = Greed.

(Fear of Competition is a hidden Fear of Loss or Losing)

Subsequent to this: Love – Power (+ Greed) = Chronic Anger

Armstrong had no real power in this story. He controlled his people, he had doctors sorted to supply the drugs, he had chemists on side, but he had no actual power. If he was found out, he was cast out. This adds to the fear of loss. It all added up to a chronic state of Anger, one that completely possessed his heart and mind. Please note the addition of the CHRONIC condition. Conditions that are stuck and fixed in a person are usually those where several passions have gotten locked up.

Armstrong also lusted for success. Let's face it, winning so many Tour De France competitions, possibly the most gruelling experience in the known world you could willing subject yourself to, was no natural desire. Armstrong set aside all compassion, he rejected his natural self, and embraced a routine solely focussed on success.

LOVE + NEED - COMPASSION = LUST: Lust is a lack of Compassion added to a normal extension of the Baby Self (Love plus Need is a normal extension). All the above ferments into a toxic, heady brew that completely overtakes the senses. All these driving forces combined in a fierce, burning desire until the fire of his passion became utterly selfish and totally disrespectful of another's rights.

But the point is not Armstrong: Are we starting to see that all the things we think and feel have a basis in human mathematics? Can we see that when we identify the elements that drive our actions, we are in a position to change the elements at work, that change the course of our actions?

Let's stop and have a quick look at the basic Passions that drive us.

When natural caring and the need for affection devolves into a carelessness and lack of compassion for another's feelings, it becomes Lust. Lust is a grasping form of affection that has the effect of making you deaf and blind to the Love you really need. It also turns away the natural love another may have felt for you. The result is that you end up just wanting more. It makes the consciousness pig-like. But even so, if you take any pig, love it, care for it and put it in clean surroundings, then it can change. This is to say: Teach a pig to use the toilet, and it will generally stop shitting over everything.

I use this analogy for a reason: Lust, curiously enough, is one of the main causes for people SHOULDING on other people. It is a lust for power that creates this condition, and when you meet a "shoulder" you are almost certainly meeting a sexually frustrated Soul. Sex them, and watch the shoulds vanish. Then will you see the wild, lustful, mad person emerge.

Vanity is Love, plus a need for Affection, plus a Fear you are not good enough. This causes the over-compensation of the NATURAL sense of Identity, and people often act out with a sense of superiority. Vanity is a state of false self-esteem, regardless as to how it expresses itself. (low or high can equally create a vanity issue) It is a complicated whirlpool that pretty much will cost you everything worthwhile in your life.

Patience is the best cure for Vanity. Take your time before speaking. Take your time and inspect your thinking, and give others more space to be themselves, and you will find that your Vanity quotient will drop off immediately.

ATTACHMENT is the most insidious of all the passions, because it lurks in many hidden ways. It is the corner stone to all the other passions. The true child of attachment is Procrastination. Have you left things incomplete, or undone? Then you are suffering attachment. It is the fear of progress that is putting the spanner into the machinery of your life. Attachment is the original Luddite.

Anger is everywhere. People are frustrated and angry, in part because we are all disconnected with the land. Humans are not designed for cities. Take any angry person, and put them beside the sea, with a coconut, a pretty girl, and some good music, and see how angry they seem then.

UNDERSTANDING PASSION

We all know vices are a passion. Most are taught that if we practice the Virtues we will cure ourselves of our Vice. This is completely false, yet so typical of the Western mindset. It is another variation of the same centrist thinking that once put Earth at the centre of the universe.

If you have a passion that is out of control, the generally accepted wisdom is that what you need is a control factor, a VIRTUE, to dominate it. In point of fact, we have set up an entire process, called religion and ethics, based on a solitary notion that we can contain desire and control our own emotions!

It is a remarkable thing, religion. We pay money to the richest institutions in the world (religions far outrank industry for wealth) and we bow low to some imagined being with the back ground fear that "God is Watching". Every Church has a "God is Watching", and the reason is simple: It instils FEAR. By putting fear into the mix of emotions people experience, they become more controllable.

In the modern world, many have left the church, but the residue of their upbringing lingers on. Most substituted religion with political beliefs, social values, new age concepts, or good old fashioned beer. Beer is probably the most honest choice.

Regardless, we conform to the standards of behaviour prescribed to us by whatever authority we recognise. Yet our religious past has bled into the social present. Tell me when rock stars and football heroes were required to be role models for good behaviour, and there we will find the cross over point where religion jumped into the political correctness.

This is not to say that our religions and their virtues are bad, but like political correctness, they deny the REAL truth: Our Passions are not so evil, and our Virtues are not so saintlike.

Virtues can become a trap just as surely as any Passion. An example: We believe consideration of others is a Virtue. It is, but consideration for others added to a lack of self-worth can quite easily add up to a martyr complex. This then becomes a passion, hidden as a virtue, which turns into a habit, one that stops you living your own life.

We are taught that it is better to give than receive, which is to counter the evil of selfishness. But if you cannot receive love from another, you cannot form a genuine relationship with them. Therefore you cannot really give UNLESS you can receive. Get it? Virtues are but one side of the coin, and we need both sides to spend it. We need to find the edge that connects our virtues and our passions if we are to make any of them work.

Let's look at the classic Virtues. (from Wikipedia) Please note we include the Ancient Greek text for these, to demonstrate that these things are OLD conditions. We have been trying to control our Passions for a long, long time.

The four classic Western cardinal virtues are:

- temperance : σωφροσύνη (sōphrosynē)
- prudence   : φρόνησις (phronēsis)
- fortitude   : ἀνδρεία (andreia)
- justice   : δικαιοσύνη (dikaiosynē)

Now Temperance is seen by many as the "cure" for Anger but really it just covers it over and smothers it slowly. The fire is calmed, but the carbon that fuels it remains. The embers linger, waiting to spark into life.

It would appear to do the job, but here is the part almost all fail to grasp. All our Emotions have their OWN reality, and their OWN survival instinct. The smothering of your Passion ignites ITS survival mechanism. It goes quiet, then births a different passion in order to survive. You might think that with all the medical research, and all the money spent, we would have the psychology of denial and repression pretty much understood in our society. There are some that do, but inside most of the religious and medical institutions on the planet, any sort of real life comprehension of what control and smothering do to the psyche is pretty much non-existent.

The understanding of how Passions work is the cause of the Medusa Myth. Cut off its head and it only provides another one. But REFLECT Medusa upon itself, and you solve the problem. This is one of the reasons the Psychologist will seem to say nothing, and allow you to unwind. The idea is to give you room to reflect, and this is why he/she often repeats a portion of a phrase you say. Reflection is a tool, but in practice this tool has become narcissistic. Very few people are going anywhere useful within the current regime of psychiatry, and the good doctors know it.

Temperance, as an ideal, wants to hold up a mirror to your desires and wants. It is not meant to to repress, but to enlighten. Temperance works when it gives you the space to see things more clearly. The virtue of itself is not wrong, but the application of how it used often distorts and inhibits the individual. Temperance is sold as a control factor, not as a mirror to see yourself more clearly.

Rather than reflect on, most will argue with their desires, and try to control them. Again, the Medusa Principle applies, and the desires will breed. Your PASSIONS will have babies of a sort. For Example: Your

ANGER, when smothered or argued with, will give birth to GOSSIP. Deny yourself your LUST and it will compress and shift sideways into slothful behaviour, or it mutates and turns into sexual deviancy.

All we are doing when applying virtue as a cure for passion is to cause the passion to shape-shift. It wants to live, and will do anything it can to continue. But understand your lust, and you can educate it.

Left alone the Passions do not compress and shape-shift within us. (thus re-expressing themselves in new forms like Medusa's head) Once we ACCEPT our animal nature, the arguments stop and it becomes easier for us to express our natural self. It is best to allow your Passions to co-exist with you as, in the end, denial, control and repression only cause far worse expressions of negative values.

Prudence is supposed to balance Vanity, but again, when this passion is smothered by Prudence it will morph. Most often it will generate children with a passive aggressive demeanour. You will LOOK and ACT sweet and kind, but underneath the dragon burns hot. We have many of this type in society today. The shape-shift happens in many ways. As a small example: Vanity shifts to Anger in order to get around the repressed expression of self. Thus we find issues with road rage, etc. (How DARE he move in front and cut me off like that!)

Fortitude is a noble trait, and if used on its own is a wonderful thing. But it is generally used to cover up SLOTH, and so Sloth creates children called "Distraction" and there are many of these: Drugs, pointless conversations, etc. Sexual perversion generally comes from Sloth, not Lust as you might imagine.

Justice is seen as a counter for GREED. But we all know what REALLY happens in the justice system. It has become one of the ultimate Greed machines. Greed is smarter than most of the Passions because it is a calculating, active force that only seeks gratification. Feeling *morally* superior is the ULTIMATE gratification.

One of my favourite examples of how passions hide in us comes from Somerset Maugham, where he portrayed what he called the Forth Temptation of Christ.

"Do you remember how Jesus was led into the wilderness and fasted forty days? Then, when he was a-hungered, the devil came to him and said: If thou be the son of God, command these stones be made bread. But Jesus resisted the temptation.

Then the devil set him on a pinnacle of the temple and said to him: If thou be the son of God, cast thyself down. For angels had charge of him and would bear him up. But again Jesus resisted.

Then the devil took him into a high mountain and showed him the

kingdoms of the world and said that he would give them to him if he would
fall down and worship him. But Jesus said: Get thee hence, Satan.

The devil was sly and he came to Jesus once more and said: If thou wilt
accept shame and disgrace, scourging, a crown of thorns and death on the
cross, thou shalt save the human race, for greater love hath no man than
this, that a man lay down his life for his friends. Jesus fell.

The devil laughed till his sides ached, for he knew the evil men would
commit in the name of their redeemer."

Jesus thus falls for the Forth Temptation.

Virtues are good in principle, but when used to counter the Passions
they usually end up as fuel for propagating them. Despite the religious
rhetoric, your passions love the virtues. Nobility is so often a disguise for
arrogance. Respect is so often hiding debauchery. Frugality is but a step
away from miserliness.

Ethics are seen as the bastion against the evil tide of satanic influence.
Having Ethics means you stand on a pillar of strength, but so often the
ethical become the pillar itself. As the emotional heart dries out, the
ethical man stiffens and watches as his childlike joy of life passes him by.
Slowly their wooden gestures turn to stone.

Out west in Australia there are places where wood will fossilize within
30 years. The area is rich in silicates, and the heat and dryness of the
climate will turn the area in contact with the ground into an opalized
stone, while the rest stays as wood. The pillars of our society are so often
just this: Wooden exteriors with a stone cold heart.

Let it go. Let it out.
Let it all unravel.
Let it free and it can be
A path on which to travel

NEGOTIATING VIRTUE and VICE

There was a sign on a service station when I was a child. It once read "Service is Our Business", but the "Ser" had broken off, and now it said "vice is Our Business". Of course, the business world in the current climate has become the hotbed of Vice. The world financial crisis, as we know, was an act of greed on a grand scale.

But the real message from this sign was very profound. If you want to get past your Vice, be of SERVICE in some way. Be USEFUL in some way, and the energy from your internal negatives will morph into a positive force.

This is the message: *You cannot beat your negatives with positives, or vice versa. No one wins in an argument between vice and virtue.* All you can do is to find something you prefer to do. Affirmative Action towards a better life is your best solution to any and all problems that besiege you.

Habits? You don't like your present habits? Then get moving in the direction you prefer to go. Your habits will let YOU go when the environment they like to live in changes. Someone is a smoker not because they stuff a cigarette in their mouth, but because they have a habit of smoking. However, when you get fit, get oxygenated and get moving we find the desire to smoke lessens. Why? Because smoking does not fit well in your new environment. Like any argument between Vice and Virtue, oppose anything and it grows stronger. But go in a new direction, and find something you PREFER to smoking, and you leave the habit behind.

It is like when you move to a new fancy place and your grunge relatives think it is too high brow for them, so they stay away.

Consider your emotions like those relatives. You have some that are good to have around, and others better off outside the door. How do you get rid of them? The trick is MOVING your CONSCIOUSNESS to a place where that particular emotion does not like to go. I make it sound easy, and it is, but at the same time, it is so damn hard. Why? We get very attached to where we are, emotionally and mentally. And we are basically too lazy to want to do anything about, which is another sort of attachment.

Attachment is the big one. It is the most powerful of all our passions, because it is the most invisible and untouchable. It hides in many disguises, often dressing up as carelessness, habitual procrastination, and dreaming.

Attachment is the most insidious of the Passions. You can conquer them all, but this last one will always remain. I know, because despite all my rationales and virtues I still have too much crap laying around.

Attachment is Love plus the Love of Love, usually transferred into the love of some "thing". Attachment is the hardest to get around but it can be done in the simplest of ways, by tricking it. You simply hold onto something greater inside yourself. Finding the greater path sets you free, but of course, you have to get past your slothful attachment to the present in order to get up and go look for it.

The person leaving for overseas is a good example. The relatives that stay behind are all left holding onto memories, while the one that is moving forward is set free to experience. John Denver wrote "Leaving on a Jetplane". It's a sad song about attachment disguised as love. "Oh babe I hate to go" the song says. Then why leave? The cure for all forms of attachment is simple: Start living in the NOW.

If you are really leaving on a jet plane, and living in the moment, you are up and away on a new adventure, not singing about everything you have left behind.

So too, all our Vices and Virtues can be negotiated using this simple, time honoured technique: Live in the NOW and have a sense of adventure. Living for the MOMENT, containing our life and love in the NOW, changes everything. All Virtues align to a useful purpose, and all Vices flip internally and help your focus by providing balance.

So now we get to the best secret in RATOLOGY, how to find the Big Cheese. This is the secret self the Rat within yearns to find.

FINDING the BIG CHEESE

Everyone wants the biggest and best things. The biggest house, the best car, the prettiest partner, the most money. Fame, success, and happiness can all be yours, and if you are to believe the new age preachers, it all works according to the Law of Attraction.

We all heard about this in "The Secret", and it was an interesting enough read. But really, at it's core it is saying that God is an eternally free to withdraw from ATM. The book spoke about the Law of Attraction, and how you can magnetise yourself to the blessings of life, etc. And while this is true, it is also false. Really, the book is saying that life is just some mechanical process designed to give you whatever you ask for.

Apparently God WANTS you to have everything you can imagine. One thing that is never mention, however, is the word "Payment".

The message of the book was about USING your desires to get what you want. In this regard, it is in accord with Ratology, but otherwise, it's a good read that fails to understand the underlying Law of Cause and Effect. Nor does it show you how to find the Big Cheese, the hearts true desire. It is about getting what you WANT, not waking up to what you ARE.

So what if you get what you want? What we WANT, is rarely what we need. We NEED Freedom, Clarity and Purpose. This is the way that leads to awareness, internal power and a deep sense of charity towards all of life, but this is something quite different from what the book "The Secret" offers. We want many things, and in all honesty, any bunny can manifest what they want. But what we NEED is a state of being where our LIFE buys us more LIFE.

And this does indeed come about through the Law of Attraction, but not as it is promulgated by the New Age Eclectics. Most of the N.A.E. Sayers (do you like the pun?) tell you that God is some sort of limitless ATM, one you take whatever you want from, as long as you have the password. (your mantra, etc.) The whole "God as ATM" does work for a while, but everything needs to come into balance, and there is a cost for every withdrawal. Ratology tells us there is a simpler, more refined way to grasp the nettle of life, and come out the better for it. Seeing the obvious.

If we persist in looking for the obvious we train our minds and hearts to see what IS. When we strip the varnish from our thoughts, and we learn to see what IS, it leaves us in an extraordinary place. *We come to live in a state of permanent arrival within the destination point of our Being.*

It will take a while for the above sentence to sink in, but it is another way of saying we live as participants in life, and within the moment.

Now I will tell you the real secret, the thing that answers the question of Vice versus Virtue, Idealism versus Hedonism, and all the natural arguments of morality versus wild, native abandon, etc. An understanding of this next statement will release you from all inner tension.

The secret is something that may not be immediately transpartent to you: *The only REAL emotions we can have are those that assist with our survival.* These are the emotions that have a purpose inbuilt into them. We can also verse this as a vice versa.

The Mystic Rat Says: ***Any emotion that does not help us to survive, is inherently false. It is hiding a lie.***

It is just this simple. Now it is also important to understand that ALL the emotions contain, to a greater or lesser degree, false beliefs. All our emotions are constructs of various elements based around one single and simple energy, the dynamic of LOVE: The Child Self. The question of what an emotion really is comes down to us understanding the Spiritual Arithmetic of: *Love plus WHAT?* First we figure out the "what" and then we can sort out "what" this equals.

We are all a study of Spiritual Arithmetic trying to add down our complication, seeking to solve our ONE self, the state where we are singular, not plural. We are a chemistry of elements seeking to find a solution. We are a LOVE looking for an echo we can make real. And this book is your course, your pathway, to this.

We are a Love, our emotions are an echo of this love, and by understanding these, we become real. The understanding of this simple truth changed me forever. From this came an understanding of beingness, and a deeper and clearer grasp on a great principle of life emerged. We are mammals with emotion, and this runs through every culture, every family, and all people who walk the face of Planet Earth. And the true purpose of our emotions is to help us survive

The effects of emotion on us is a very real thing. They affect us physically, with the endocrine system, the adrenals, the whole body being governed to some extent by our emotional state. But emotions ALSO affect and create our BELIEFS. Our beliefs affect our body chemistry, our relationships, our thinking, and everything in our life, just like our emotions. But they can be completely wrong. The difference between our natural emotions and a state of belief is that the pure state is not subject to an arithmetic more complex than the addition of "Love plus what?".

When we see the elements involved in a belief, and break this down to core elements, we see the "what". False emotion is always a series of additions. As an example: *Child State + fear + upbringing + frustration = Panic Attack.* Or the upbringing factor might create Narcissism, etc.

Pure emotion, the emotions of survival, and singular in nature. They are not a gestalt of parental or social influence, they are core elements within the child self.

This can be difficult to understand. But consider: Coca Cola in a bottle will look like it has a specific shape, but pour it into a glass, and everything changes. Yet it will taste the same. But, try to pour the beliefs of one religion into a different religion, and they will not fit. Jewish guilt is completely different to Catholic guilt, even though the guilt is the same. What we need to resolve is the difference between the true feeling that propels us, and the false emotion that is driving us.

The difference is that the complication of false emotion creates a fixed bubble, a sort of rigidity, and has little benefit to our ongoing survival. Our natural emotion changes to suit the environment, and allows us to move with the chaging tide of circumstance.

So how do we work out what is a false emotion, and how do we find our real ones?

Do we sit and sift through every thought and feeling we have, asking ourself if this is real? Of course not. In fact we do not need to do anything other than focus on feeling more intensely this moment. One day, some years ago, the most striking truth entered into my heart. It is the most dangerous truth, the most fearsome truth, and yet the simplest truth anyone can hold. And the Truth is this: *We do not need to let go of Desire, we simply need to LOVE more clearly.*

Whatever we feel, whatever we think, whatever habit drives us, the secret to happiness, the universe and everything is simply to love more clearly. And to be clear, we need to let go. To truly love, we need to let go. To live in the moment, we need to let go. There is nothing to defeat, no devil to escape, no heaven to attain: There is only kindness and discrimination to discover.

If you have a feeling arise that confuses you, ask "Love plus what?" Anything left over from a sense of love is what is confusing you. Let it go, with kindness. Are you worried about what someone thinks? Let it go, with kindness. Are you concerned you are not good enough? Let it go, with kindness. Be kind and aware, not kind of aware.

Kind Discrimination is the cure for all trouble, most especially emotional illness.

Forget trying to BEAT your Passions, and especially stop trying to defeat them with Virtues. Your mind is not stupid, stupid! It knows that you are exercising your so-called Virtues because you are really trying to cover up something you believe to be wicked. All that happens is that your mind will go looking for the wicked. What is more, it will think this game you are playing is fun. This is when your own mind starts to bury passions in your virtues and virtues in your passions, then waits for the fireworks when your ardent passions burst through, screaming "We're BACK!"

Virtues are fine and noble, but they can quickly become your worst enemy. Your RAT will show you through the maze of passions NOT by repression or control of things, but by identifying the real goal. That's the secret, knowing the direction, and knowing what you are looking to achieve. That's the Real Cheese.

At it's most basic level, you see someone you like. You want to be near them, but your mind enters into a battle zone with itself. You argue over inner feelings of worthiness, and other issues you cart around like baggage. Rather than going up to say "I like you" you go through a gamut of options, trying to negotiate the mine field you have created inside yourself.

But when you are close to your REAL emotion, there is no battle ground. You just see what you want, and you reach out. How do we get to this state? How do we cut through the mire of false emotion?

Trust your RAT. Your RAT smells where the Real Cheese is before you even know it is there. It KNOWS (nose pun) the way to go, so trust it. And while you are at it, go for the BIG Cheese. My friends, why stuff about with half measures and stale crackers?

So what IS the Big Cheese? It is many things to many people, but overall it is the loving heart that is ALIVE. The Big Cheese is that part inside you that really swells with delight, no don't be dirty, it MAY be that, but usually it is something more like achieving recognition from your peers, etc. When your heart feels the love pulsing in every moment you have found a Big Cheese.

Think of the child in the sand pit, forgetting of everything but the imagination and the play. All of life is but the moment NOW, and all else recedes like the spent tide. This was the goal of Picasso, and for him it meant relearning to paint as a child. (At age 14 his works were indistinguishable from the Masters, and as a result he felt he missed his childhood in his pursuit of being perfect) Picasso was focussed on the Big Cheese with all his heart. Therefore all his emotions, all his passions and all his virtues were put to work in his pursuit of the greater state of being he sought.

In the end, this is the only solution to your false emotions. It doesn't really matter what you believe, because external reality rarely changes to suit your preconceptions or beliefs. You may believe that Jesus will come along and draw you up to Heaven on the last day, or that the Moon is made of Green Cheese. This doesn't make it so. We all have lots of small, and often downright weird beliefs, that are essentially false.

When I tell people that their emotions are constructs, and essentially unreal, they think I am the fool, but the truth will dawn, one day.

Regardless of what you presently believe, we can at least agree that what matters is how we deal with our emotions, and in particular how we deal with the FEARS that cause the negative emotions to take over. I offer you a simple concept: *A greater purpose dissolves your fears.* Your FEARS are part and parcel of what create the passions that constrict you, while a greater purpose helps us get past fear, and loosens the passions and the things that dam us.

Ratology really is the *"Way of the Un-Dammed"*.

I know how presumptuous this will sound to some. It may seem I am telling you that Buddha, Jesus and Krishna were all incorrect, and that all their teachings are flawed. This is not so, what I am saying is that what has happened since they left this place is that their message has been distorted, and their truth perverted. What I am really saying is how they were PACKAGED was spiritually incorrect, and that the subsequent religions based on them are really marketing exercises that succeeded.

Do you really believe the ads on TV? No, but you buy the stuff anyway. That's the sum total of religion, people. It is advertising that worked so well you believed it.

I also know how ridiculous it may sound to some when I say that all we need for spiritual freedom and heavenly understanding is a greater purpose, but it is true. The truth is simpler that we have been told, and we are simpler than we believe. The path to joy and happiness is really very straightforward.

But first, we must get past the duality of vice versus virtue. If you take nothing else from this book, please remember this incredibly simple truth: *Vice may be able to defeat your Virtue, but Virtue will never cure you of Vice. Only a greater purpose takes you past this conflict within.*

Vice Discussing Matters with Virtue

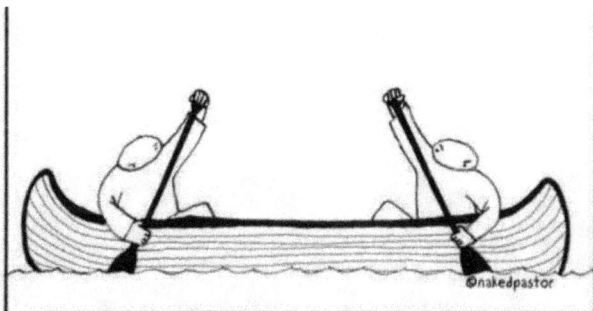

DEPRESSION Versus PURPOSE

It is such an ugly word, depression. It indicates a place into which rain must fall, and it does. Depression is as it sounds, depressing, flattening, dull, onerous and sad. Yet it can also be a symptom of the building up of the water behind the dam, just before it bursts.

Beethoven and Mozart are well-known composers, and little-known depressives. Before every single great symphony that Beethoven produced, he went through a significant and deep period of extreme difficulty with anxiety and depression. The signs of depression are many, but the fruits of it are what is important. Yet these are barely recognised. Ask a psychiatrist what the FRUITS of depression might be, and precious few will have much of an answer.

But ask ANY creative person, and they will shrug. Really, if you don't understand that the creative process is a natural roller coaster, why should anyone explain it to you? The only reason I am trying is to convince you is to set in motion the notion that you need to take up something INTERESTING that is also CREATIVE.

When you do this, you will start to discover that the highs and lows of your life are the same wave, and that rather than drown in it, it is far better to surf it. But you need to have a project that will keep your head above water. Churchill, as we have already mentioned, called it the "Black Dog" and depression plagued him how whole life EXCEPT for when he was caught up in his purpose. It does not stop the "blues" when you have a purpose, but when you find meaning and direction in your life, the blues will no longer own you so completely.

Dealing with depression is no laughing matter, and it is a plague in the Western World. I personally believe one major reason it is so prevalent is simply because people are not fit. In simple truth, when your body is well oxygenated and your health is vital, then depression plays far less a role in dictating your moods.

One culture that fully understood the swings and roundabouts of depression were the Romans. This was a culture of extremes, rulers of the world, yet their own city of Rome was full of dispossessed citizens. The ruling class put on shows of unbelievable savagery in the Colosseum in order to distract the mob. The goal was to entertain, and direct the frustrations of poverty and uselessness towards external matters.

Rome was full of shows, horse racing, gambling and general time fillers. It's coffers were full from all the countries she had conquered, but the people were empty. One of the reasons Julius Caesar was so worshipped and adored was that he sent back his beautifully written missives on the progress of his war in Gaul, or wherever he was fighting at the time. The people loved them, and they were the first best sellers.

He beguiled the people's imagination, and affirmed their natural superiority over other races. He made a Roman feel good about being a Roman. His famous Veni, Vidi, Vici was not really "I came. I saw. I conquered." While this is the exact translation, it potentially sounds boastful, and this is how jealous Senators sought to portray the words. There were discussion how it SHOULD have been written to include all of Rome, and used the plural form "We Came, We Saw, We Conquered".

But it was not a boast. Caesar sent the message to the Senate in the First Person Perfect Tense, and not as the generic Venire, Videre, and Vincere for a reason. Those words would have been boasting, but putting in the PERSONAL tense as he did Caesar was communicating a message on many levels. It was HIS army that did it, they belonged to HIM. HE was the force to be reckoned with, and he was telling the people this.

Why is this important? Caesar knew he was dealing with several classes in Rome. The Patricians (Ruling Class) and then the Merchant Class (Knights), followed by the "Head Count" (Common People). What he was really saying to the Patricians was "I am the one who owns this army, and don't you forget how formidable it is."

But to the common people the "I" aspect of his quote was like the "Royal We" the Queen uses. To the basic Roman Caesar he was saying "Look what we can do people. We are winners. No one can push us about!" He was writing to boost their spirits in the midst of a War. This proclamation on its own turned around a fragile economy and gave great confidence to business and the people. This was a real Rat at work.

Rome had sunk into depression, and Caesar pulled it out of the mire by simply doing what he did best, he won wars. Success brings us together, unites us in a common purpose. This is what he did with the Roman people. He showed them his winning ways.

He snapped the people out of depression. This is why I include the story in this section, because the concept of Depression goes way beyond yourself. This was the state of their economy, but Caesar single handedly changed it all. He won wars, he proved Rome was still strong, and his confidence broke the tide of discontent. Rome flourished once more.

This applies to you as well. You can surge forward against all odds when you align yourself to your greater purpose.

Each individual is like a city divided, for the most part. We need to be able to take charge of it, and we start with being in control of at least one moment every day. This is another aspect of "Seize the Day". If you want freedom, we really must take charge and OWN this moment, at least once a day. If we can do just this, we find the effects of depression and other negatives will lessen significantly.

To pull yourself out of the depression cycle do simple things, like clean the house, organise a room, change the furniture, mow the lawn, write a poem. Maybe even write a book? It is all about not being defeated, and just being able to DO. As they say in the Nike ad: Just DO it.

DO IT! Soon enough the rhythm of useful activity will create a hum that will overrule the buzzing annoyance of depression. And yet at the same time you must be prepared to walk through hell, literally. Now I am going to suggest something you will rarely hear: Consider if you will that your depression is really a call for you to walk through the underworld of false emotion, and discover the meaning behind the dark aspects of your being. It is a gift wrapped up as a curse. Depression is a John the Baptist to your Jesus Rat.

Winston Churchill suffered incredible and debilitating depression. He called it the Black Dog, and for a good part of his life it utterly immobilised him. His depression owned him completely, and as he sank lower into the darkness he could see no solution to this bane of existence that had overtaken his life.

Yet when he came into his role as Prime Minister during World War Two, the misery of his negative emotions lifted. He still suffered it, but had a greater purpose, and as a result there was simply no room left for lesser emotions. Yet here is the important part: BECAUSE of his personal darkness, he could understand the deep and vicious motivation of the Nazi. He knew about the murder and mayhem hiding behind respectable appearances, because these thoughts had run through his own mind.

Churchill was a master marksman. How do you think he managed this? He spent a lot of time on his estate, shooting things. He spent a lot of time discarding (in private) the "nice" person and cursing the confining lies of society. In doing so, he awoke the rat within, and in doing so recognised the dangerous CAT (Controller and Terrorist) in the Nazi.

We all walk our own road to our point of self awakening. I cannot tell you that a zig zag path is incorrect, or that walking in a circle is wrong. All I can say is that if you are thirsty, what you need to do is to each over, grab the glass (whether it is half full or half empty is irrelevant) and DRINK. Your RAT will show you WHERE the glass is, and even how to reach for the glass, but like leading the horse to water, you have to DRINK it to discover your freedom is already here.

Depression is an internal block that stops you from reaching over and drinking from the Fountain of Life, and there is NO solution to this depression. But reach over and sup from the fountain, and it is gone. Yes, recognise that it exists, and that there are better things to discover each day than profit you more than sitting with Chateau Cardboard (the cheap cask of wine) as your friend.

The Black Dog is that part of you that recognises you are missing an intimate connection with your Baby Self, your source of Love. If depression has you in its jaws, what you must first understand is that you have been trapped by a a fear of some sort. Your job is to escape this fear, and the only escape from those jaws is to get out and make a difference.

Only a lack of purpose is holding you in place. You DO have a lack that haunts you, but it is nothing like what you imagine. It is simply a lack of direction, a lack of purpose and a lack of meaning in your life.

If it is this easy, you say, what is stopping me? Far more than you realise. You have the weight of ages against you, and the tyranny of distance before you. It is a long hard journey out of the Nothing Trap of Depression. However, the choice you need to make is simple: Love or Fear? Move forward with love, or retreat into fear.

We have, in a sense, only TWO genuine emotions: Love and Fear. Every day we either go forward in Love, or we retreat in Fear. This choice can only be made by the genuine self, the real person inside all your concerns. But where is this? Who is this? What is this? How can we start to recognise it?

To do this you first must recognise the MEMES (memory patterns) that are running your mind and emotions.

NB: Clinical Depression is a very serious, and life threatening disease. This chapeter is a guide, only. Please seek treatment with a qualified professional if you have been diagnosed with this illness.

THE MEME MACHINE

The Meme Machine is the title of a book by Susan Blackmore, and it is recommended reading. Memes are the hand-me-down imprints of family and society that "stamp" our being. They work on us at an elemental level. You may find it odd, but do you realise "you" are a carbon copy? To begin with, "You" started out as a single cell, and "you" biologically photocopied yourself to the state you are in today.

Your Stem Cells went to various parts of your developing baby body, and they "knew" what to become. A kidney here, two lungs there, a brain at the top, and toes at the bottom. What is more, all humans are stamped out in the same way, because we have an organic copy code called DNA.

So why do so many people refuse to believe they are carbon copies of something or someone else? Despite everything science tells us, that we are an assemblage of genes in particular constructs that create specific and repeatable genetic forms, we still refuse to believe we are copies stamped out of the great sausage machine of life.

As the Monty Python crew expressed: We are all individuals! Chant it together folks, and hopefully you will one day believe it. Yes, you are an individual, but you are an individual mix of jig saw pieces that came from somewhere else, with other people's pictures painted on the pieces.

Imagine that there are a series of sausage machines, and the mix being prepared in one of them is YOU. Dollop by dollop the general collection of bits that are to be your future self are squeezed into the chute, ground up, squashed together, and then they all pop out as a whole sausage.

Each machine makes a particular type of sausage and even though the ingredients vary from sausage to sausage, a pork one remains pork despite the changing herbs and spices because this is the main ingredient.

But let's go further. As a sausage emerges and joins a sausage family (the shared experience of the meat grinder firmly embedded in its cellular memory) it discovers that the other sausages have little stick it notes over them. One says "Good looking sausage" another says "Fat Ugly Sausage". These notes osmose inward, and imprint themselves on the sausage, slowly becoming part of the sausage itself. These are the flavours of belief that are GIVEN to each sausage as it matures in the outer world.

Now you are a Pork Sausage, with other flavours added. The cooking in the fire of life's experience merges all the bits inside, and it now forms into what seems to be a whole. The flavours all come together, and you become the Sacred Sausage of Self.

This is how we are formed. We have a basic nature, but onto this is grafted images of how others perceive us. Often these images we receive are really photocopies of how people see themselves, and they have simply used another as a hook to hang things on, but even so, these energies osmose into us and become part of our belief system.

To quote the old paradox: *There are two types of people in the world. Those who believe in types, and those who don't.*

I am terribly sorry if this offends you, but you are a TYPE. You are a photocopy. You are like a letter of the alphabet, cosmically speaking, and only by being in the right place at the right time will your life start to make any sense at all. To find contentment and purpose you must first come to understand what TYPE of person you are, and only then can you come to a deep, inner agreement that this is OK.

At this point of "OK with Self" you begin to sort out what is NOT you in the jumble of images and emotions that run through your head. This is a much harder thing to achieve, because the Sausage believes it is ONE, and not an assemblage of bits. But let's just presume you have found your RAT and come to the point where you see the add on tags, and have accepted that these are OK. Now you are ready to get on with life.

Yet all of this is just words. None of this will have any meaning to you, and you will continue to believe these your hand-me-down's jigsaw puzzle pieces are the real you, until something dramatic comes along to shake you from your tree.

Your Humpty Dumpty needs to fall from the wall, and break.

That's how it is on planet Earth . We all pick up patterns and images from our environment, and this dramatically alters our natural state. But to recognise things after they have been subsumed and made into a personal reality is a little like reverse osmosis, where the saturated salt is removed from the water until only the pure essence remains. The process of seeing ourselves as we are is rarely simple, and always painful.

Science thought that with the Human Genome all sorted out, things would then be simple. Once you had all the pieces to the jigsaw, it would be easy to put it together. Ideally you could see what type someone was, and figure out in advance if they should study in the sciences or the arts, or go dig ditches. But this didn't work as expected. Twins were found to have widely different responses to the same stimuli, and utterly different levels of aptitude despite having almost identical genes.

So the science of Epi-Genetics, based on the once despised Lamarckian concept, came into a new form of recognition. This is that external events shape the way our Genes respond, and life stress itself it part of the individual evolution. It turns out that the body of itself seemed to choose "Protein Coats" to cover certain areas of the gene strands. This affects how a gene acts, and what it does. This study will go on and on for years, but let's keep it simple: *You are more than your genes.*

You are more than the DNA of your parents twisted into a new life. You are what you are, but you are also the aggregate of your life experience, which includes the "grafting" process of socialisation.

However, you are also extremely resilient BECAUSE you are a TYPE. We also have an in-build degree of self awareness. You may be not fully realise you are a pork sausage, but you already know you are not chicken or beef. This means that you will not necessarily take on board any or all tags you are given. The Pork Sausage doesn't necessarily absorb the tags that a chicken one would. In a sense, right from the get-go you have a "type of" choice in the matter, to some degree.

Just as an acorn will never grow a willow, you are a basic type, and no matter what influence you have, you will still grow up into the nature of the specific characteristics of what you are. However, the soil you grow in and the water and sun you receive determines how well you grow, and how long you live. It's the parable of the seeds: Some fall onto rocks and wither, others get shallow soil and sprout for but a short time, while others take deep roots and survive.

The "Deep Roots" in the parable is the symbol of your Consciousness. Consciousness of itself is the key to life. Genetics and experiences have a strong influence, but the way we understand and work with what we are comes from a deeper well. A well that is inside each of us.

The very greatest miracle in life is that a person, crippled with anxiety, fear and depression, can get up and WALK into the sunshine. A person reaches within themselves, finds the well of their being, and draws it up to the surface. It is a true miracle that this book got written, and an even greater one if you grasp what it says, and make it real in your life.

Now, how to find this well! This is where your RAT comes into play. It smells out the water of life underneath your being. It is your dowser, and if you pay attention to where it points you will discover the spring of your being far more easily.

Chemistry-wise there are many different types of "type". There are Emotional Types, Mental Types and even Mineral Types, as well as any combination of these. As an example: Some people have more calcium than others, while some have more iron, and so on. This affects the way you perceive the world, how you metabolise food, and how your hormones will react to stress, etc. The "Mix" of the sausage changes from person to person, but if you are a "Calcium Type" you will share similar traits to other Calcium Types.

Do not doubt this: *You are a TYPE. You have a basic pattern.*

Just as the month you are born in gives you a Star Sign, the type of body you receive gives you a destiny according to your DNA and Epi-Genetics. As one example: I come from a family on both sides of very long lived people. Some aunts went to 114 and many relatives lived past 100. I can reasonably expect to live to an old age. This no doubt contributes to the fact I am still alive despite the fact that the good doctors have said I should have been dead many times.

It does not matter if you believe or disbelieve me regarding mineral types, star signs, or anything else. The point is that you are a TYPE. And on top of that, you have been programmed by the images placed upon you by others, and by society, and you WILL act in accordance to the way you have been trained to by these images/energies, that we call MEMES.

If this interests you, read "The Meme Machine" by Susan Blackmore.

I emphasise, it comes back to the notion that, while you believe your thoughts are your own, they are NOT. All your thoughts, all your emotions, all of you is in some way part of a general jigsaw. Think of it as if every single part of you is an atom from somewhere else that has been ASSEMBLED to make the person you are today.

More importantly, you can REASSEMBLE the various parts of your nature that you wish to change. By rearranging your perspective, you see things in a different way. When you see things differently, you act differently. When you change the way you act, you change the reaction you get from others. When you change the reaction you get from others you alter the TAGS they put on you.

Change your TAGS, and you change you life. Your RAT will help you with the perception area, and allow you to see things differently. If you are already starting to think differently, your RAT has started to wake up.

Changing your MEME's is a little more difficult than changing your clothes, but it is essentially the same thing. Your RAT inside already knows that most people are wearing the "Emperors New Clothes" when it comes to reality, and that the tags we think are important are really insubstantial pieces of nothing. But what matters is that YOU understand this. You can, and will, if you trust your RAT to show you the way.

Learn to respect, venerate and cherish your RAT, and you will discover the path to Freedom and Power is within you. *If you want to be truly happy, if you want to get REAL, allow your RAT the room to breath.*

The niggle in the back of your thoughts? Pay attention to it. That feeling this is not such a good idea? Listen closer. When you are about to go into a new job, ask inwardly what your natural sense of this is. Start a dialogue with yourself, an intimate dialogue, where you learn to trust and open up to your own fears, beliefs and shortcomings.

When you do this, your RAT, your Reality Awareness Trigger, will be become clearer, and stronger. Just as you tune in to a radio station, the better you focus, the more clearly you will hear the inner whisper.

And the first thing your Rat will do is STOP you. It will stop you looking at the pictures of your past. It will stop you pretending you are something you are not. It will stop you from stopping yourself being free.

In conclusion on this section, the core understanding we need to achieve is that we are all many things. We are multiple, with many aspects to self. By accepting this, and learning to see the various elements, and in particular, identifying where our real emotion lies, we can apply Spiritual Arithmetic, and start adding ourselves up in newer and better ways.

Our future self is decided by every step we take NOW. What we are learning here is how to be mindful, and step more carefully in the direction our heart wants us to go.

No Photos Allowed

India is a funny place. All over most of the museums and tourist venues are signs saying "No Photos allowed". It was strange to think in the modern day there appeared to still be this belief that a photo might steal the soul of some object that held a passing interest to a tourist. But it got me thinking: We ALL take snapshots of our life experiences, and we put them up on the walls of our inner being.

This is the role of the subconscious self. It is like a video camera that records every passing experience, and files it away in a bank of memories that can be called up when required. As an example: During hypnosis, people have even been able to accurately recall how many telegraph poles they passed by on the way to that meeting. This is what our subconscious does, it records EVERYTHING. As a result, we are chock full of PICTURES in our heads. So many pictures.

For most of us, we can no longer see the walls, or doorways, or windows, or any aspect of our true being, because we have too many pictures on the wall to see the reality upon which they hang. So a greater part of discovering freedom is removing the clutter of images that surround us. To be truly happy, we need to find the natural reality behind the images that fill up our life experience. How can we do this?

Simply put, *we need to find the place inside where we have no photos on the wall.* Can you imagine a space in your being where there are NO images from the past affecting you? The mind is a series of pictures, so you can't go there. Your Emotions are images of sensation, so you can't go there. So where? There is only one place.

No matter where we look inside ourselves, there will be pictures from our past hung up on the wall. Yet we CAN find a "No Pictures Allowed" place inside us, but only by not looking there. We put our total attention onto the present moment, that which is all around us, and through us.

Can you imagine living so much in the moment that the ONLY image that counts is HERE NOW? Can you imagine a state where your thoughts, imagination, feelings and beliefs all line up to experience NOW? It can happen, but only when you let go of your pictures and the internal dialogue and ignore all the stick-it notes you have all over your mindscape and emotional playing fields. And to do this, you have to not give a Rats!

Only when we detach from our conditions and live absolutely in our present moment can we find the "no pictures" space.

There is no "how" to do this. There is only an imperative that comes from deep within that you MUST. How do we find the motivation to even start? Generally, life steps in and pushes us. Stuff goes wrong, and we want a solution. Or we want to know why we are depressed, and can't move forward. It is all of the above and a whole lot more.

This is just how life works. Its message can only be heard in the present moment, because it speaks to nothing else. Life will push, pull and prod us until we FIND that space where we can hear it.

Have you ever thought to ask yourself three questions?

1. *WHY am I not happy?*
2. *WHY am I not free?*
3. *WHY do I feel confined?*

Answers are not important, unless it is "But I am happy free and unconfined!" We are just looking to comprehend what the questions mean to us individually. They are designed to help you you understand that you are being propelled by your misery, not your joy. When we accept that inertia, fear and self-loathing are driving our bus, then we may stop and be prepared to start looking past our internal "Rule Book of Should and Should Not". Then we start asking "Why not?" to any new experience.

Imagine this for a moment: FREEDOM. Complete freedom.

Substituting "Why Not" in place of "I should not" will help you discover greater freedom, and this will lead you to the present moment. And there is a plus factor: When we ask questions with genuine curiosity, we are given a sort of invulnerability shield that allows us to walk through our own self-created and externally imposed hells.

Even if we don't get an answer, the fact that we ASK helps to sets us free. First, try and set up a space inside where there is only the present moment. Then ask a question about anything that is troubling you. Why am I poor? Then listen, listen and ask how you FEEL. You may be surprised to discover that you don't mind being poor at all. If so, now you don't have to worry about that aspect of your life. If you find it bugs you, ask, "What is the best way for myself to move into more money?"

Sit in silent listening, and an answer will arrive. Maybe not right away, but your Rat will line things up, and it will come, often when you least expect it.

RULES Are NEGOTIABLE:

A lot of people think there are too many rules, and there are. I firmly believed this when I took over the running of a spiritual organisation in Byron Bay, Australia. This was just a local job, akin to that of a parish priest, and in a fit of open-hearted grandiose flamboyance I decided that we were to suspend all the rules, and that everyone would have to look to their own heart in order to find the correct way to act.

Yes, well, as they say good intentions pave the road to hell. Slowly but surely enough people acted in such a way that it required the reimplementation of rules. I didn't want them, the people in the group didn't want them, but in the end we NEEDED them.

While I was inspired by the notion of responsible anarchy, the practice itself left a lot to be desired. People felt naked and bereft without some sort of boundary to define HOW they should act, and so Rules become clothes we wear that make us comfortable in public. And this is all that Rules are.

Rule are part of the fashions of our life, and they can change like fashion. In particular, you can renegotiate your relationship with the current rules when you understand how ALL authority wants to rid itself of the trouble that comes with enforcing them. Enforcing rules in a pain in the butt, and, as most authorities are lazy, they will take every opportunity to excuse themselves from this arduous duty.

I say most, not all. There are always dedicated monkey-minds who believe rules are Gods, but there is nothing anyone can do about this. Let's focus on how to NEGOTIATE your way around rules.

One day I was pulled over by a policeman, and asked why I was exceeding the speed limit. Note, this standard first question calls for you to admit guilt. First Rule: *Never admit guilt.* I said *"Was I officer? I can't say because the light to the dash board went out as I was coming off the freeway, and I have no idea what speed I was travelling, other than I truly believed I was doing the speed limit."*

Now, there was some truth to it. The dash lights HAD gone off. I had switched them off. Now a policeman has specific things in mind. He is looking at how you admit guilt, and if not, he is then looking at his options should you argue the fine. There is degree of effort and pain he goes through if he has to turn up to court, etc. Yes, he will do his job as required, but he is also considering if you actually pose a threat to society, if you are cocky, or rude, and if you have a bothersome solicitor.

If you seem ok, and it's a minor offence, the decent officer will prefer to let you go. He checked the dash lights, they were off, so he said "Well, ok. But take care and get those fixed."

Now if I were eighteen years old, with an attitude, and driving a junk box I would have been fined. If I sounded less than earnest, I would have been fined. If he had felt that I would have just paid the fine without going to court, I would have been fined. But I was driving a Porsche, was well spoken, and this type can, and do, pay solicitors. This makes life hard. He and I understood pretty much the rules of how this all works, and all of it forms a silent communication. The good officer wisely decided to let it be.

It was obvious that I was not a threat against society, that I was well spoken and that I had a good excuse. All this adds up to getting let off with a warning from the judge, so really, was it worth the bother? I also drove a car that was not known for its stupid drivers. If it had been a turbo-charged Supra, I would have been fined.

You want to know something ridiculous? Once I went through a speed regulated spot on a highway with an unregistered trailer at TWICE the nominated speed (I really was exhausted and didn't see the sign) and somehow the good officer on that occasion decided to give me a misdemeanour for the trailer, and let me go.

It has happened SO many times that it gets ridiculous. Then one day, driving a Toyota I had bought for my Mum, I go through a radar camera held 500 meters away by a Gestapo member. No negotiation, cheap car, slightly over the limit, here's the fine Sir. I was not seen as anything but a bunny for slaughter.

We break rules all the time. We can't help it. There are so many of the damn things that all of us will break some of them at some point. And tell me, what happens when a Rule is broken? Absolutely nothing unless there is someone to enforce it. It is like the fellow at school drawing a line in the sand, saying "I dare you to cross it!" If there is a big tough bully on the other side, you don't. If it is a weak-willed whimp, you do.

The Mystic Rat Says: *Rules are like locks, they are for honest people.*

I break social boundaries all the time. I always seem to end up talking to people I am not supposed to, and say things I shouldn't, but generally it is funny, and mostly they are laughing.

True story, I made some smart-ass comment to a guy who was a professional killer, and even his friends said, "You said WHAT to the Hitman?" A big smile is a shield when used properly. Or maybe it was the time when I was chatting to a local tough guy, encouraging him to keep a diary of how he felt: "You were sitting chatting to THAT fellow in THAT Bike Club, the one known for the most murders in the country?"

But it's not "me" doing it, it's the RAT inside.

Here's the secret: *The way your attitude and expectation is set often determines how the rules will be applied.* If your attitude has an inch of victim in it, you will pay a three inch fine. If you break rules and feel guilty, you will attract retribution. Sad, but it this is how it is. If you love Rules, then you fear Freedom, and you will never understand what is REAL. I recommend a reading of the "Velveteen Rabbit".

"What is REAL?" asked the Rabbit one day, when they were lying side by side near the nursery fender, before Nana came to tidy the room. "Does it mean having things that buzz inside you and a stick-out handle?"

"Real isn't how you are made," said the Skin Horse. "It's a thing that happens to you. When a child loves you for a long, long time, not just to play with, but REALLY loves you, then you become Real."

Rules Addiction, and things like a belief in science and technology as life solutions, are the opposite of being Loved and Being Real. We tend to have a victim mentality and guilt consciousness that binds us to a need for rules, but when we allow life to embrace us, it changes. When we learn to let go of the man-made notions, which is enforcing a mechanical order in a fixed society, we understand that only natural is 'right".

But if you must have Rules, go back to Book One and the Rules for Rattyness.

They will work much better for you.

Get Real or Get Ghettoed.

L et's talk for a moment about the unreality in our life. We THINK our life is real, just like we think money is real, but let's not look at the "thing" itself but the consequence on our participation with it. Reality in the consequence of choices, or the lack of choice we hold. If you are chained in a dungeon, this is reality. You can do little but suffer it. Yet things like money have no great reality to those who have lots of it. It is like a tool in the shed, you use it when you need to. Money only becomes real when you don't have it, because the CONSEQUENCES of this will make your life hard.

Here's a secret: Our life will only become real when we lose our current set of patterns and beliefs. The consequence of losing fixed beliefs is that we are free of them. When we are free of beliefs, we become real.

On impulse I walked down the only ghetto in Sydney one day. It wasn't much of a ghetto by world standards, but at least we had one. This was a place where the Aboriginals and drop outs had moved to, a place called Everleigh Street. Of course today the "Down and Outs" are getting priced out of the place, but in the 1980's there were lots of street people and it could be a violent place. Why did I go there? Something said to check it out, so I went.

I met some lovely people, great kids, and a few nutters. Quite pleasant really. But then something said it was time to leave, and I could see a couple of dark eyes gazing at me from behind windows. The part of you that says "danger" is your RAT, but it can take a bit to hear it clearly. This is usually because our paranoia is shouting and drowning out our inner whispers, so all you hear are your fears. How do we tell the difference between a genuine insight and paranoia? Silence. Paranoia is noisy.

We also have to be careful. This means to be full of care as well as taking care not to be stupid. But more than this, we need to have enough experience of reality to know the difference between the voice that comes from our still, certain point and the madness of our paranoia. If we are to understand the message of our RAT we need a little inner silence. If we are stuck in Rules, we will never get there.

Over the years I have stopped and chatted to many street people. While their life was hard, it was also a treasure to be valued. Yet life was valued in a different way than you might imagine. You see, many street people are living in the homeless world because, in this reality, they finally found a lack of two face lying bastards. They have found the company of lying bastards with just ONE face. It made a real difference.

I worked near Everleigh Street, in Sydney and got to see many of the goings on. It was interesting but on the whole, it was not a pleasant place. People preyed on each other: rape, violence, mental and verbal assault as well as physical attacks were common place. Alcohol, drugs, petrol sniffing were everywhere, and a sense of apathy hung over everything.

Sounds dreadful, yes? Well, this is where YOUR consciousness is going if you fail to discover things of truth and reality in your life. You may not end up in Redfern, but without moving forward in freedom, the mind will slowly turn in on itself, becoming isolated, alone, and in danger from negative moods. I often see a ghetto in a mansion full of gold. Riches do not stop it from happening, and indeed, sometimes wealth CREATES poverty. Where people have become spiritually bereft, and there is no harmony in their hearts, there is a ghetto..

The richest suburbs can be poverty struck, consciousness-wise. Down the road from me most of the houses are million dollar plus homes, and there's row after row of them. This does not mean the people who live in them are free. Money offers no promise of freedom, just more illusion of choice. Most people are trapped in the mill wheels of their circumstances just as solidly as extreme poverty can chain you to servitude. The truth is that ANYONE (Rich or Poor) can be free, regardless of circumstance. The fact is, most are not. Why? Perhaps most people are pretending their life is something it is not. They are not being REAL.

How to get real? *Stop telling lies.* People tell lies to HIDE something, or to pretend, any number of reasons. The rationals we give ourselves for our actions may not seem to be connected to the internal lie, but they are.

I used to lie about what my father did as a kid, for no other reason that I wanted to feel as if I had a father who was not an alcoholic on prescribed pills who continually walked into walls. The fibs I spoke of regarding his actions were not really connected to what HE was. They were about how I felt. Pretending I had a real father made me feel better.

When he later improved and came more on line as a Dad (As in, not staggering from wall to wall, hitting his nose) I felt less of a need to pretend he was fine. The lie I spoke was really wishful thinking. I had spoken "as if" it was already real. Believe it or not, THOSE types of lies are beneficial in achieving your goals. However, I was still hiding the fact that I had a problem. I was lonely and wanted to fit in.

The Mystic Rat Says: *Everyone who is telling a lie is hiding something.*

Of course there are exceptions to some degree with the habitual and pathological liars. While they are also hiding something, this is often not related to the lies they tell or live. This type are living a disconnection from reality that is so complete that the lies BECOME the reality they exist in. There is no negotiation, it is their way or the highway. Many leading executives and a number of politicians are pathological liars.

The habitual liar is generally hiding his or her sense of worthlessness (and there are LOTS of these about) while the pathological liar is hiding his arrogance and hatred of others. Yes, they have created the state of being because of some issue inside them, but they have also disconnected from this, and created a "bubble" of thought that they run around in, much like a mouse on a circular ladder.

The pathological liar simply enjoys the process and fuss they create with lies. Over time, the polarisation reverses, and there is a collapse. The hatreds they created invert and become their worst enemy, but prior to this inversion the projection is absolute. The curious thing is that their mocked up belief in the reality they project will ALWAYS convince weaker minded people that it is truth.

I lived next to one in a country area. He had always been quite odd, yet had remained pleasant until I saw him one day, head in hands, clearly desperate. There he was on his verandah, totally lost in complete, desperate misery. When he realised he had been seen for what he believed he was, I started to see the nasty side. From that moment on, he hated me, and with an absolute vehemence. Humans are fascinating creatures in this regard, and they can be quite troublesome.

We generally accept that the art of lying runs in a scale from

1. *Little fibs or white lies, to*
2. *Lying to get what you want, to*
3. *Habitual lying, through to*
4. *Pathological Lies.*

I am saying that, while it is all different, it is also all the same. The psychology of lying is essentially to HIDE something. That's it! Most people think we lie to get something, and while this may be the motivation, it is not the cause. It is always to hide something. The Art of Lying is the practice of obfuscation.

The psychologist will tell you the desire to lie is generated from a million possible causes, but I am telling you plainly, it all comes about because you are trying to HIDE something. What's more, it works in reverse. When you stop telling lies, you lose the need to hide things. That is when we START to become clear and direct. This is the first step towards reality.

What's more, when you stop lying you will discover that your Good Luck improves enormously. You find you have $20 in that drawer underneath that hidden thing you once had there.

You may even find some of those missing socks.

CREATING OPTIONS

We have approached the subject of Choice many times in this book. The difficulty of choosing when you are not aware of having a choice is obvious, so here we will discuss a little on how we CREATE choices. And, in simple terms, this is to be bold.

The Mystic Rat Says: *The Gods favour the Bold.*

Bold and adventuresome people do not need to create stories to fill their lives. There is nothing they need to hide because they are happy to stand true and proud. Other people feel this when they walk into the room, and a natural luck energy flows towards these folk. Opportunities open up, and their life appears to be LUCKY.

People who live in the ghettos of unconsciousness are always unlucky. Even when rich, they can have a poverty consciousness, and, because of low self-esteem, come to believe they are a lesser person. Yet they wish to hide this fact, and so they live a lie of pretence. This distorts the energy around them, and these folk do not attract the good vibes.

As a result, they tend to make negative associations and develop friendships with those who share this disturbed energy. Their life wraps around the lies based on their fears, rather than the truths of their Soul. The most common lie is that they do not have enough of something, and they want to HIDE this fact. The lack is hidden by a need not to look poor in the eyes of their peers, and so the poorest people often drive the most expensive car they can find, or seek to wear lots of gold. I knew one man who had crates for furniture, yet a cabinet full of antique Dolton china.

Kids, on the other hand, rarely live in Ghettos of Consciousness. We know children have no pretence when they are very young. If they want something, they just want it. No reason given, no reason asked for, nothing to hide and everything to gain.

Later they will learn to lie in order to get what they want, but it is still an innocent fib, until they get to puberty. Then you lie through your teeth in order to get sex, money and everything you feel you need to be an adult. It all has consequences, because one little lie can start the snow ball rolling, and the energy of illusion builds.

Remember that old nursery rhyme about the woman that swallowed the FLY? Think of it as she swallowed a LIE. "I don't know why she swallows that Lie. I think she'll die!" The Nursery Rhyme goes on about the consequences, and that is how it is with ourselves. The lie that WE swallow, either from some belief of unworthiness, or a fear of loss, or even a fear of success, grows. It is a LACK that drives us, and if we swallow it whole, it starts a process that, in time, kills consciousness.

Some of the greatest liars are at the forefront of the New Age movements, often shouting that God loves you, or that the Law of Attraction will provide everything. After which they will brag about how much they earned on the stock market. Any number of obfuscations and small deceits are used to hide the fear they feel.

I went to a seminar on Options Trading that was run by a man, who a professional liar. This was something you paid to look at, and if you liked it, you paid for training on how to do it. The funny thing, and the simple truth, is that the first thing the guy said was, "This is a Zero Sum Game!" In other worlds, there is no "plus" element. Whatever money goes into the pot is what is split between the players.

A Zero Sum Game really means there are some winners and many losers. Of course, the gambler in you will whisper that YOU are the winner, for sure.

At the presentation he shows us pictures of himself and his family smiling at a picnic, with a red Ferrari parked beside. This is how HE lived, and he said "That is my car, and this is our mid-week picnic." Yet he lived in the same valley as I did, and I noted no Ferrari in his drive. So "his" car was one he rented for the photo shoot. Sure, it was "his", for a few hours. That's how the real liars lie. They speak an ounce of truth diluted with a gallon of fib.

He bragged about how much he paid his stockbroker, spoke loudly of how great his life was, and the impression was that generally everything was marvellous. The problem for me was simple: If he is making so much money why is he only charging $1500 to teach others how to make money? So I asked him this.

He responded saying he loved this business so much that he wanted to share the wealth. He said he would happily do it all for nothing, but that he needed to charge people because otherwise they would not value what they learned. So, I popped up and said, "Seriously, thank you for the offer, and I accept it." He quickly back pedalled on the "I am happy to do this for nothing" line. What really got me was that people were swallowing this BS, and he got some people signing up for his course.

That is the thing with professional liars, they will blatantly appeal to GREED (or any one of the passions) and they use this as leverage to extract dollars from their clientele. There were people at that seminar who desperately wanted an easy life, and they would pay money to get it. This made them an easy mark.

The guy and myself got on quite well, however, and he stayed in touch. Maybe it was because he knew I really did have an exotic car, and large acres at the end of the valley, and I presumed he hoped that he might be able to get some dollars off me. But as time passed, I discovered it wasn't that at all. One day he came out, and said he would appreciate my advice on how to make money in real estate, because this was where the REAL money was to be found.

I suspect he also wanted to be friendly because he knew I knew that he was a fraud, but liked him anyway. The odd thing about most liars is that when you nail them, and yet allow that this is their nature, they love you for it. (Disclaimer: But not the Pathological ones! Their entire existence hinges on EVERYONE believing them.)

Liars appeal to people who are in LACK. Liars are in a State of LACK, and as like will attract like, they bring in lack-minded people. Why do people live in Lack? The answer is simple. It is convenient.

People continue to live in a state of Lack because it suits them. It is a set of clothes that fits their consciousness. But please do not imagine that a BMW in the garage, a suit on the rack and a highly paid job in some way immunises you from this state. You can be rich and still have a consciousness that begs for acceptance. You can have high respect in your profession, yet still grovel in the gutter looking for something to appease your needs and desires.

The paradox is that all of this LACK, which drives the need for the LIE, is created and propelled by the LIE that runs you. That's just how it is, a total circle of wasted energy. It's a Catch 22 and we are either in it, or we get out of it. STOP LYING! That's the answer.

The ILLUSIONS of SELF

O ur entire life is generally run in accordance with the stories we are told in childhood. We live with and inside the consequences of the stories we accept as our reality. Jesus will save me. Mummy will feed me. Then you discover Santa Clause is a lie! You get over the shock, but a little part of you inside still echoes with the question, "How many lies have I been told?"

Well, quite a few. The Hindu Vedas talk about MAYA, or illusion. This is the Santana and Sanyana of existence, or the flow of images that paint a picture of false reality. The MAYA, or illusions, are the inner pictures and beliefs that control you, (and there are quite a few of them) They take up residence and constitute the jig-saw puzzle in your mind. The common illusions are as follows:

1. *I am not Good Enough*
2. *Other people are looking at me*
3. *I need approval from another to feel whole*
4. *The grass is greener over there*
5. *I need to hurry or I will lose something*
6. *If I love everyone, they will love me*
7. *If I love you completely, one day you will love me.*

There are lots more. These belief patterns are part and parcel of the "Sins of our Fathers" or what we call the Karmetic Chain. They are most often handed down through the family lineage. The Bible sates that these "sins" take seven generations to wear off, and curiously, if you note how dynasties take shape, they seem to last roughly seven generations.

Your RAT can sniff out gnaw through the chains of your past, if you let it. It will find them, and nibble them away strand by strand, until they give way. Sounds easy, yes? It isn't. The reality is that when your RAT gets active, at first it feels like YOU are being attacked. As a consequence, we shut down our awareness, because it hurts. What's more, other people feel you escaping from your prison, and will want to lock you in. Just like crabs pulling back another crab trying to escape the pot, our family, friends and business associates start trying to wall us in.

Why is this so? I often wonder about this. Why do people want to confine others to THEIR limitations? Well, fear of course. I suspect that in part it is because the jealous or negatively polarised person cannot trust themselves to heal their life, or repair their heart, so it is better to have everyone in the same boat, thank you very much.

Why do people block others from freedom? Why do they lock

themselves up in mental and emotional prisons? I certainly cannot pretend to hold all the reasons. However, I can say, absolutely, this one fact: *Every single lie that runs anyone is based, firstly, on a fear of some sort, and secondly, that this lie is hiding something.*

I don't have all the answers, but here is the good part: We do not NEED an answer to all of this. We just need to become REAL and stop hiding. When we practice this, our natural truth will begin to emerge from the shadows, where we have stuffed it like a smelly old aunt, and it will tell us what we need to know.

The steps towards this state are simple:

1 *Stop the LIES and you stop the FEAR.*
2 *Stop the FEAR and you REVEAL YOURSELF.*
3 *By revealing who you are to yourself, you experience Reality.*
4 *Reality is Truth. When you are REAL you are TRUE.*

The truth SHALL set you free. But you have to SEE the lies and fears that are presently driving you to be able to counter them and find a greater reality within.

In all honesty, this is the hardest part. The patterns of lying within us are generally so ingrained into our inner landscape that we often have no idea they are there. When we stub our toe on one, we usually blame someone else for our troubles.

Do you remember the Simon and Garfunkel song "The Boxer"? It's about a punch drunk former boxer, lost in the past, and about a young man, who is lost in the present, seeing this. It is all about LOSS, and the chorus goes "Lie lie lie".

In the clearing stands a boxer, a fighter by his trade
He is wearing the reminders, of every glove that knocked him down
And cut him till he cried out, in his anger and his shame,
"I am leaving, I am leaving." but the fighter still remains
Lie la lie, lie le lie lie lie lie lie, lie la lie, lie lie lie lie lie, etc.

It's a stunning and insightful song about the nature of the lie that drives us. It is about people living in the ghettos, and how they are places where the LOST go. Here you find companionship with other lost souls. Unless you discover REALITY in you life, you too will eventually become lost and confused, and unable to get out of the maze that is your head and your emotions.

By the same Laws of Attraction that supposedly treat God as an ATM, you draw other lost people towards you, and because being lost is now a majority sensation, no one in your group will realise how totally and completely lost they are. Did they mention this in "The Secret"?

There is no one so lost in falsehood as a member of a delusional group.

There is no one so certain of their rightness as a member of a group.

Some years ago a husband and wife I was working for stopped by their warehouse, before they headed off to a new life in London. The couple had bought in Knightsbridge, and done so at the right time. Already their house was worth a million dollars more than it had cost them.

Business was booming and with $1.5 Mill a year in clear profit all was looking rosy. What is more, they ran their business with precision and focus. Even the efficiency experts, who had come in for three days with the promise that they would only charge 20% of what they SAVED the company, were amazed. They were still there two weeks later, saying "We are learning more about true efficiency every day!"

It was a tight ship, a profitable, fast-paced importing firm that was, as they say, rolling in it. So do dogs, I might add.

Unfortunately, on that one particular day before the bosses left, I stepped into the verbal equivalent of that special something a dog leaves behind in the park. I stopped to speak to the wife who was, of course, utterly perfect in every way. I want to say upfront that it was NOT my fault! It was my Rat that did it: something came over me. This was not the first time it has happened, but this was the first time I was completely conscious of the fact. My RAT took over my mouth.

I suddenly saw in fine detail the life she would be leading in London, but my brain had not engaged before my mouth started to work. My mouth described her new life with clear precision. It said, "I can tell that you will have a marvellous time. Tennis in the back yard, friends over for morning tea, new shoes every week, fashions shows, boutiques, coffee at Harrods in the morning, then over the Chelsea for lunch, and after collecting the kids from their private school, drop in to see friends."

What I cannot convey to you in words is what was REALLY happening. As I was watching all these images roll past, it was like a movie unfolding. It was a story of a little rich girl, one who is completely bored by the monotony of the high life. Every word I said seemed to echo the fact that this woman was going to a luxurious hell. What is more, she knew it! As I spoke she seemed to get the images herself, and I could see the blood drain from her face. So realising my job as at stake, I changed tact. Or I thought I did. My RAT was cleverer than I.

"Of course, if this seems a little trite and boring, you can always join a charity and do something for others, or take walks in the country, or maybe even the odd affair, or perhaps ... " Opps. Did I really just say that?

I stopped myself. I should NOT have said the word "Affair". What's more I really could have been more diplomatic, and thought of something else to say rather than stop there, but a huge weighty pause ensued. It just stopped everything in its tracks. Somehow, without actually saying it, we both understood that the entire course of the woman's life was moving towards an existence of nothingness.

I cannot explain this, but in between the words, the images were flashing bright and clear that she would NOT be an Artist, or a Writer, or a Politician, or a person of note. She was fated to a life of rich-bitch smug mediocrity. We both saw how the threads of her dull destiny was going to pull tighter and tighter with every new million dollars her husband made.

SURELY my RAT could have stopped at this point. But it would not. "Look, seriously, on the bright side of the equation, you will be closer to your cousin (Name deleted but the woman is a famous actor with many awards in Britain) and this will make life far more interesting, I am sure."

Note to self (and you, dear reader): Do not offer options of comparison unless they are flattering. Why I should NOT have said this is fairly straightforward. Did it really matter that her cousin was a famous actor? Yes it mattered. It mattered a LOT because this dear wife of the boss had quite a sore point, which I had forgotten until that very moment. She too wanted to be a person that mattered.

So far everything I had said had tilted her into the dung heap of faded dreams, lost hopes and wasted expectations. And what was more, all that lovely, lovely money was actually becoming the train ticket to her personal uselessness. (Note to self: People do NOT like reality when it does not favour them in the ways they hope for.)

I was fired mere days after my mouth opened. No explanation was given, nor was it expected. I have since learned to pause before speaking, because that DAMN Rat cannot be trusted. As it reveals all in me, it will do this to others, because this is its true delight. Watching people squirm is simply a bonus. But I have learned to be more careful.

Well, I like to think so, but really, no. Like the time I was speaking to a beautiful woman at a meeting, with my then wife beside me, and I stated the obvious. "My God you are just so beautiful. Does it cause you problems with men?" I might add, on one level there was nothing in it but an observation of the obvious, and a wanted to know that side of the feminine fence. Apparently, as I am now divorced, I was not supposed to be interested in discovering anything on the feminine side that I was not supposed to. I remain curious to this day, however.

The Mystic Rat Says: *Reality is always obvious.*

I guess it is obvious that my then dear wife would have taken my comment amiss, and so I am not encouraging you to spread the truth. That is far too expensive. In relationships too much truth means you get a new residence. (Sometimes if comes with a hillside nice view, complete with free nails and a cross.) But it IS a good thing to stop the lies. To stop the lies, obviously you have to be able to RECOGNISE them. This is not so easy. These fictions are buried deep in your thoughts and erode your dreams, a bit at a time, like acid water wearing down a rock. Yet when they have done their work, it seems so normal you believe this is the way things are MEANT to look.

Here is the Paradox. When you learn to NOT tell lies, and as a result stumble into the truth about yourself, you also learn that to survive you have to (wait for it) ... Lie. Are you scratching your head on this one?

I would have been bankrupt years ago if I did not know how to lie to the bank to get a refinance. The person filling out the forms knew I was 'probably" lying, but to get the finance, certain boxes HAD to be ticked with the right ticks. And they were.

Ratology does not say lies of themselves are wrong, only dishonest ones. They can be extraordinarily useful things for survival because, in a world of liars, this is the language they speak. You do not go to France and expect to speak English. Likewise, you do not go to a liars world and try to communicate truth.

HOWEVER: Getting lost in lies and believing they are truth is incredibly harmful to your spiritual freedom. Saying you have been good to grandma, in order to get a cookie, is a perfectly acceptable lie. Why? Because you get a cookie, and it makes Grandma happy, that's why.

The Big Bad Wolf died because he wasn't a good liar. "My my grandma, what big teeth you have got!" and what does the wolf say? "All the better to EAT you with!" This starts Red Riding Hood running about and it gave time for the hunter to come and kill the wolf.

Stupid Wolf. He should have said "I have a sore tooth dear, could you come closer and take a look at it?" and that way he could have eaten her easily. But no, he chose to be smart and tell the truth. Now he's dead.

Hopefully this book will help you in some small way to find the right balance in this area. In the end it is between you and your RAT to sort it. Your RAT can sniff the lies out, dig them up, and in the end, like the Big Bad Wolf, you will find you have to EAT them if you are to stay alive. Raw, undiluted lies are often hard to swallow, but you must because at the core of each lie is a great truth.

I can promise you, finding a lie that has been running inside you for years, and realising that you can kill it, and eat it: this is a very satisfying thing. Find It, Kill It, Eat It.

Please note the *Paradox of the Liar*, which is that if you ask a Liar to tell you the truth, and he does, then he is no longer a liar. It is a classic bit of good old fashioned nonsense philosophy that I will outline for you.

Principle ONE: An honest man cannot lie.

Principle TWO: A Liar can tell the truth

Problem: A Liar that speaks the truth is no longer a Liar, yet he can still lie, just as an honest man may believe he speaks the truth, but lies.

- If you ask a Liar if he is telling the truth and he says "NO", has he stopped being a Liar, because he is being truthful?
- If you ask a Liar if he is telling the truth and he says "YES", has he stopped being a Liar, because he is being truthful?

Both answers form an unsolvable conflict.

An old Monk once offered me a simple thought. When I asked him a question about life, he simply said, with a look that he had said this a thousand times to a thousand young truth seekers, *"If it is not obvious, it is not worth it."*

We just need to see the obvious in any situation, and only then will the course of action we must take becomes clear. Running around trying to solve things you don't understand just means you run around in circles.

And there are things like the Liar Paradox that just make a permanent loop of logic. *Blessed are they who run round in circles, for they shall be known as big wheels.*

Tired of dawdling pedestrians blocking the footpath and slowing you down? TIME IS MONEY! Shift those boring nuisances with the new, eco-friendly, solar powered PEDESTRIAN SUPER TOOTER from HORN BLASTER TECHNOLOGIES — THE HURRY EXPERTS.

HAPPINESS:

W e all have moments of happiness, but why don't they last? Why are most people generally not all that happy? We were mostly happy as children. Not all, but most, had reasonable stretches of happiness. So where did this natural state go?

There are moments where happiness is possible in our lives, but we often sabotage them. We let our fears step in, or we forget to be kind, or we ignore another person for no particular reason. Why? What is wrong? Nothing is wrong, it's simple a choice we make. I can tell you that as much as YOU are the problem, YOU are also the solution. The simple truth is that we are happy when we are not lost in complication. The question of finding happiness is really a question of rediscovering simplicity.

The Mystic Rat Says: *Your solution for yourself is yourself.*

Have you ever asked yourself what a solution really is? It is a liquid into which things have been dissolved. In this sense, when we are looking for a solution, we are seeking to re-solve by dis-solving. It may sound silly, but think about it for a moment. Take salt, take water, mix, and the solution is salty water. A solution is something we get when we unite different elements into one.

But any solution you are looking for can only come about when you know what you are trying to solve. And when you do, there is a unique RATOLOGY solution that will apply. Let's say we used Spiritual Arithmetic and discover what the core issues are that are creating the problem. What next?

Well, just dissolve the problem in something it will dissolve in. That may sound stupid, but in practical terms iron will dissolve in acid. If you have something that is hard and sharp in your life, some acid wit might work, get it? When we understand the nature of the problem, we can work out what solution it will dissolve it.

So how do we discover the true nature of the problem? How do we take the notions about Spiritual Arithmetic and apply them in real time?

We need nothing but ourselves and to accept this particular, powerful, piece of advice: *Celebrate, articulate and become commensurate with your Inner RAT.*

Do you want to break free of your isolation, your prison, and that self-imposed exile from life (generally created by your personal sense of guilt and shame) that we all suffer to some degree? Get to know your Rat.

YOU are trapped in your own dream. This is the sum of all your concerns and the core of all your problems and blessings. This is why you have the partner you have, the job you do, and the house you where you live. Everything is part of the DREAM (or nightmare) that runs you. It is not your fault, because your personal dream is not even yours. It is the manufactured reality of countless generations before you that imposes itself upon your thoughts and presses you down.

Being happy is a momentary state of balance. Have you ever seen a tight rope walker? They live in this permenent state of temporary balance, and because of this, they survive. Be happy when your life is a tight rope walk, because this is all it will ever be, a momentary state of balance.

Most people's unhappiness comes from their desire to stay away from the edge of danger. They trade freedom for security, in other words. There is very little I can say here, other than we do wheat we feel we must, but if you are not happy with your life, why do you keep doing what you are doing? Why not try and be a little bold, and do things differently.

Yet if, after reading these words, you STAY in your rut, then you will have only yourself to blame. RATOLOGY can indeed set you free, but you have to want your freedom enough to let go of whatever is holding you. Let your Inner RAT guide you. Trust it, but please, not too much because it bites. It is a little tricky getting this right, because, like my mouth that lost me the job, it can and will cause ripples and concerns in the comforts of your personal world.

The Mystic Rat Says: *One thing is certain, if you are UNHAPPY, if you feel you are not achieving, if you believe you are a worthless minion, you are NOT accepting your RAT.*

Why Do Some Get , and Others Starve?

We all share similar issues, and whether we are a native roaming the plains of Mozambique or an Astronaut walking on the Moon, we have certain things in common. The obvious is that we all eat, we all crap, we all breath and we all want something we don't have.

Yet some people seem to get plenty! Why is it that some people just seem to get what they want so easily? Why does it seem so hard for US to get ahead while others seem to surge forward without anything like the problems we face? Most answers come when you can see the obvious, so first, we need to discuss the OBVIOUS.

The FIRST obvious reality is that God is not part of the story regarding what you get or don't get. Being kind, obeying rules, kissing babies: None of this works. It is OBVIOUS it doesn't work because utter bastards who shoot ducks, kill friendships and massacre subtle emotions often do quite well, thank you very much.

Forget God being within, throw away everything you have been taught about love and kindness. These things are neither good nor bad, but they CAN be a hindrance. To discover how to get what we need in a way that works for us, we need to start rearranging our notions of "Good Versus Bad". The first surprise here will be that the good you think you are doing is so often the very evil that is holding you back.

The Second OBVIOUS point is that you always get what you EXPECT. If you work hard enough for something, get past your fears and learn to EXPECT and feel you deserve what you have worked for: It arrives. But really, you can also work just enough to get what you want, because as long as you EXPECT to get, you get.

Expectation is a powerful thing. Most people in the West expect a flushing toilet and a shower, so they GET it. In Africa, this is not something many people expect to get, so they don't. It really is this simple. You can work harder in Africa but the overall level of expectation there is SO much lower than the US, that people just do not GET what they desire so easily. Get it? EXPECTATION defines your reality far more than prayers, hopes and wishes ever will.

Why is this important to understand? Within the Psyche of every individual there are a hundred voices. They are many desires, whispers and beliefs within, and they can easily become subtle traps that weld you to a life of pseudo-pleasant non-states of waffle and rhubarb. When you clarify your Intention, this polarises you to a specific course of action. It chops out the waffle and gets right to the cream.

You may WANT certain things, but opposing this, inside you are thousands of small devils and angels seeking to stop you. You may WANT that second cup of coffee, but that miserable angel tells you not to. Then you want to be good, and leave the café but that nasty devil says "You DO want cake!"

We need to find that sacred space of freedom within ourselves where the many voices grow still. There are MANY states within (and without) you that defy and define both your desires and your detestations. There is also the call of nature, your natural desire to be REAL. So how in all this cacophony do we find the Omphalos, as the Greeks called it, the belly button of being?

Well, you can sit and go through every single thought and emotion you have, and decide if this one leads to true adventure, or not. Or you can do it the easy way. Relax and clarify your INTENTION. Just as we spoke right up front in this book about subtext and understanding what another is really trying to say, why not try and do the same for yourself?

So, how do we do this? You guessed it: Your RAT! Your Reality Attention Trigger is a truth inside your heart that shines the light on your Path to Reality and Freedom. Your RAT sounds out the alarm. Your Inner RAT is swinging on the bell trying to get your attention. It it may well be ringing loudly right now, trying to warn you that you are heading towards dullness, death and lack of distinction. Whatever the message, it is trying to tell you to get focussed on what is really in front of you. It is asking you to look through the vapour of dreams and fears that currently control your head and heart, and see the obvious.

Your RAT: It is the closest thing you have to a true friend, and yet how many are ignoring it? Most of us are trying to pat our life down into comfort and convenience while at the same time we are internally screaming for purpose, a life of consequence and the crashing down of convention. Well the GOOD news is that you CAN have your cake and eat it to. The bad news is: Because of your conditioning, you will try to stop yourself from achieving this.

The Mystic Rat Says: *I reveal to all in these pages an arcane wisdom. This secret was known in Ancient Egypt, spoken of in Crossroads Temples of Rome, and practised every true Celt, by every native warrior, and by all who hold themselves as FREE men. It is this: Doubt everything.*

So if you want to be HAPPY, (you DO want to be happy, yes?) STOP whatever it is you are currently doing. Stop reading, stop thinking, stop everything. Just put your foot on the brake, stop the emotions, stop the wondering about tomorrow.

STOP tying to be Nice. STOP trying to be pleasant. STOP trying to be the good guy, the perfect wife, the white knight, the saving mother, the forgiving lover, etc. and START waking up your Doubting Thomas. Start exercising the one who doesn't believe ANYTHING unless it's proven, and even then it thinks twice.

That is all you have to do to awaken your Rat.

Sorry if, after all this rhubarb, that all I offer is this stupidly simple advice, but that's how it is. But the real point is, once you have the mechanical ability to do the Spiritual Arithmetic, once you grasp how people live in bubbles, then doubting everything is not a negative thing at all. It's like the builder preparing to build a house, he doubts everything will work easily, so he plans, organises, and cover the negative possibilities so he CAN build the house easily.

Which brings us to the next section, where we get to the serious stuff of Rattyness.

But right now, remember the STOP principle. It is time to celebrate, embrace, and extol the powerful creative force that you have largely forgotten about. Being "nice" destroys you. It proves you have come to agreement and acceptance of the Social Lies that run this planet. Defy it. Wake up that hidden part you are afraid of, that part of you that is your Power. By ignoring this you have killed your Freedom. By ignoring the self-centred bastard within you have ignored many of your options to LIVE. It is NOW time to reach for the RAT inside and LIBERATE yourself.

The Minister for Big Things listens as the architect presents his plans for the amazing new building.

BUILD:
And the Law of Life will never repay you in a Negative Way

Why is this true? Have you ever seen a builder approach a job? He always looks at everything that can go WRONG before he starts thinking about how to actually get the building underway. In his mind, he has assessed whether his workers are up to the task, if the money is sufficient, if the ground is right for what he wants to build, He has gone through a thousand possibilities of what can go WRONG before he even begins to think of what will happen to make it go RIGHT.

ALL builders go to Bastard School. They know what it takes to become a good builder, and part of it is the certain knowledge that a large chunk of pure negativity and disbelief in EVERYTHING is required if you are to survive. You may be surprised, but the real secret of creativity and success is found in doubt. Learn to approach things NEGATIVELY and life will go easier on you.

I knew one builder who was a genuine Nice Guy. He really wanted to do the right thing by everyone. He truly believed that by building good houses at good prices with lots of nice extras then everyone would love him and he would succeed. Eventually he faced bankruptcy, and it took this financial death to awaken his Inner RAT. He was certain to go down the tubes if he didn't do something fast, so he started growing Marijuana inside the houses that were not selling to survive. Then he got rich and forgot about building anything but rooms to grow more of his hydroponic crops in.

Do you see where being nice got him? He became Drug Baron. Think about it, if he had been a big enough bastard in the first place he would never have been driven to becoming a drug Czar. He wanted to build good houses, but this unfortunately didn't make him as much money as the far simpler and cheaper brick boxes that got churned out like sausages by Bastard Builders.

Are you beginning to see how you can RUIN your life by not practising and embracing your Inner RAT? I spoke to a builder about how they priced jobs, and the answer was "Well, I add up all the costs, and then add 10% for mistakes. Then I add a 30% profit margin, then I add another 15% on top of that to be sure."

"SO," I asked "What percentage do you actually end up with as profit?"

"Usually around fifteen percent.".

I questioned him: "15% was IT after all was said and done?" He just shrugged. With a sense of world weary experience he explained that it always takes longer, costs more and pays less than you plan for.

I had a Feng Shui consultant come to advise me on a house I had bought. His first question was, "Who owned this prior, and for how long?" I explained it was a respected builder, and that he and his wife had lived in the house for 25 years. The fellow said "There is little need to look any further, the place is already proven."

I asked him to explain more, and he said, "A person who added to his community has spent 25 years in this house, and remained happily married? It is obvious. Just the history alone tells us the energy here MUST be good."

Build and the Law of Life will never repay you in a negative way, but if you build in negative way, life will only repay you in like coin. Build too cheap or too expensive, or worry about what others will think, or lower your quality too much, then all you will get is bankruptcy and derision.

WHAT we build also counts. It is not just houses and material things. You can build up BS and waffle as a way of life, and in due course this is what you will attract to your life. Or you can build up reality, perception and clear intention. If nothing else, understand that it is your choice. You CAN choose a different path to the one you are currently walking. Or can you?

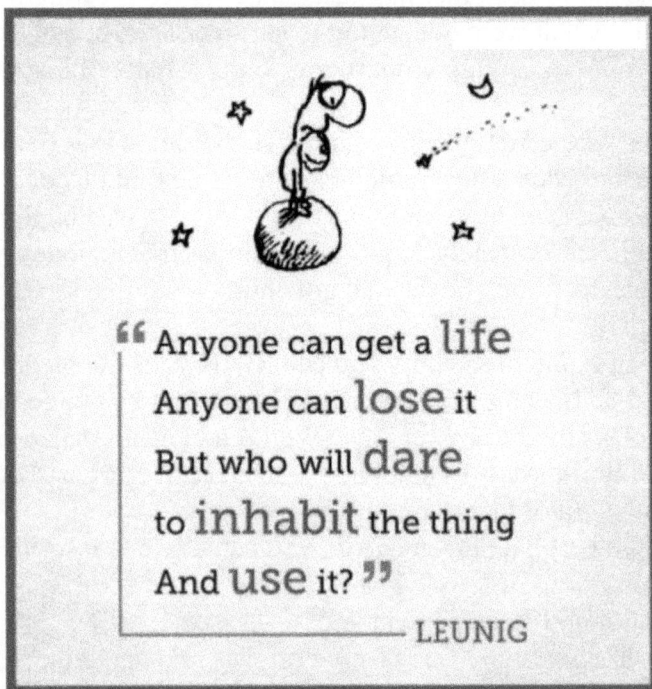

" Anyone can get a life
Anyone can lose it
But who will dare
to inhabit the thing
And use it? "

— LEUNIG

Un-Stitching the Patchwork Quilt

Your mind is like a patchwork quilt. It takes the snip of this and a snap of that, gathers a hundred different pieces of experience, and then stitches them all together like a jigsaw puzzle with the thread of belief. This is how everyone's mind is built.

Mostly, the core patterns, the canvas, is set in childhood, and we are just adding bits that seem to fit the jigsaw picture as we go along. In this sense, our mind is not ours at all, but a collection of images lined up to make some sort of sense.

If only it all made sense. Socrates proved how vulnerable people's thinking process really is, and that at the core of most thinking are wrong assumptions and prejudice.

Do you recall those funny "bobble head" dogs they put in the back of cars? I always have this image in mind when I see people mechanically agreeing, or disagreeing, with what another is saying. They are like the bobble head dog in the back of the car. They are outwardly saying yes or no, but really they are just not thinking about things.

We hear so often the phrase "Follow your passion!" but most people are just following their inertia.

Let's get back to Bubble Thinking for a moment. We all have fixed beliefs of some sort, but are they truly immovable? It depends on how honest a person is. APeople will go to fairly extraordinary lengths to keep their bubble of belief intact. People will invent total nonsense, thoughts and beliefs in order to keep their cherished notions. It does not matter that life serves up a reality that opposes their wishful thinking. An example: The KKK believes in white superiority, and the fact that there is a black man as the US President is proof, to them, of everything they stand for.

"This is why we believe what we do, to stop the blacks from taking over!" It doesn't make any sense, other than it is an escape clause to keep the bubble intact. Yet, lack of common sense is what people do.

Why do we do this? For the very same reason we have white and black notes on a piano. Did you wish to know why we have these white and black notes? It's a facsinating insight into human nature.

The reason is quite extraordinary. The Catholic church BANNED what are now the black notes, because of its belief in the Devil. You could create what was called "Devil Chords" when you incorporated what are now the black keys on a piano. These are the odd tones you hear at every horror movie. IE: The spooky chords.

The belief was that for every one of these chords were played, a devil would be released from Hell to walk upon the Earth. So logically, if you can't play the chords then all the devils will stay locked up in Hell. Simple! So the Church BANNED five of the twelve notes of music, and saved the world.

This is how we got the white notes. You were only allowed to play what we now call the "C" scale. Things were "of God" (the "C" scale) or "of the Devil". (Every other note) During the reformation, common sense started to prevail. It was argued that, as Pythagoras' mathematics were what was used to build the church temples, he could not be "of the Devil".

Yet his Music WAS classed as being of the Devil. How could he be of God, and of the Devil all at the same time? The Germans were already doing the Lutheran thing, and making music with "all" the notes, and Henry the Eighth had put his name to the popular song, "Greensleeves". (which had an evil Devil Note in it) Finally the Church relented.

Reluctantly the "new" notes were allowed. We called them names such as Bb, Db, Eb, Gb and Ab, and these notes were now able to be incorporated into instruments. This is what sparked off Bach, Motzart and the Symphonic period. However, there was a problem: Where do we put the notes? A spinet had only the white notes of "C" scale, and after much discussion it was decided to put the notes in the right order as Pythagoras had them. But not, as logic would determine, by going from One to Twelve. Much fiddling (pun intended) had to be done. Rather than restructure the keyboard to be chromatic, the "new" notes were just stuffed into the places where they used to be.

What we ended up with in the piano keyboard of today, which is actually an entirely illogical instrument when compared to a fretted instrument such as the guitar. It made absolutely NO sense to have stayed with the "C" scale as the basis for everything, and trying to put "black" notes into it that were NOT DESIGNED for this scale. But his is what was done. The musicians of the day made it all fit with convoluted Music Theory, but it is a logical framework build over an illogical reality.

Now, try and tell a classically trained musician that they have spent 18 years learning something that is completely illogical. They will think you are MAD. They have trained their mind to wrap around the impossible leaps of logic. Using a different fingering for every scale is normal, and these folk are all quite certain that THIS is how music is MEANT TO BE.

It is not. True Music is simply a series of Patterns that are generally harmonious when locked together. Music is mathematics from 1 to 12. It is form, shape and perfection. But Music Theory (incorporating Sharps and Flats) of itself is a twisted mess of logic that has been concocted to make the illogical logical. However, once trained in the illogic, it seems perfectly right to the mind immersed within it.

This is EXACTLY how bubble consciousness works.

It's completely wrong, and yet it works. And a good thing it does, because no more symphonies could be played until everyone relearned how to play in this "new" way.

Human inertia determines human evolution as much as new invention will seek to change it. When our mind is challenged with a new reality or paradigm, it generally takes what it will from the past, and shapes a reality that conforms to what it has already inherited from society and experience.

But in this case there is a practical reason as to WHY this musical illogicality has been allowed to continue. In the 16th Century one smart cookie had the notion to REDESIGN the keyboard, in order to make the white and black notes function in a more logical manner. It was proven to all the established Music Schools of the day that with this rearranging it would take the current 9 years of music training and allow a student to achieve the same result within 18 months. Obviously, faced with so HUGE a loss of revenue the Music Schools ALL rejected this notion out of hand. Money, therefore, is the real reason learning music is such a pain in the butt.

The Mystic Rat Says: *Your mind will concoct and fully support completely false images in order to keep your current reality in tact.*

SMART people know how to manipulate this in others. MEDIA, as one example, is all about manipulating and rearranging the images that form the quilt of your belief.

Constantine: Bubble Maker Extraordinaire

Emperor Constantine understood that the Medium is the Message, long before Marshall McLuhan wrote about it. He started the Catholic Church and built one of the most glorious Bubbles the world has ever seen. He knew how to play the minds of people to his advantage, and specifically a particular group called the Christians.

In order to make this new idea acceptable, Constantine had to incorporate enough elements from the old religions into his new one. He basically reformed Mithraism and other Roman beliefs, and called it Catholic. The name itself means "universal".

There was nothing "new" in the new church, other than it was wrapped around a historical figure called Jesus. Yet Mithra, who was largely followed the the Roman Legions, had 12 apostles and died a martyrs death, and he is raised from the dead as well. Add to this the Attic Goddess, who as an intercessionary agent between the Gods and Man, was very much like Mary, and you get the basic framework. The basic patterns of other teachings were copied and revamped in the new Catholic Church.

What he did, in effect, was to create a package of SYMBOLS and IMAGES that could unify people to a collective goal. None of them individually were that much different from what was already known and accepted, other than the concept of ending animal sacrifice. This, and the notion of ritual cannibalism where you pretend to eat the body of someone, were the hard points to sell.

Ideas and beliefs had always ruled the hearts and minds of people, and, for the Romans in particular, religion was always a smorgasbord of choice. Another religion was just another religion, as far as they were concerned. What Constantine did was unify the PUBLIC SERVICE of his day, which was largely Christian, into a single force. He understood that governments and rulers come and go, but that the bureaucracy lives forever. His religion unified disparate elements of the Christian faith into one focussed church.

This solidified the power structure and gave it stability. Constantine himself worshipped the sun, right up to the day he died, whereupon he converted to Catholicism. And in due course, as we know, the Roman Empire evolved into the Holy Roman Empire, or the Catholic Church.

How did Constantine sell this concept? The Romans were very superstitious, and whole heartedly believed in omens and messages from the Gods. Constantine, on the eve of a large battle, speaks to the troops of how he sees this CROSS in the clouds. Now, keep in mind that his particular army had lots of Christians in the ranks. Most of the Roman legions were Mithra, but his was strong in Christians, who joined because of his opposition to the Christian purges by Diocletian. He KNOWS this imagery will stir up the men and give them a will to win. So he tells them he has had the vision, and it is clearly a sign they will overcome. He is blowing up the bubble of success in their hearts. The men accept it, willingly, and they DO win. From this point on, Constantine uses the Christian Militia and its related organisation to help run his empire.

But he went a lot further than this! He had to BIND this religion to his cause and so he created a SET OF RULES everyone could adhere to. This is the GLUE to cement the Bubble. What did Constantine do? He invented the Nicene Creed, and put into place the basic principles of the Catholic Church. The Council of Nicea ran for YEARS, and during the course of this process all the various texts from the Torah and New Testament were stitched together to form what we currently know as the BIBLE.

In other words, Constantine MANUFACTURED the Catholic Faith and the Bible itself in much the same way that an editor sorts out the final publication of a book. But when you point this out to a Catholic (and in particular how references to Karma and Reincarnation were specifically EXCLUDED by the later Emperor Justinian) and the good Catholic will reply, "That may be the case, but WE believe ..."

That is just how it is when a Bubble gets fully established as a reality in the mind of the believer. Logic, reason and common sense will do little to affect it, but your Inner RAT can whittle it down to size. Your RAT can see through to the OBVIOUS.

The Mystic Rat Says: *I and the Rat are One.*

We all can see the obvious when it does not challenge our beliefs. When it does, it is oblivious to us. Your Rat will insist that you see the obvious, therefore it needs to shatter some beliefs. But your Rat has to WAKE UP first, and in most cases, your Rat is sleeping soundly in the passive world of convenience. Your RAT is stitched up with compromise and locked away in a small room of acceptable behaviour and, if you want to burst ANY of your personal bubbles, if you want to change the course of your existence, you will have to wake it up and put it to work.

The Mystic Rat Says: *There are many hundreds of Bubble Types. You live in some of them, and you are sharing Bubbles with many others.*

Bubbles are really AGREEMENTS you have made. There are Trans-Personal Bubbles (Where you share similar habits) there are Collectivist Bubbles (Where you have similar goals) and there are Enforced Bubbles (Where you are given a set of rules without your apparent consent). It may be that you drink, and your shared Bubble is at the bar down the road, or it may be that you do NOT drink, and your shared bubble is at the coffee shop, waiting for your friends to come in each day.

You may have a MIXED Bubble, like when you go to an Evangelical Church that fills an emotional need (Personal) a Social Need (Trans-Personal) with a Spiritual Goal (Collectivist) yet which also fits in with indoctrination as a child (Enforced).

So it is not all cut and dried. Your Bubble Mix is generally an overlay of many types, with varying thicknesses and many other variations. Often we modulate other people's Bubbles, and graft them onto our own.

We not only have Bubble Consciousness in our personal beliefs, but we also have different bubbles of consciousness waiting for us in:

1. *The places we frequent,*
2. *The habits we indulge, and even*
3. *The types of food we eat.*

We are CONSTANTLY walking in and out of a thousand different bubbles of consciousness, every day, every hour, every moment.

Take the respectable judge, so upright and honest, but on the side he has his B&D Bubble where his favourite Madam is waiting to whip him. The extraordinary thing is that Good Judge will not see any contradiction in this, at least until he is photographed by the local journalist and his bubble gets burst in public scrutiny.

People generally HATE to have their bubbles burst, and for the life of me, I cannot really see why. It should be a relief to be removed from the falsehood, but it is not. People avoid change, and this simple avoidance seems to be their only rationale, which is of course completely irrational.

The mind generates a quilt of belief, and generates Bubbles for reasons of its own. It really has very little to do with YOU, other than you have to live in these "houses" created for you. Things will stay this way until life or yourself does something to move on from the old ways of thinking and feeling. But here's a heartening thought, all you need do is change ONE feeling, ONE thought, and you have started the bubble bursting process.

However, bubble bursting in one area doesn't really change anything. Some (like our good Judge) will simply modify behaviour to avoid further scrutiny. One Bubble gets burst, and another will be generated to replace it. We will blithely continue to do whatever we want and desire, and convince ourselves that we are CHOOSING our path in life. Our only real choice comes with awareness and seeing the obvious.

As we state in the Chapter after next on FREE WILL "You never do what you WANT, you simply WANT what you DO". Burst One Bubble and you will simply go build another. Why? Because that will allow you to do whatever satisfies your urges.

Shared Bubbles

S hared Bubbles comes in many forms. The Trans-Personal and other main groups we have already mentioned, but there are many more. There is also the Zero Tolerance Bubble, where you have an absolute conviction that everything you do is right, and you gather with similarly intolerant people. There is a Gossip Monger. (Self explanatory) There is a Cynic Bubble, a Science Bubble, an Anti-Science Bubble, a Contradictory Puzzle (Philosophy) Bubble, a Conspiracy Bubble, and so on. There are innumerable and diverse cultures of Bubble Consciousness, as many as there are grains of sand on the beach.

However, there is ONE common thread that unites them ALL. That is an acceptance by and with the people who agree with you. The classic example: Put a batch of soldier crabs in a bucket, and they all get on. All is fine until one disagrees. If it wants to get out of the bucket, and move on, the others in the group will haul it back, and EAT it. People are not so very different to Soldier Crabs, they seek to kill, stop, immobilise any associate that tries to get out of the shared bucket.

So it is serious, life threatening stuff when you start thinking about addressing your pre-set Bubble Beliefs, and waking the RAT that will burst your bubbles. Anyone who SHARES a Belief Bubble will get on with others of the same belief. Anyone who alters their belief, once they are in a shared bubble, will be attacked.

Bubble Types are another way of speaking about the archetypal conditions that are descriptors of all aspects of the human condition. Just as atoms choose connections to other atoms, or reject them, Bubbles develop relationships with other Bubbles that are in agreement OR in opposition to their nature.

There is one defence against Bubble Consciousness taking over your life. If you are completely disinterested in what someone is offering you, or trying to project onto you, then you become invulnerable to the influence. If you are completely disinterested in your OWN imaginings, you are then free of your own Bubbles, or at least that is the theory.

It is almost impossible to be disinterested in your own imagination.

Buddha spoke about desire being the source of all suffering, but this is not exactly true. Your BUBBLES are the source of your problems, your inflated opinions that have become fixed ballooned beliefs are the things that are causing you grief.

But here we discover the Paradox of the Martyr. This is that you can be the word's best martyr, and get yourself up on the cross and even nail in your feet, then one hand, *but you need someone else to drive in the last nail*. You just cannot do it on your own. So too it is with Bubble Bursting. We need someone else to help burst the stubborn, ingrained ones.

Why? Many of the Bubbles you carry are what you believe are your own thoughts. They are NOT. Your Bubbles are mostly HAND ME DOWNS. Almost every single one of them is a condition that has been passed to you like a torch on an Olympic Relay. Society, Parents, Siblings, Friends: They have all given you the bubble baton and you believed you had to run with it.

Because you are part of this invisible race of Humans, you inherent belief is that you must not drop the baton. This is just another Bubble. Bubbles exist within Bubbles, beliefs exist within beliefs, and you will NEVER sort them all out. What you CAN do however is to CALL UP YOUR INNER RAT, and your RAT will help you see the obvious.

The Mystic Rat Says: *Only by allowing yourself to see the OBVIOUS can you set yourself free.*

Your RAT is the prick who bursts your bubbles. This Reality Attention Trigger is the call to common sense, the sharp eye that sees the wood from the cheese. It is your Clarion Bell that rings in the CHANGE of the GUARD.

While you habits are gnawing on wooden plates and calling it dinner, your RAT knows what real food is, and it will kick your butt until you start to feed on what it needs. You MUST feed, cultivate and care for your RAT, otherwise it will get bored of you, and fall asleep, thus giving you no guidance.

In current society, the Inner RAT has almost been extinguished. You are required to be polite, to behave, to not speed on the road, to do your homework, to always speak the truth, etc. Even though most people are living a lie, they somehow believe they speak the truth when they say political correctness is good.

The REAL truth is that it is all largely a lie. When your RAT is wide awake, you will see the lies, and you will see them everywhere. Otherwise it is a case of Eyes Wide Shut. And here is a perfect example of how Bubbles will censor us. In the US edition of this last Kubrick movie the director digitally painted in little things to cover up any sight of pubic regions during the orgy scene. Why? He knew the US bubble would not allow it, though the European version was left intact.

I remember when I was 4 years old, and went to the Catholic Church for the first time. At the end of the incredibly tedious nonsense they call Mass, I went outside with my family, and to my horror everyone who was speaking had TWO FACES. One face was uttering polite nice words, but the other was a darker, evil face that was acting almost opposite to the image on the good, pious face.

I was shocked and dismayed when I realised that everyone was two faced! This in good part was the trigger for Ratology, the fact that most everyone is living a life in consequence to the LIE within themselves. Later I was to realise that the RAT is the bridge between the liar/Humpty Dumpty person, and the sincere Soul.

It is hard to hate someone when you see them as poor, broken Humpty Dumpty. People who live an internalised lie are all Humpty Dumpty. They are broken minds and emotions that have "fabricated" a glue to hold themselves together

Now, your inner Humpty Dumpty, the self you patched together, is merely the reflection of the Bubbles in your inner mind. Are we seeing the long, drawn out connection between your Humpty Dumpty self and a Bubble yet? While you cannot fool yourself when your RAT is awake and functioning, your mind can, and will, confuse you with images (Maya) until you learn to see the obvious.

The way it works is quite simple: If you try to say "I am RICH" but your inner mind knows where your bank balance is really at, then the reflection it creates in response to your attempt to direct your life creates a conflict. The mind knows it is a lie. You are trying to convince yourself you are RICH, but really, inside you know you are poor. Therefore, you remain poor. And secretly, you never expected it to be any different. Change your EXPECTATION, however, and you don;t have to chant any positive mental thinking slogans, because everything changes and shapes itself in accordance to how, and what, we expect.

Forget all that crap you have been told about how the subconscious mind simply accepts what you feed it. We are told if you simply believe that you are rich, then money will come to you. And when it doesn't it is your lack of belief that was the problem. People like to believe that magic and miracles will happen, which is why they buy into lotteries. And occasionally, someone wins a lottery, but the majority continue on, penniless and dreaming.

This all comes down to multiplication versus addition. If I save one dollar every day, then at the end of the year I will have 365 dollars to spend. If I dream of having a million dollars I would have to save 2379.726 dollars every single day. Most people cannot do this, so they try to live a life dreaming of multiplication. If I buy this lottery ticket, or do this "get wealthy" seminar, or whatever, then this factor will become a MULTIPLYER in my life. I won't have to save single dollars, it will all just multiply and I will become rich.

You wish. If wishes were fishes, beggars would eat seafood every day.

Every property bubble comes about because people live in multiplication world, in dream world, rather than simple addition. People rush into the property market as it surges upwards, trying to get in and get a slice of the self-creating money the real estate market will give them. Then it bursts. Same goes for the stock market.

I knew a farmer, a man who did things one step at a time, who bought a property, and when the money was in cattle, he bought bulls. When asked why, he said "Everyone wants cattle, and bulls are cheap. But a drought will come, people will have to sell off the cattle, and bulls will be needed." Sure enough, inside five years when all his neighbours were going broke, he was selling bulls at a premium price.

And with this money, he built sheds. When asked why, he said "The drought is over, this is why people are buying bulls. But another one will come, so I am putting up sheds to store hay. That way I can feed my bulls during the next drought." Sure enough, another drought comes, and he can keep even more bulls, and sell them for more money next time it rains.

And with this money, he bought a huge bulldozer. He put in flood proof raised roads, using the soil from one of the largest private dams in Australia, which he created using his huge bulldozer. When asked why, he said, "There will be another drought, and I will now have a permanent water supply on my land, and when the rains come I will be able to get my bulls to market quicker, because I would be locked up on my property. And because of the raised roads, my bulls will also have a place to go to get out of flood water, which means I lose less livestock to flood."

He worked with addition. One plus one equals two, but he did so knowing that life has a multiplying effect when you add things up right.

Your Subconscious Mind may well accept the images you feed it, but your SUPER CONSCIOUS Mind is fully aware of when bullshit is being spread on the garden. And here's the rub: It lets it happen. But in doing so it steps back, and so your dreams and wishes now effectively create a distance between your inner knowing and outer understanding. But the Super Conscious self also knows that the BS your outer consciousness has spread can help the roses IT likes to grow.

But it will not put up with it forever. If you are going to try and force you're your mind with images it knows to be false, it will rebel. Eventually the Super Conscious breaks out and wreaks havoc in your life, so here's the warning, if you are going to try affirmations and positive thinking (Which is really bubble creation), make sure you set goals you can get to QUICKLY. Get there QUICKLY and your inner mind will allow things to be, but if you take too long about it, Humpty Dumpty

WILL fall, and the pieces will never get put back together.

In the end trying to CONTROL your mind never works. Your BUBBLES, your hand me down beliefs and patterns, these are what are running your life. Unless you have made a conscious effort to awaken the heart, and have (in a sense) slept with your Inner RAT, then you will have no chance what-so-ever of breaking free from these patterns that have become your chains.

So how do we do this? Indeed, this IS the question. And really the very first step any one can take in to direction of true freedom is simply knowing what you want. And how do I find out what I really want? Listen to the Mystic Rat!

The Mystic Rat Says: *If you wish to be Free, Free the Rat Within.*

You have to unleash your pre-conditions, your hero complexes, your martyr strategies, your "good person", your struggle self, your blind belief in authority, your false confidence, your hopeful self, and just start each day wanting to be REAL. Mostly though, we have to let go of our faith in the God of Good Deeds and completely toss the notion of "Salvation through Good Works and/or Faith".

Here I pass along a warning: In order to find what you really want, you tend to have to go down a whole lot of blind alleys and dead ends. We call this failure, your Inner Rat calls it exploration. Your curiosity and your enthusiasm will be tested, and your heart will suffer many losses, but persist. Defeat is really a removal of false dreams. A blind alley is really a rut you got out of. But your inner guidance will always be there. It is a matter of silencing the outer noise of beliefs and emotions.

You cannot trust your mind, your mind is a trickster. You cannot trust your emotions, they are programmed to tell you lies. You cannot trust your Priest, your Counsellor, or your Parents. They have all, by and large, rejected their RAT therefore they cannot guide you to the point where your RAT can be recognised and accessed.

Your partner 'may' be able to help you if they are raw enough, and true enough to the purpose of discovery. But most partners want a compromise between their wants and your needs. As they tend to prefer their wants to your needs, most relationships become a Battle of Get, rather than a Suffice of Needs.

Knowing what you WANT is more important than sufficing your NEED. When you KNOW what you want, it is easy to fulfil a need. But trying to fill a need without knowing your true desire is like pouring an ocean into a pipe that connects to another ocean. So HOW do I discover my true WANT? After all, having Freedom to choose doesn't count for much if you don't know what you want.

FINDING OUT WHAT YOU WANT

What do I want? THAT, dear Yorrick, is the real question. Something precious few grasp is the fact that if we do not know our true wants we run on automatic. This is the reason why our patterns run us. How so?

There is a gap inside, an empty space we feel, and as nature abhors a vacuum (which hardly explains Space at all) this nothing zone draws in "fillers". Usually these are beliefs, emotions of need, or a variety of control factors. The net result is: *We never do what we want, we simply want what we do.* And this is a *best case* scenario. Many people do not even want to do what they are doing

People love to talk about free will, choice, choosing your destiny, etc. It is a LIE! Unless you know and understand the base impulse, the core WANT within, then all the options and choices in your life count for nothing. You are blind to the obvious.

Adam and Eve didn't have Free Will. They had no choice but to do what tempted them, for the very reason that, given a limited range of option, people go for temptation every time. You cannot defeat your imagination. As soon as they saw the bait, the imagination got to work, and their mind took over. Everything else was simply a delaying process until the inevitable arrived. And what is more, both God and the Devil KNEW this was going to happen.

Where is the Free Will? Certainly not in the Garden of Eden. Self-determination comes in knowing what you want. It is so simple to say, but not so easy to achieve. Yet, until we find true self-determination, we never do what we WANT. We do not even do what we WILL. At very best, we will just WANT WHAT WE DO.

Extraordinary research in the US has demonstrated that a deep impulse within us makes a decision milliseconds before your conscious mind chooses. Brain wave patterns peak immediately PRIOR to the point where a person believes they make a decision, therefore the simple conclusion is that YOU are not deciding. Something else is, something that comes from a deeper point than thought.

I include an unabridged quote from the American Scientist magazine that paints the picture fairly clearly. If you can manage all the words, the summation is remarkable simple. Something within us is choosing before we have any sort of conscious volition.

COGNITIVE SCIENCE: FREE WILL AND THE BRAIN

The following points are made by S.S. Obhi and P. Haggard (American Scientist 2004 92:358):

1) In 1983, Benjamin Libet and his colleagues at the University of California San Francisco published a profoundly influential paper on the source of human control. In this study, participants watched a small clock hand that completed one full revolution in 2.56 seconds. While fixated on the clock, a participant voluntarily flexed his wrist at a time of his choosing. After the movement, the clock hand continued to rotate for a random time and then stopped. Then, a participant reported the position of the clock hand at the time when she first became aware of the will to move. Libet and his colleagues called this subjective judgment W, for "will". In other parts of the experiment, participants judged when they actually moved, and Libet called this judgment M, for "movement". The timing of the W and the M told Libet and his collaborators when, subjectively speaking, a participant formulated a will to move and actually moved.

2) In addition, Libet's team measured two objective parameters: the electrical activity over the motor areas of the brain, and the electrical activity of the muscles involved in the wrist movement. Over the motor areas, Libet recorded a well-known psychophysiological correlate of movement preparation called the "readiness potential" (RP), which Hans H. Kornhuber and Lueder Deecke first described in 1965. The RP is measured using electroencephalographic recording electrodes placed on the scalp overlying the motor areas of the frontal lobe, and appears as a ramplike buildup of electrical activity that precedes voluntary action by approximately 1 second. By also recording the electrical activity of the muscles involved in the wrist movement, Libet precisely determined the onset of muscle activity related to the RP.

3) Libet and his colleagues examined the temporal order of conscious experience and neural activity by comparing the subjective W and M judgments with the objective RP and muscular activity. First, the investigators found that, as expected, W came before M. In other words, the subjects consciously perceived the intention to move as occurring before a conscious experience of actually moving. This suggests an appropriate correspondence between the sequence of subjective experiences and the sequence of the underlying events in the brain. But Libet also found a surprising temporal relation between subjective experience and individual neural events. The

actual neural preparation to move (RP) preceded conscious awareness of the intention to move (W) by 300 to 500 milliseconds. Put simply, the brain prepared a movement before a subject consciously decided to move. This result suggests that a person's feeling of intention may be an effect of motor preparatory activity in the brain rather than a cause. As Libet himself indicated, this finding ran directly contrary to the classical conception of free will.

4) Considering all the existing data, the brain is apparently going full speed ahead well before a person experiences the conscious intention of moving. Consequently, no role appears for conscious processes in the control of action -- or so it might seem. Although research casts doubt on whether conscious processes cause actions, the data remain consistent with the idea that conscious processes could still exert some effect over actions by modifying the brain processes already under way. The fact that conscious awareness of intention precedes movement by a few hundred milliseconds means that a person could still inhibit certain actions from being made.(1-5)

References (abridged):

1. Haggard, P. 2001. The psychology of action. British Journal of Psychology 92:113-128.

2. Haggard, P., and S. Clark. 2003. Intentional action: conscious experience and neural prediction. Conscious Cognition 12(4):695-707.

3. Haggard, P., S. Clark and J. Kalogeras. 2002. Voluntary action and conscious awareness. Nature Neuroscience 5(4):382-385.

4. Haggard, P., M. Taylor-Clarke and S. Kennett. 2003. Tactile perception, cortical representation and the bodily self. Current Biology 13(5):R170-173.

5. Haggard, P., and B. Whitford. 2004. Supplementary motor area provides an efferent signal for sensory suppression. Cognitive Brain Research 19(1):52-58.

Extracted from American Scientist   http://www.americanscientist.org

In other words: Eve was already reaching for that apple, even before her conscious mind said "OK". There was no conscious choice: We WANT and ACT before we consciously choose.

What happens inside most people is a little more complicated, yet just as simple. We want something and start an action, but our ACTING gets caught up in the performance, and we often forget our original desire. Baby wants love, acts to get love (waaahhh) but baby gets nappy changed. Oh, that's a new sensation, and Baby likes it! Whaaaah, change it again! Baby gets caught up in its acting.

Put this way, it seems fairly obvious, and it is! Essentially, we start out with a sense of want, but in the process of getting what we want we get sidetracked by our habits and patterns. The problem here is that we forget about the original desire, and fall into what we call secondary needs. Remember original desire, and we can get back on track to our core purpose.

As a child, there is no great conflict. But as the individual matures, this small gap core wants and artificial ones grows. When we forget the originating impulse, we get easily sidetracked. It's a little like Homer Simpson saying he going to do something, but then he sees a doughnut, and completely forgets his original choice.

To be able to be free of tension, we must be connected to our natural wants and needs. All true choice is determined by our WANT, not our WILL. Our WANT sends a signal to our brain, and it acts to fulfil the want. But when the gap grows inside, when the pieces first start to break as Humpty Dumpty falls, our actions get confused. The curtain of forgetting falls over our initial impulse. The result is that an ever large gap appears between originating wants and the mind.

An example: The notion "I feel like watermelon" comes from a deeper desire for fluid, one that existed before you were aware of watermelon. But with the discovery of watermelon in hand, the mind jumps past the original motivation, and now thinks it originally wanted watermelon.

"Yes, this is what I wanted!" your mind says to itself. Our CONSCIOUS mind believes IT has made a decision for watermelon, and generated your physical activity to achieve that decision. IE: You go cut up the watermelon. But the mind only acted on the deeper level of WANT.

When you fail to recognise this, it means you are not doing what you WANT, you are WANTING WHAT YOU DO.

It sounds like splitting hairs, but it is very important. The reason is the gap. When you are connected to original wants, there is no internal gap. Nothing appears to be BROKEN inside us, therefore there is no jig saw puzzle to assemble. The picture is simple and complete. When you move away from original wants, into dreams and imagining, the cracks appear in the psyche. This makes you far easier to manipulate with external influences.

The perfect example is the younger sister of friends of mine. Her older sibling started a relationship with a man that she rather fancied herself. She wanted a man for herself, and she painted a picture over the gap she now felt. NOW this charming handsome man, who was so nice to her, was clearly her soul mate. He became the one she always had dreamed of. Of course, he was just fascinated and amazed by the young girl talking about karma, spiritual subjects, and the fact she had no notion of modesty when changing clothes.

In the course of time, it becomes clear that the older man is with her sister, but she has forgotten that the original want was a man for herself, because now she wants THIS man. The gap between her original, and natural desire, got fixated into the notion that in front of her was the Soul Mate. The logic loops that follow are where the real issues get created. Logically, this made her sister a thief. The net result was the girl became very bitter, and after 30 years will still not speak with her sibling.

This is a TRIANGULATION PATTERN. You are not connected to your original impulse, and come to believe your secondary reaction is your original choice. You no longer know what it is you truly want, which means you have lost the focus of your true heart and your free will. You, your originating impulse, and the action created by both, are separated. With no understanding of the core motivation, your supposed choices that follow are not choices at all. As one issue adds to the next, adding layer upon layer of complication, this is when the pain starts.

It is like a three way love affair with two mistresses, each either side of the mind whispering into its ears. You become double minded an unstable, because without knowing your core want, there is no solid ground for you.

If you do have a devil inside you, this is where it lives. And what did DeNero say about the Devil? *"The greatest trick the Devil pulled was to convince you he doesn't exist."* Well, we now know it is the Censor pulling the strings, and we call back to how to get past this creature. Knowing your true wants is the first step.

This may not sound like a terrible evil, forgetting the original want that started your action, but if you are not connected to your natural wants, you are never going to understand your natural needs. This is a very specific "hole" in human nature that has been exploited by every mind predator that has existed. Specifically, organised religion specifically places itself as the authority figure in your mind, should you accept it. Lack of clarity in the area of your genuine wants leaves an opening for other forces to control your thoughts and feelings.

Religion uses this "break" in the mind, the area between your want and your action, by inserting notions such as guilt and shame. Now your original wants get filtered through a guilt habit, and all your actions have a filter of guilt they have to work through.

Your Inner RAT will free you from this. It brings you back to the Immediate Moment of Decision. (IMD) How? Simply by accepting that you have natural desires, want and needs. Accepting these means you no longer need this artificial barrier between yourself and your wants.

Acceptance means the gap inside vanishes. The space where guilt and shame lived no longer exists. As this is evicted, the strings that bind get snipped, and problems that have run through families for generations all come to a close.

It is essential, if we are to be free, that we live in the Immediate State of Being, which we call the spontaneous, natural self. It is very important to have no curtain between you and your natural emotions and thoughts. Why?

In one fell swoop, you remove fear, eliminate the gap in OH mind, and come closer to understanding your natural wants. Just by accepting you have natural wants, desires and needs. Here is where you find your RAT, and where your RAT finds you.

The Mystic Rat Says: *Accept your RAT. LOSE THE CURTAIN OF FORGETTING. Become aware of the IMMEDIATE MOMENT. Relax in the presence of NOW. Your actions become ONE only when you are ONE with your RAT.*

RAT TRAP

LOOK, *CHEESE*!

HUMAN TRAP

LOOK, AN *INTERNET* CONNECTION!

SINGER +AVIDOR

Reprinted from Funny Times / PO Box 18530 / Cleveland Hts. OH 44118
phone: 216.371.8600 / email: ft@funnytimes.com

The CAT – Controller and Terrorist

T he only way to know what you truly want is to live in the present. To live in the present, you have to remove the curtain of forgetting. Trust your Rat, and learn.

However, we must always remember that your RAT is not perfect. It loves its cheese and it adores its chocolates, and this means that any cleverer RAT or in particular, a passing CAT can, and will, set a trap to catch you. Being truly ONE with your Inner RAT generally means an exponential increase in life awareness, and the likelihood of getting trapped grows increasingly less as you unify your inner being.

I need to point out that your inner CAT exists in opposition to your RAT. This creature lives inside you as well, and every time you try and control things outside of your immediate moment, there you will see it at work. Some people like control so much that they "become" their CAT, and live their lives according to it's dictates.

The External CAT is a Controller and Terrorist. They are the rules people, the ones who "Should" on you, and who try to manipulate your good self to do things that help them survive. They have absolutely no consideration at all for your well being. A Cat considers people they can order about to be fools, and servants of their will.

The CAT inside you is that mental program that is your Caustic, Atrocious Terrorist. It is a Catastrophically Awful Tear-jerker. It is your Callous Attractor Trigger. The experience of the CAT, as it appears in its various disguises, has one single response. It generates a FEAR MAGNET inside you that creates the shadows and gives them dimensional existence. IE: It makes you feel small, and the world big.

This is what causes you to hide from yourself. The Sleeping Cat of Love is the worst of the CATS inside you. It is the one that convinces you that LOVE is the cure for your pain, when in truth, your misplaced love is often the CAUSE of it. Your NEED is what the CAT re-frames as your LOVE, and has this trick of converting your sexual need, taking it away from its natural state, into a state of duality. Now, rather than just having an intimate connection, you feel the need to BE loved and TO Love. This "Sleeping Cat of Love" feeds off your fear emotions.

The duality of the need to be loved, and the need to love, often form a short-circuit in the emotions, one where you start feeling an inability to accept love. You have all this love inside, but when someone offers you the same, you shy away. This is another reason why simple acceptance works better than any pill to cure the heart.

Now, here is the tricky part. Your CAT, like your RAT, will bring you to a point of awareness in the NOW, but it can take you no further. Your CAT will align up your inner bodies so they all act in sequence, but it does this to hone instinct. It like to kill, and being aligned makes you a better killing machine. Have you ever seen those vicious girls in a sorority tearing strips off everyone? That is the CAT at work. You have seen the ice maiden, staying calmly collected through every mood, never showing an emotion? That is the CAT at work.

The RAT, on the other hand, is a family creature. It is a loving Soul that wants to live in the NOW in order to appreciate life, not kill it. Surely the RAT wants the cheese, but it does not want to intentionally harm another in order to get it. Mind you, only a fool comes between a RAT and his/her cheese.

Oddly enough, what we are really talking about here is attaining a consciousness where there is no DELAY in your decision making. Both the RAT and the CAT inside you can remove the curtain of forgetting. Both can bring you to a more spontaneous place where you either: DO or NOT DO, SPEAK or NOT SPEAK, ACT or NOT ACT. The difference if that the Cat inside you tries to control the situation to achieve this end, while the RAT seeks to liberate your experience. The CAT works but requires you to be truly self-controlled, to the point you are like the robot that achieves the single goal put before it. No thought, just do.

However, when it comes to a decision between two equal possibilities, the CAT will fail to respond properly. It sees alternatives as things to kill, not options to consider. Given two paths, it will travel the one with the most food, money, fame, etc. Not the one that will please the heart.

Let's say you have a CAT wife, and a pretty girl turns up at a party. The CAT will immediately talk about
 what a trollop another woman is. She wants to ELIMINATE options. She is doing this to sort out her partners reaction before the other woman makes a pass, after which the CAT has a bigger battle on her hands.

The paradox is this: Obey the CAT and things go along OK. It is DELAY, the old vice of procrastination, that is causing the pain and suffering in your life. The CAT removes this, but demands total obedience. If you have a doubt and want to explore other options, the CAT will attack. It will actively go out of its way to hunt down and kill alternative possibilities for your future existence.

The Cat fears and hates all forms of doubt. It demands single minded focus, with no other consideration.

Yet doubt is not your enemy. To the RAT it is your best friend. True doubt is a way of standing back to get a better view. Mixed with fear, it becomes a paralysing experience, yes, but doubt with courage liberates you. Doubt is what you use to pierce the shadows, to question the path, it is not a fear that is holding you back. But the Cat whispers, "He who hesitates is lost" and urges you to reckless behaviour.

The CAT attacks and kills an inadequacy. The RAT accepts and works with it.

So, how do you accept yourself?

1. *To accept yourself fully, you need to know yourself.*
2. *To Know Yourself you need to Relax.*
3. *To Relax you need to know your needs and wants, and then TRUST your desires and wants.*
4. *To Trust your desires and wants, you need to Integrate Your RAT with your CONSCIOUS MIND.*

So the goal in accepting yourself is to really become CONSCIOUS of yourself. This book is in part a "How To" course for this very purpose.

Ever thought about enlightenment? Well, just accepting the cracks, the dark places within, means we let the light through and stop hiding. No more hiding means we stop lying. No more lying means we start to know our truth. Obviously, you need to integrate the areas you believe are "dark" inside you, in order to achieve a functional enlightenment. It is all about ACCEPTING YOURSELF, even your perceived INADEQUACIES.

And now we need to venture a little further into the physical side of things, and discuss the fact that you have more than one brain controlling things in your body.

It will most likely surprise you to find out where it is.

> "NEVER FORGET THAT
> ONCE UPON A TIME, IN AN
> UNGUARDED MOMENT,
> YOU RECOGNIZED
> YOURSELF AS A FRIEND."
>
> — ELIZABETH GILBERT

Your HEART is a BRAIN

Let's look sideways for a moment, and take a preview of super-stress situations, and how these can change the way you act. It's important. I also recommend having a look at heartmath.org where the insights as to the brain/heart connections in this section started.

When it comes to those emergency life-saving decisions, we have an extraordinary evolution inside us that accelerates our instinctual responses. We have a completely different brain that kicks in, and it is your heart. The heart itself is full of neurons that are 'supposed' to be in the brain. But it is different. Heart based neurons remove the "delay" process in reacting to danger. Where normally you go through a want trigger, to a brain activity, to a thought action, to then physically acting, when the heart/brain kicks in it is instant. This millisecond delay disappears. Your adrenal glands and your pituitary sideline your brain, and amazingly, your HEART becomes your brain for a short period of time. The Heartmath Institute proved that the Heart, of itself, can overrule the brain at any given moment, and that the nerve fibres in the heart are itself a form of Brain.

When under real threat there is NO ROOM for indecision, and the body becomes UNIFIED. Incredible feats of strength and endurance have been performed when the adrenal functions/heart-mind take over the body. The impossible is achieved.

I have seen for myself. One day two very old very fat cats, very surprised at finding a bull terrier on their doorstep. It was then that they DEFIED GRAVITY. These very fat cats ran up a wall, along the ceiling, then ran through the top of a doorway. (while still running on the roof) It was an utterly impossible feat, but three people witnessed how they managed it, in order to hide on top of a cupboard. These were fat cats that ordinarily could not even manage a leap onto a ledge, and insisted on the door being opened for them to come inside the house.

This image has stayed clearly in my minds eye for decades, how we can defy the laws of physics when we let go of all indecision.

It goes to show what can happen when your heart and mind are unified, but we have more. We also have another brain in our body.

Just as your heart will act as a second brain in times of extreme stress, you also have a THIRD Brain. This is the ganglionic nerve mass back of the intestines, the area we generally call the Sympathetic Nervous System. This is the area where your TRUE WANTS exist and your TRUE INTUITION also coexists with these wants. Our sense of empathy comes more from this region than any specific section of the brain. This is a sort of sounding board that "hears" the environment through feeling. It is where our natural sense of intuition and our natural wants reside.

And behind this, your RAT awaits. We must get to the true and natural intuition and the natural wants that come from this place before we can uncover your RAT.

In most ancient cultures your RAT is in some way recognised as the primordial funnel for spiritual power. It is seen as the MAGNET for the currents of Light and Sound that pervade the ethers. It is the attractor for those foundational energies that create Matter, Space, Energy and Time. The Hopi call him Coyote, the Trickster. Your Rat goes by many names.

Your Sympathetic Nervous System is a sort of "finger" that can touch and feel the pulse of the arcane current of life. You know when you get butterfly's in the stomach? That is the Sympathetic Nervous System (SNS) responding to the influence of a variety of energies that are in the ether around you.

Technically speaking, this is the result of a signal sent from the fight and flight response (located in the Cortex at the base of the brain) through the MANAS or mind proper, down the Vargas Nerve, and into the SNS. It is all triggered by a sensory input in the Spinal Chord, which is really the house for your reptilian brain, or the primal sensory organ.

You, surprisingly, are a highly sophisticated machine, fine-tuned by aeons of evolution, to survive on the planet we call Earth. Or should I say, you WERE. All your sophistication is currently inverted to a process of self-doubt and questioning because your natural flows of energy have been stymied and caught up in a thousand preconceptions of SHOULD.

This is the whole problem in a nutshell. Your natural and magnificent super-self has been squashed into conformity, expectations, and low self esteem. And all this is held in place right where your bias, or blind spot, cannot look.

Harvard has designed a series of tests on your "Bias Level". This is in simple truth your "Should" level. There are a range of these, and you may be very surprised at how you score. Very few get a neutral result. If you have a chance to go online go to: **https://implicit.harvard.edu/implicit/demo**

What do tests like this prove? It is very simple: You are constantly SHOULDING on yourself. Thus you are disobeying the PRIMARY Rule of the Rat, *"Stop Shoulding in your Own Nest."*

But how do we stop Shoulding on ourselves? Your self-shoulding is invariably disguised as something that you currently believe is necessary for your survival, and which, if you stopped it, would give you some sort of major issue. Beliefs such as: If I stop worrying about what the neighbours will think, my life will fall apart. Of course it won't! The fact that it doesn't is not important, we believe it is important and we fear the consequences. The notion of not being concerned about neighbours is shut down before it sees the light of day.

There is a small truism I have found in life: The expectations of how we feel others should behave, act or appear, are really expectations we have about ourselves. Accept this, and you will soon adjust to a more positive mindset. Do not accept it, and you will keep shoulding on yourself a while longer. Keep doing it and you will most surely suffer severe psychic congestion, due to the excess consumption of other people's opinions.

If you are concerned about what the neighbour thinks, stop thinking about your neighbour. When you do, you will no longer be concerned about what they think.

THE CENSOR REVISITED

We touched on this subject in Book One. We all have an internal controller that colours how we see things, how we think, and how we feel. I have approached it from a different angle this time, calling it the thing that fills the gaps in the Humpty Dumpty self, but it is also closely associated with your CAT.

Your CAT, despite all the rhetoric I have used, is really the trained pet of your CENSOR at work. It is, in truth, the *Censor Action Trigger*, and it uses a variety of measures to keep you under it's thumb. The Censor already knows the predictable habit patterns that it knows you will follow, and it seeks to arrange your life experience to fall inside the pattern. It does not want you breaking your habits.

However, eventually you must BREAK THE HABIT if you are to be in charge of your life! The easiest way to do this is to learn to be RANDOM and to do things outside your Box. A classic novel on how to stop shoulding on yourself is "The Diceman" by Luke Rhinehart (AKA: Prof George Cockcroft)

I like the concepts offered by Professor George Cockcroft. We have been writing to each other for many years, and he is the perfect example of a Soul who has integrated their RAT. He can be very sharp, very pointed, very plain spoken, and when he sees that you can accept his direct approach, he can also be very kind and thoughtful.

But you do NOT get this attitude at first. You always get this last. He uses his RAT to test you, to see what you are made of, and when he decides that you are OK, you can be his friend. His book, the Diceman, is a MUST READ if you are to explore the nature of breaking boundaries, and getting to open the door to your Inner Rat.

A brief summary of the Diceman is that a Psychologist finds his life to be meaningless, his work useless, and his existence every day a suffering. There is no reason, other than he feels stifled and conformed by forces beyond his control, so he uses the random casting of the dice to determine what his next action in life will be. Simply, he stopped trying to PRETEND he knew anything about what was best for himself, and he threw his fate to a higher force, the forces of chance, fate and destiny.

So finding your RAT is a little like Caesar crossing the Rubicon, when he shouted "Iacta Alea Est!". (Let the Dice Fly High) Can you do it? Can you dare to be Free, can you dare to challenge convention, do you dare to be YOURSELF?

LISTENING, SEEING, KNOWING

The greatest problem we suffer when we are not in charge of our Censor is that information from the outside world is muffled. IT is controlling what you see and hear, and this means you are missing all the natural survival signals that nature sends.

The world is radiating non-stop energy from thousands of sources. There are a myriad of psychic radio stations pumping out "Buy Me!" There is a cacophony of noise, to the degree that most to shut down and seal themselves into some comfortable rut where they feel less affected by the push and pull of existence. But life is ALSO broadcasting important survival messages, things we need to hear.

How do we determine the difference between man-made noise and naturally generated communication? Your RAT knows, but you have to give it breathing space. You know how, start not giving a Rat's. There is SO MUCH media and BS that we have to filter it. By not giving a Rat's you stop getting caught up in the spin, and you learn to watch the river of moments flow past. A miracle then happens: As you focus, each moment individualises, and you step in a personal experience of NOW with the universe. There is a curious benefit to this: You worry far less about what others think, and focus far more on what you DO. This is important.

By not giving a Rats, your Censor has less control. You start seeing things as they are, and not through the filters of your various bubbles. We start to live in the moment, and enjoy what life will bring.

When we start focussing on NOW and what we DO, we ALSO start picking up more correctly the signals to the brain from the Sympathetic Nervous System. You know the term "I trusted my gut"? This is what we are speaking of, and developing a mix of being present and being active gives this area of your psyche a tremendous resilience.

When we learn to just do, over time we develop competence in what we do. Developing physical competence and mastery of ANY skill changes you. It toughens you. It develops the edge you need to cut through the crap. It also trains you to listen to the signals around you. Get both of these things working together, and you will be amaze yourself.

A master woodworker can feel through his fingers when the nature of the wood changes. They KNOW when they meet a spot that will not carve easily, because they get a feedback through their nervous system that speaks to them. A combination of being present in the moment, listening closely, and being in charge of what you do creates a matrix of awareness where attainment and success become second nature.

When you can let go of the crap to tune in and hear what is being broadcast from the world directly to you, your entire perspective on life changes. You can tell the difference between manufactured media and true nature, and a remarkable thing happens. You just KNOW what is coming.

All of nature is already doing this. Ants know when it is about to rain, for one. Animals move inland when a Tsunami is coming. How do they know? They LISTEN to the internal broadcast of Life.

LISTEN and you will start waking up the instinctual reflexes. Stop thinking so much, and start feeling a sense of freedom. Stop imagining what will go wrong, and start a moment to moment act of listening to your environment. As a sensory animal, I am always receiving information from the world around me. I have discovered that there is ALWAYS an alarm sounded for those who are awake to the pulse of life.

When you realise this, and learn to trust it, you start to relax, and be what you are. This is where the "Magic Rat Space" opens and your instinctual self begins to marry your higher self. You line up the inner ducks and your life starts swimming in a straight line. You see more, you feel more, and you just KNOW more.

As a healer, I look at a person walking in the room and often can tell you EXACTLY what was wrong with them. How can I do this? My nervous system attunes to the universal state of being, the natural archetype if you will, and I can see and feel the areas where a person is out of balance. I cannot say HOW I know this, but all I have to do is rest within the knowing space, and it comes.

The problem is that, in attuning ourselves, we can lose "self" in the world of sense reality. We fall down the rabbit hole of out own imagining. It took many years to refine and define my space, which meant learning to live in two worlds. What would happen to me is that I would be in a group of people, and suddenly feel seriously ill. I would be wiped out and need to lie down. Or I might have an unwarranted fear emerge, and it would take all my will to not collapse on the floor.

These were not anxiety attacks, they were sensory overloads. These were not things I imagined happening, this was "stuff" that WAS happening to people on subtle levels, areas in which I was swimming without a boat, without a paddle and without a clue. Finally I learned to connect with my RAT, and the message it told me was that this continual experience of overload that I suffered was not MINE. It was someone else in the room, and I was picking it up. Finally I got the message clearly.

One example of how I grasped this: I am at a seminar, and I fell this constriction in my stomach and neck. And I looked up to see an old friend sitting down, his back to me. Without words I know this was coming from him so I go up, and starting freeing up the tendons and muscles in his neck and shoulders, yet not saying a word.

Neither does he. he just accepts the gift, and says nothing. After 10 minutes I felt the severe stress attack I had picked up fade away, and finally my friend spoke. "Thank you. I do not know HOW you knew I was in such pain, or WHY you chose to help, or WHAT brought you here, or even WHO you are. And what is more, I am so happy that I do not need to. Thank you."

With that, my friend then looked up, and recognised who was behind him. He said "You know, I KNEW it was you. You are the only person I know who has enough sense to act clearly and shut up at the same time."

But we are talking the circle of life here. Many, many years ago I had been suffering a slow crisis. I did not even know what it was, but I was in the middle of it. This was when my friend from the above story turned up and started playing a song. It was no great song, and his voice was no great voice, but something in it snapped the crisis and I started to feel happy again. So it was a favour returned.

The difference now was that I was AWARE of it. I was staring to connect to my Inner RAT in a very real way. I could see, act and deal with moments as they came on a ONE to ONE basis. Just me, just the moment, just the reality I experienced. If other people were involved, their reality no longer impinged on mine in a way that I could not control. I still FELT their reality, it still AFFECTED me, yet I could keep my own moment intact.

JUNK SCIENCE

Dan Agin wrote a book called *JUNK SCIENCE: How Politicians, Corporations, and Other Hucksters Betray Us.* (St. Martin's Press/Thomas Dunne Books, New York, 2006). It's worth a read to see how you are lied to, cajoled, and tricked with statistics by those that you believe can be respected and believed. Real Science is getting submerged in a funding race that abuses statistics for political and financial gain.

The Mystic Rat Says: *If you are not listening to the evidence, and seeing it clearly, then you can never know anything with certainty.*

Virtually everyone who wants power and/or money is telling some sort of fiction in order to get it. No one wants to be a liar, but the reality is that if you are completely yourself, you get no funding. You are required to lie, or let's say "massage the facts", in order to present things the way convention requires. This paints a picture that everyone with influence is not to be trusted. But there ARE lots of really good people working very hard to create better society. However, they are getting submerged.

A perfect example was given in "Less Than Words Can Say" by Richard Mitchell. In this utterly excellent book on the power of Grammar, he gives an example of a how you might get a grant to research placing a blackboard at the BACK of a class. Obviously no one is going to fund this, but if you title the funding application: *"An Experimental Research Proposal to Study Pedagogical/Instructional Outcomes/Behaviors as Related to the Unconscious Symbolism of Traditional and Non-Traditional Spatial Placement of Individualized Learning Stations within the Primary Learning-Facility Location."* THEN you got a chance.

That's how it is people. Accept it. Political Correctness has gone mad. But before you criticise too much, accept that YOU are not so perfect either. YOU are really a mishmash of jigsaws put together by a loose knit collection of assorted experiences to form a generalised concept of something you call yourself.

Sounds a little similar to the above title for a grant application, yes? The basic issue is that we have lost a connection to the heart, forgotten the power of child-like curiosity and exploration, and have instead substituted concepts that are acceptable to our peers. It creates bad English and Junk Science.

DENIAL:

(Showing NOW at the Picture Theatre in your Head)

You may believe that your depression, your sense of failure, your inability to complete a task, your doubts about yourself, and/or your fears for the future are an internal problem. They are, but this is never the whole picture. If we wish to move around these issues, we need to know what they hang on. This is an extension of our discussion about pinning, and it is core to the secret of resolving all personal issues.

Inside most people there is a "hook" called DENIAL. This is where many of our negatives hang up their coats. This Denial Hook usually gets created out of the consequences of small decisions made in childhood. To paint the picture: When I was a 3 year old, at kindergarten, I was asked what peg I wanted to hang my things on. While the weight of this decision was not immediately evident to me, at the time I chose a Purple Dinosaur. Why? It seemed nice and friendly. Your locker, your peg, your place at the table, your bed for sleeping: Everything at kindergarten was based on the purple dinosaur from that moment on.

However, because so many things are associated with this simple choice, if someone steals an apple from your locker, or takes your coat from your peg, or messes up your bed, your mind then associates this negative experience with the Purple Dinosaur. The image can go from being a friendly fellow to a Tyrannosaurus Rex in our thoughts. And I do not want a Tyrannosaurus Rex running around in my head, so I just pretend it isn't there.

So often, the pegs for placing things inside us gets associated with not-quite-so pleasant consequences. This can turn the peg into a place where our negatives get hung, and it becomes a peg of denial. The peg of denial is where hidden, dark and nasty creatures come to feed. Vindictive, venomous, evil and cruel, the peg of denial attracts and attaches itself to our FEAR. This fear creates an energy picture, one we all have in our denial "zone", and this denial zone becomes the place where our greatest fears and most wicked moods learn to hide. Why? Because you don't want to look there.

A perfect example is falling out of love. When we fall IN love, the person is just perfect. The picture before us is a wonderful thing. But as love sours, the image becomes tarnished. You wonder when they changed, because who could have ever loved THAT creature! Yet is it the same person you once loved.

The tension between what you see and what you hoped for turns slowly into a denial. Where once we hung our love with hopes for the future, now we see drab resentment and depression dangling before us. But the changed image of the once loved one is swinging on the same peg we placed all our love, hope and future wishes on. Confusion! Nasty nasty and not to be looked at. Bury it.

The next one we meet, we are more careful. We remember that we still have the gruesome image to deal with, and hold back. Or we do the opposite, and leap towards the new love with careless abandon, denying the gruesome image is there at all. Either way, we deny reality, which is that life is a process of change.

"When I was a child I thought as a child, yet when I became a man, I gave up childish ways." What do you think Saint Paul is really talking about here?

At the core of our being, when we associate our thoughts and feelings to our natural wants and needs, we have no desire to deny anything. We have nothing to hide, and nothing to hide from, so we need not lie about anything. But life is not perfect, and things do intrude. We start to associate things, we start to add up things, incorrectly. To "be a man" we step back, and face the world front on. We accept what we are, and deny nothing

Most of our life is indeed a process that follows on from the childhood choice of a "peg" that through wrong association becomes a place where denial. Do anything enough and it becomes a habit. The simple consequence of denial is that we hide from ourselves. Here's the problem: Once this is established as a pattern, we seek to avoid our problems by looking for "acceptable" pegs to hang our "nice" clothes on.

So we look for the "right" job, the "right" partner, the "right" address, etc. These become the goals for people, and being aware takes a second place in the race to the "right" thing. *This is a denial of the natural self.* In doing so, many people make a job their religion, their family into one of their possessions, and their life becomes mimicry of fashion. As a result, our personal world breaks into pieces and becomes a staccato series of connecting events, something that we loosely call our fate.

The problem is, because of the hidden denial peg, nothing in our life works properly. We become a dis-connected jigsaw. We paint our face happy, but under the clown mask the smile is sad. We most often choose to deny the denial, pretend it is all OK and just hope that it will all work out. *We put the bullet of discontent into the gun of external activity and get a suicide of circumstance.* People start doing things to self-medicate the problems caused by the disconnection they feel

Accept things, stop denying reality, and it all stops.

Denial is insidious and affects everything. Communication becomes confused, because we are deaf to the obvious. Relationships suffer because our internal happiness prevents us from experiencing the moment, which destroys intimacy. So many people are DENYING themselves a fuller existence of life. Why? Who can say, but I have noted over the years these symptoms of denial:

1. *Unreasoning faith in your Profession and/or Religion*
2. *Ownership issues with your family*
3. *An inability to accept change*
4. *A lack of creative thought and feeling*
5. *A tendency towards isolationist thinking*
6. *The inability to accept contrary viewpoints as valid*
7. *A refusal to admit fault, even when you say you are sorry.*

Denial is not a river in Egypt. It's a river of images swimming through your head that got caught on a hook of fear.

One of the most poignant examples I can offer come from a school friend, who runs a medical research laboratory. His specific area of focus is Cancer, and I noted that a simple and old remedy using herbs, which was proven to have had direct and significant effect on cancer cells. I suggested he follow this up, but he just laughed, and held up his hand.

"If I even SUGGEST anything like this, I will lose my job. I have to approach everything from accepted norms, or funding will stop, and my job will be gone."

Denial of the natural order has become second nature in the scientific and medical communities. Despite the fact that some 98% of drugs are developed through the observation of a natural compound having an effect, only an extract that can be synthesised is considered as a likely candidate for drug trials.

Science, which started with natural curiosity that was as an affirmation of humanity, has lost its way to a degree. It has become the new religion of denial.

"Good Practice" in science now is to get good grades and good jobs, and the best way to get these is to agree with whatever people want you to agree to, and publish papers that support it.

Science is now training its acolytes to develop self-critical behaviours that effectively stop the growth of INNOVATION, because every step you take is now full of questions of how others will see your concept. There is great fear in stepping away from accepted norms. Galileo and the Moons of Jupiter is a play running in a scientists' mind near you!

The lies, deceptions, illness and fatigue that is currently running inside your brain can be overwhelming. If you are not strong, and willing to persistent against the disapproval of others, stop now. Just agree with what you are told, and vanish into the mill-wheel. Don't ask questions about how you can stop the erosion of your being and the theft of your truth by the accepted norms around you.

Deny it. Deny it even as your reality is being shattered and dismantled by the process that grinds on outside of ourselves. And yet, it is this very process that forms the basis of your introduction card to yourself. The very destruction (De-structuring) of your beliefs is what gives you the chance to meet and deal with your Inner Rat.

Think of it as MINING. The machines of inquiry need to grind through the blind, deaf and dumb rock in order to find the gold that is hiding in the mountain. Your destruction of the patterns, and fears, and denials within will be your liberation.

Finally I say: Accept your denial. Just allow yourself this luxury, and stop pretending it isn't there. Fighting it only makes it stronger.

There is nothing wrong with Denial as long as you do not deny its existence. Like all elements of our persona, it has its purpose. The trick is finding the right place to use it. Sometimes we need to stop the flood of emotion, and that's fine as long as we remain aware of what we are choosing and how we are acting.

The unspoken paradox of denial is: *If we deny something we have been accused of, we are in denial. Yet if we fail to deny the accusation, we are also in denial.*

Rat from Mouse, not Vice Versa

There are a lot of people out there who will not be able to recognise their RAT for the reason that it is still a MOUSE. This is not a problem if you recognise it. So how do you recognise your Mouse? Simple: Look for the CAT (Controller and Terrorist) inside, which is always easy to spot because it is trying to control things. Then look at what is most scared of the Cat. This is your Mouse.

You need to give your Mouse the time and room to grow. It is that part of you that is scared and frightened, yet inside this fear lies a true Rat, wanting to escape. A mouse survives by hiding from danger, and you need to accept that this is part of your journey. There is nothing wrong with hiding if it means you survive. But many people sacrifice themselves on the altar of some Cat, thinking this is the noble thing to do. They accept external authority because they feel this ends the fear they are afraid of.

One example of this is my brother, who was put under the thumb of his new wife right from day one. He was a drummer in a popular band. Now the day the honeymoon ended, as they were moving into their new house, she insisted that the drums stay outside. It was the drums or her, she said. Foolishly my naive brother, not truly realising that this was a pure control measure, threw himself onto the Altar of the Cat. He sacrificed himself in order that she find her happiness in controlling him.

His mouse was exterminated before it managed to find it's true nature as the Rat within. However, he still can on any given day go buy another set of drums, and start practising the Way of the Rat. But will he? Not very likely.

The flip side was my oldest brother. He passed away when I was nine, but I learned a lot from him. He was wild, unpredictable, fun, intelligent, wise and foolish all at the same time. People loved him for his spirit, his intelligence and his innate sense of judgement. He never gave in to Controllers. He remained aware of the games people would play, and steered clear of them. He wanted only to get his car running, and get some freedom. What you did was your business, what he did was his.

What is more, he is the one who introduced me to the Rat Within. How? Through stories when I was a young child. He was Goofy, I was Mickey Mouse, and we would go on marvellous journeys to all places you might imagine.

I completely identified with Mickey, the wild free spirit who could do anything, go anywhere, and who loved his life. In fact, by Age Three if you called me anything else but Mickey Mouse, I ignored you.

On one occasion when I first went to Pre-school a Cat tried to pounce on me. I was just Three, and had gone there a year early because I wanted to be with my older sister. Now this is one of my earliest and clearest recollections: I must have been out of my body watching this, because I know adults do not speak this way with a child present in the room. I clearly saw Mum talking with the woman who ran the place, explaining that I was called Mickey Mouse, even though my birth name was John.

Now here let us stop here for one moment. I must deviate and explain to your good self that I came to this planet with the CLEAR agreement to be called Michael, but my father (The same one who gave advice to a 47 year old on shaving) decided at the registry office that the name Michael would mean that I would be called MICK, which in his mind was an Irish fighters name. So he decided to reverse this agreed on choice of Michael John, and make me John Michael. Ironically, the only person in the world who calls me "Mick" now-a-days is my father.

I was NEVER a John. It just isn't my nature. Mickey Mouse suited me fine. However, the woman who ran the pre-school obviously thought different. It is fair to say I was pre-warned, because I had seen her face, and in the Out-of-Body State I could read her thoughts quite clearly. She was thinking "We will break this one and get him in order right away"

"Nope" I thought. There was no way I was going to give in to this controller. When it was time to go in for nap, all the kids were called in from where they were playing outside. But I stayed where I was. It was time for a showdown.

She called out to me from the porch, "John! Nap time!" I ignored her. My name was Mickey Mouse. "John" she called louder. Then again, "JOHN" even louder. By the seventeenth time she called "John" she was SCREAMING.

As I listened to her, it just further reinforced how it was such a dull and unsuitable name for myself, and so I continued to ignore her until, finally, she said (under her breath and very quietly) "Mickey Mouse."

I immediately hopped up, bright as a button and said "Yes Miss?"

Have you ever trapped a Cat? They look at you with pure venom and feel their entire ego has been destroyed. They want to kill you. But if you prove yourself bigger than they are, they are completely stymied.

That was the first time I saw a woman hate a child. I mean, venom was not something I actually understood as a word, but I could FEEL it. This extremely nasty control freak female left the day care facility within a couple of weeks, I don't know why, but I was glad to see the end of her. I suspect that other people hearing her screaming at a child might have contributed to her departure.

Your RAT starts as a Mouse and grows bigger through the trials of life. My oldest brother somehow knew all these things, and though I cannot remember him ever saying anything, I always remember the sensation of being free to be ME when he was around. With most people it is the opposite. They want you to conform to THEIR comfort zone, and to do this they seek to control you in some way.

Controllers are CATS. (Controllers and Terrorisers) They love to play with MICE, but fully grown Ship Rats are more than a match for them. (Let me diverge and point out that there are small and big rats, but the Ship Rat is often bigger than a Cat, and seriously dangerous when cornered)

My mother was a controller, and Brother Peter showed me that you can be free despite the desires of others to tie you down. In many ways, he was not really of this world. He was always "elsewhere" and I do believe his passing on at such an early age spared him a great deal of hardship.

I digress. We ALL have a scared little child inside us, but not many of us have an older brother who can train it to be brave. I was lucky, and for most they have to find, then train their own mouse to become what it is destined to be. However, if you look inside your heart and see misery, sadness and loss. If you look inside and see small, meagre passions and deep unworthiness: Take heart. You are looking at your MOUSE. You will not realise it straight away, but this is the part that grows up to become your RAT.

Now the flip side to this is my other brother. He had courage, he was out there playing in rock bands as a drummer and discovering life and its freedoms really well. But then he fell in love and decided to get married.

Of itself that is fine, but what happened was that he married a really powerful CAT, one that never let you realise you were being eaten for supper until it was too late. As mentioned just before: The first day after the honeymoon, when they started to move into their new home together, and my brother was getting his drum set from the van: His wife says very sweetly, "If that comes inside, I leave."

I would have said "Nice knowing you" if some woman had tried to tell me I could not bring my guitar into my own house, however my other brother crumpled, left the drums outside, and lived a life of every increasing enslavement from that point on. I mean, the HIDE of the woman, to say a man cannot do something he is both good at, which gives him enjoyment, and which is a creative outlet.

Her reasoning is transparent, but only when your RAT is awake. Drums mean Band, Band means late nights, late nights mean parties, parties mean girls, girls mean temptation, temptation means guilt, because everyone gives into temptation. And THAT was the problem she was going to SAVE him from.

Now, to put this in perspective, my brothers band had only one other band in town that gave them any competition, and many believed HIS band was better than them. What was the name of the other band? ACDC. You may have heard of them? I am guessing you never heard of his band, Head West? No? I didn't think so.

My brother was waking up to life, with his RAT coming along nicely, but he fell into the grip of a CAT, and she forced his emerging true nature to become stunted. She did this through simple, yet effective control measures. She trained him like a flea in a flea circus to only jump so high, and after enough time elapsed he didn't even THINK to jump out of the glass cage and find freedom.

Your MOUSE is the insecure, frightened person. Do not hate him/her, do not ignore him/her. This is your RAT in early stages. But equally, do not allow your MOUSE to become dominated by other people's beliefs and control measures, unless you like being henpecked, that is.

The Mouse within you need to GROW, and to become all that it can be. The nervous, shy, insecure little mouse is your RAT in disguise. So if you look into your heart, and hate what you see, this is a good thing. Why? Because you are starting on one of the Paths to discover your Inner Rat.

Self-hate is, at least, a recognition of some sort of self. You can grow your understanding of self-hate and at some point act to counter it. Then your RAT will start to germinate, and your self-awareness will blossom.

I was fat as a kid, and I detested this. In time I came to understand it was a protection technique, but before any such truth came to my thoughts, my heart got ACTIVE. I got onto an outdoor gym, I got into sport. (and when you have a triple chin at age 13, this is not an easy thing to do) I got BUSY going where I wanted to go, and stopped focussing on what I hated.

But the self-hate was the fuel for the fire. It was the fiery water that caused the seed to sprout. Bitter water you might imagine, yes? That is true, but life IS bitter sweet. Life IS Yin Yang. No one will teach you this at school, but life really IS a jungle of opposites and our job is to somehow get it all walking in the same direction.

It can get confusing when you are out in the jungle on your own. It can be incredibly difficult finding your way through both the psychological and the very real obstacles you will face. This is why we now give you clear guidelines to keep you on the rails, and we come back to the core of Ratology: Rules of Rattyness.

The Rules of Rattyness are, in case you forgot:

1. *It's Not About You*
2. *Do Not Should in Your Own Nest*
3. *Always Keep One Eye Open*
4. *Ask No Favours (Do Not a Beggar or a Lender Be)*
5. *Keep Your Teeth Honed (Be Prepared)*
6. *Always Have a Bolt Hole*
7. *Do Not Expose Your Vulnerabilities*
8. *Pay Attention to Your Brother's Activity, But Not Their business*
9. *Pick Up and Dust Off*
10. *Shoot the Pope (metaphorically speaking)*

RULES OF RATTYNESS: Ancillary Notes

Second Level Considerations

Let's review the Rules of Rattyness, and look at the ancillary aspects and principles that flow from these.

The Rules are self explanatory when you understand them, and invisible barriers when you do not. We covered these in Book One, but for now we must visit the subsequent follow-on considerations that reinforce the rules. These ancillary principles are an adjunct to the Rules of Rattyness, and represent the application of Right Thinking.

It is a given that most people's concerns arose out of wrong thinking and false emotions, and this next section is to help you refocussed the minds eye, and see the ordinary things of life more clearly

The Titles are:
Play the Third Man
The Meta-Rat
Touchani (The Art of Perception)
Courage
Inuet: Pure Intention
Filters
Are You Experienced?
Law of Reversed Effort
Our Life is the Lesson
Understand the Meme, Remove the Fear
Your Third Brain
Round Up

PLAY the THIRD MAN

D o you remember when we gave an example where the solicitor asks if someone was "Gilding the Lily" and we suggest that the person says, "I certainly believe I am telling the truth, and I would hate to say anything that would hurt another unfairly, but surely it is up to the Honourable Judge to decide how much truth is in my testimony?"

You did not use denial, or blame, or any excuse. You simply shift the energy to a different focus, the THIRD MAN. If you deny, and say "Certainly not!" the judge doesn't believe you. If you agree, and say you have, you are a liar. There is no solution in answering loaded questions, so you shift the focus away from yourself.

It is NOT about me, it's about them. I will NOT should in my own nest and do what you expect. My eyes are open, my teeth are sharp, and what's more, my third person play is my bolt hole. There it is, the first six Rules of Rattyness already covered in a single sentence.

This is the Third Person trick. It is a diversion technique that is a submissive reversal. You are not denying anything, thus looking automatically guilty, yet you are also implying that the Lawyer is putting himself above the Judge and being impertinent. How? He appeared to exclude the role of the Judge. In other words, you are including a THIRD MAN to your argument, and distracting yourself from being the target. The Judge likes it because you have elevated him to his proper level of respect. The lawyer hates it, because the Third Man is not the one he is questioning, and overall you have effectively removed yourself from the target range.

In essence, there are times when we are being prosecuted by someone one or thing over some issue that has cropped up in our life. Usually, these things are just a social faux pas, or political correctness over stepping a boundary, but in all cases, it is time wasting. Do you need your time wasted? I don't, so I use techniques to save time, and one of the best is the Third Man technique.

There are many ways to apply a Third Man diversion. The oldest is simply to imply contrary gossip. Someone accuses you of something, based on what they were told. So you can say, with a straight face, "Well, I appreciate that what you are saying you believe to be true, but I heard a story that opposes this. Bob Johnson told me a completely different version of events. Maybe you need to check up on your facts before you go accusing people of things?"

Now this has a triple red herring bonus. One: You can be pretty sure the person will not go to Bob Johnson and double check what you are saying unless they are totally convinced that their story is 100% true. This only happens with pathological types, and if this is the case the second red herring helps, because, TWO: you WANT him going off to harass someone else, regardless.

Thirdly: Even if Bob Johnson denies he said what you said he said, it has distracted the assault and the person is now battling on two fronts. You have at the very least DILUTED the problem by introducing the Third Man.

This works particularly well with gossip, because everyone suspects gossip is a lie anyway. Often when you include the Third Man your accuser will think "Yeah, I lie, so maybe the person who said this guy was the issue lied as well. He seems to be upfront, maybe I did get it wrong?" More importantly, you have not placed yourself into the argument or embroiled yourself in their anger, plus, and this is a HUGE plus, you did not contradict the man. You are simply refuted his source with another source. Instinctively, it sets a different tone to thing. The fellow feels that you must be alright, because the natural response is to argue and fight. You were so confident, you did not have to, nor did you spike his vanity and cause him to have to defend himself. (It helps if Bob Johnson is a friend who will back up your story, of course.)

You have triangulated the problem away with a deferral to a third party.

Triangulation can also work against you. This is where the Third Party is brought in by someone else as THEIR reference point for argument. The obvious one is when your wife discovers you have a mistress, and she insists you choose who you will stay with. Now you KNOW life will be hell no matter what you choose. So you apply a different sort of Third Person. You bring a FORTH PERSON into argument.

You say, "Well, actually it is worse than you imagine. There's another woman on top of this. She's rich, she wants me, and we are thinking of moving to New York. I will miss the kids, but she is also beautiful and friendly. And so if you are insisting that I choose, well, I truly love you all, but I am not so sure."

Soon both the Wife and the Mistress will get together to plot against the EVIL other woman, and you will no longer have to choose. The best option is now to keep things as they are. Worked properly, you CAN have your cake and eat it too.

One notable case was when the TV crew caught up with a man 100% guilty of stealing money from clients. They demanded he answer to them, but he rolled down the car window, and said "Sorry, but I have already sold the story to an opposition channel." They all go "Oh, OK." and he drives away with no drama.

Third Man style arguments are a camouflage, a deflection tactic. They work ONLY because people will believe in the low motivations of others, including their own. However, the sad truth is that this applies in 95% of all arguments. As a note: People who like to argue base their lives around low motivations.

To paint this more clearly: A truly honest person who feels they may have been wronged by you will, in some way, ask for your side of the story first.

Remember, this is a technique to be used in certain circumstances, usually where there are people already immersed in wrong thinking. It is a basic avoidance trick, and designed to save wear and tear rather than offer any solutions. The majority of life's so called problems are really just rhubarb thrown up by people who are essentially abrasive. Rather than suffer the sand paper of rude egos and bruised emotions, duck them by referring everything on to a third party.

A warning, if you are facing a well researched and competent investigation, this technique does not work at all. If you are guilty, and provably so, move straight to the second form of legal defence, Blame.

Blame anyone and everyone for the situation, and the circumstance. This is second level Third Man technique. Bring in another party and say they are the ones that caused the issue, not you. If nothing else, it forces the opposing party to be better researched and more persistent.

However, let's just say they have you dead to rights, and you are well and truly nailing you to the cross. Accept it. If there is no one else to blame, apply the third level of legal defence: *Grovel and beg for forgiveness.*

If none of the above works, you either have to bribe someone or go to jail.

The META-RAT

This is a subtle and complex area of thought, yet also shockingly simple. It is a sort of Rat Metaphysics we are talking here. Life here is based on our experience of each moment. To experience a moment here on Planet Earth we need to have the following pre-requisites: Matter, Energy, Space and Time. Obviously, we need a degree of consciousness to be aware of the experience.

We need a PLACE to be aware of an experience, we need a RECOGNITION of the Moment to be aware of what we are experiencing anything, and we need a sense of CONTINUITY to retain awareness.

All these elements combine in varying degrees within us to form the experience we presently enjoy, or not, as the case may well be.

Matter and Energy are entwined in a fixed relationship. One might say Energy condenses to form matter, while nuclear physics and the Atomic Bomb have proven that Matter can be used to create energy. But there is always a third element needed to create change. More simply, the burning of wood creates heat, but this also needs oxygen. Leading on from the Third Person notion of the previous chapter, the notion of a THIRD energy being needed to bring about change is the thrust of this section.

Space and Time are related in their own unique manner. A child that gets lost in a day-dream has expanded time and space, and it slows the passage of both for that child. I remember well lying down to listen to Keith Casey, the Conga Player from Ossabissa, playing on his drums one day. It seemed like 15 minutes had passed, but in reality 10 hours had slipped by as I lived in the "Drum Zone" of his incredible playing. *Play* is the third energy that creates change in accepted norms.

Play might not sound very scientific, but consider the opposite, stress.

In times of stress, Space and Time can close in around you, crowd you thoughts, and add tremendous pressure to your physical existence. Your options evaporate, and you are left struggling to survive. The third energy here is stress, the opposite of play. But relax, and laugh, your options begin to open once more. Play has power!

Just as the fire converts Matter to Energy, your playfulness or your stress, in the form of attention and awareness to a singular focus, will convert Time and Space.

Here is the important part: When your Inner RAT is fully awake and operational, it can use the power of play to convert ALL your feelings and beliefs to a more productive experience in Time and Space. This, in turn, affects your relationship with Energy and Matter.

This improves the connection you have with your natural knowing, your innate intelligence. And when this happens you start to become this intelligence, and better able to see the patterns at work around you. Or more correctly, you become aware of a natural intelligence flowing through you and your life.

As you learn to connect your Inner RAT Nature to the outer world, and synchronise it, your PERCEPTION of things like Time, Space and Energy will change. Using the power of Fun, you will renegotiate your relationship with Matter, Energy, Space and Time, and it will seem to others that your life becomes miraculous. And it does! The ducks line up, and the world just works better for you.

If you want to bend the rules, change your place in the universe, and create a new world for yourself, you now have the tools to do so. But always remember, everything is based around seeing the obvious in what is before you. This means that you need to develop your TRUE PERCEPTION, or Touchani. When you hold this jewel, what the Tibetans call the VIDYA opens up, and everything is seen in its correct place and time. At this point, you can make the imaginary real and the real imaginary.

The Mystic Rat Says: *It's all Yadda Yadda until you make it real.*

All these teachings that talk about High Consciousness, being One with God, knowing the Divine Spirit, yadda yadda. It's all waffle from what amounts to "would be if they could be" types of people. They read it in a book, and want to believe there is some saviour out there who will make it right. All you have to do is follow the rules! It is just BS dressed in respectable clothing. What we really need is a powerful sense of play, added to pure intention, clear perception and a heart with courage.

Let's start on this trilogy of power with the notion of PERCEPTION.

TOUCHANI: The Art of Perception

In the marvellous film, Avatar, there is a powerful greeting people of that world give each other. "I see you." It means they see the heart of the person, the core of their being, and accept it. This is true perception.

The Law of Perception is held in the ancient truth called the Touchani. This is the Sword of Perception, and when you learn to wield it, all power comes to you. But remember, it is a two edged sword. It is all about recognising and developing our options, but like the great financial crisis, the discovery and use of options based purely on greed can become incredibly destructive.

How does it work? Or more to the point, how do we get it to work for us? There is a process by which ALL manifestation energy flows, and there is never an exception to this pattern:

1. *What you PERCIEVE you can CONCIEVE*
2. *What you CONCIEVE you can ACHIEVE*

The energy that flows from this generally follows a traditional path. (There are differing options with the use of a variety of different forces and tools, but most follow the patterns of tradition) This traditional "Path to Power" is that your PERCEPTION allows you to CONCIEVE which opens the options to ACHIEVE.

- *ACHIEVEMENT brings RECOGNITION.*
- *RECOGNITION Brings OPPORTUNITY.*
- *OPPORTUNITY brings OPTIONS.*
- *OPTIONS bring more openings for ACHIEVEMENT*

Inside the realm of RECOGNITION we can see many alternatives emerge, but one thing is certain, every single power base in human society comes from this step on the path to power. The step of RECOGNITION is all important, because this is the "Raising of the Flag" stage where others are attracted to your cause.

It is here that you can branch out from developing PERSONAL power to developing INDUSTRIAL, SOCIAL and/or GOVERNMENTAL power. Every individual or group that achieves a potential and is able to change things uses the POWER of RECOGNITION to set their agenda in the public eye.

This is why every corporation has a logo, a flag of sorts, by which they are easily recognised. The raising of the flag attracts the forces that are needed to achieve the goals and aspiration of the particular agenda.

In TRADITIONAL societal terms, it takes at least seven generations to form a dynasty, however the advent of mass media has accelerated the possibilities. Media allows RECOGNITION on a VAST scale never before imagined. An ordinary singer can now command huge resources of power because they achieve a little recognition with a few hit records. Some actors are paid $20 million a movie, more than a lifetime of hard work for the majority of people, because they attained recognition.

Using the 1976 book "Your Erroneous Zones" Dr Wayne Dwyer achieved wide spread recognition, and this gave him influence and power. However he stated that this was but ONE option he could have taken to achieve this end. In this book, Dr Dwyer subtly introduces the notion of gaining a handle on your life by reducing guilt and worry, and it is recommended reading.

Let's face it: You want POWER. In fact, if you want to be FREE, you NEED Power. Yet use the word "power" and it sends a shudder down the backbone. Why? Because there has been so much abuse of it in the past. Power corrupts, absolute power corrupts absolutely. But most people would agree that POWER would be good if it helped them to help others, so like the love of money, the evil is in the love of power. Regardless, to be free, you need to have a degree of personal power.

Yes, the meek truly SHALL inherit the Earth, but only after the rampaging bulls of commerce are finished with it. You can sit outside and grow your vegetables, and barter them for milk at the markets if you want to. There is nothing wrong with this, but the fact of nature remains: The passive, meek creatures are invariably living in fear of the carnivores.

True Rats are NOT meek or passive. They do NOT live in fear. Every good Rat respects powers greater than they are, and does not challenge it, (Give unto Caesar what is Caesar, dear friends) but the true Rat never seeks to live in fear. The True Rat only seeks to SURVIVE. And here is the different area of focus that sets the Rat free.

They will seek to live in a place (both physically and mentally) that is safe, and this usually means a degree of inaccessibility. They will also live in places where others dare not go, and they are also the first to desert the sinking ship. Why? A good Rat is SMART enough to know when the time for this particular cycle is UP.

The Rat Creed states: *The only good Rat is a living one.* Think about it the next time you want to bow down low to a dying man strung up on a cross. Let's look at the facts: Jesus didn't worship Death. Buddha said "don't make a religion out of me". Krishna: Well, who cares what a guy with a blue face thinks.

I am smart enough to not even think about referencing the Islam guy, because next thing I know I will have a Fatwa on my head, and I am not that stupid as to invite it. On the positive outlook, the Moslem have a sense of connection to their Inner Rat. Granted, a confused connection, but at least they know enough to protect their own.

It is all about PERCEPTION: How we see, and what we see. This is what determines our reality.

What you see may not be completely true, and, in fact I will guarantee it isn't! But the fact that you SEE at all is enough of a qualification for you to be able to graduate from this point to seeing more clearly. The Ancient Greeks saw things very differently. Vision to the Greeks was the light coming from the eye, and enlightening the object of your vision. People laugh and say this is stupid, but perhaps it is more true than we suspect.

HOW you see things inside is a little like a shadow play. We are putting internal beliefs (images) over an internal light. What is seen on the external wall or our reality is the dance of your inner vision and beliefs thrown up, like a shadow puppet play.

What happens is what creates our reality. We get entranced by the external performance, and we forget that WE are the ones manufacturing the actors and the script. Whatever you see is in part a projection, and a part perception. Sorting out the projection from the perception is one of life's real tasks.

But in the end, it is all just oil on the wheels that run down the track. It doesn't really matter how right or wrong you are, or how good or bad you are. What matters is how well you survive and how clearly you can see.

Touchani: *What you see is what you get.* It is that simple. If you see Freedom, if you can see it well enough to Taste the Experience, then it will come to you. If you have the COURAGE to face the truth within, you will discover a greater courage in dealing with life's obstacles.

COURAGE:

If you have fear in the heart, if you are scared of new moments, or change, or of differing opinions, life will fade and your inner vision will shrink. All perception of truth without true inner courage is useless. We need an externalising force, the thing we call courage, a word derived from the French word for "heart".

This is possibly the most misunderstood word in our language. People think of Courage as some great thing that stops tanks rolling in on your home. We like to think of ourselves as heroes who save the day, and we put the label of Courage on this. But speak to ANYONE who has been in war, and they will tell you that REAL courage is simply surviving the day.

Real courage is getting up when everything is lost. It is feeding the kids when you have no hope left. It is coping with the gossip from the malicious backstabber's. True Courage is seen in the SMALLEST of things, not the largest.

Antoine St Exupery, who wrote "The Little Prince", spoke of courage. In the deserts of North Africa, he faced down storming Arabs attacking his compound. He flew into the teeth of a hurricane in his little propeller driven plane, and yet he said this was not true courage. That was simply survival, where there were no other options left. What he defined as true courage was going up to two young girls at a fountain, and introducing himself. Here you face your deepest inner demons, and you do so for love, not fear of the consequences.

It is easy to be brave and courageous when you are in the spotlight, but how are you when no one is watching? How are you when the bills arrive and there is nothing left to pay them with, but you can't let the kids see because they will worry too much. True Courage, my dear reader, is UTTERLY INVISIBLE but it is the very thread that holds together your entire existence.

You get true courage from a mixture of things, but in the end, it comes from the size of your heart. As the wise man said: It is easy to fight off a barking dog, but the fleas he leaves behind can send you mad.

Real, ingrained courage comes from a place of embracing. Embracing the moment, taking on the challenge of survival, and working towards a better day. This is true courage. It is the bedrock of being upon which your Inner Rat lives.

The Mystic Rat Says: *Your Courage reveals your Tue Intention. The tests of life will come, and in them you will slowly learn to recognise yourself in your responses.*

INUET: Pure Intention

Next in the trilogy of essential elements is Intention. In an old, forgotten by almost everyone language, the person who has Inuet (in-oo-ay) is one who is transparent to the divine impulse. Having the purest of intention, they became silent vehicles for the highest truth. Many people would class such a one as mad in today's society, because they are utterly vulnerable, yet at the same time, completely invulnerable.

It is NOT the "best of intentions" we are speaking of. Those intentions are the social bricks used to pave the way to Hell. It is an inner state of expectation, and sense of knowing it will work out, along with a sense of where you are going.

It is a place where you recognise yourself as part of the whole, yet separate at the same time. It is a peculiar point of BALANCE between worlds, between thoughts, between feelings. It is a state of poise in poison, of gratitude in gratuitousness, and a relief of burdens we find in the discarded refuse of humanity. Pure Intention gives you the power of continuity, the ability to carry on regardless of circumstances.

It doesn't sound much like Intention, does it? It is really a state of core TRUST we are speaking of, added to an expectation that there is something good to be found in everything. There is no coincidence that this word is so close to that which describes the Inuit people of the Arctic, it derives from the same archaic language.

The one with pure intention is the only one who can hold pure perception, and this state of intention has nothing to do with Will or Want or Wish. It is all to do with the WAY we DO, or more specifically, the Wu Wei Wu: The Effortless Effort.

It is a way of DOING without Thought, FEELING without Emotion, BEING without what you think of as yourself being present. It is a state of being utterly singular, with no plurality of any kind affecting you.

Once again I refer to Antoine De Saint Exuprey and his marvellous book called "The Little Prince". In this small novel he placed many great secrets, seeds of truth that we might understand. If you would seek to have freedom in your life, read this book. He teaches you how to have a love without owning it, and how to have the goal without a destination. The main character in his book is called the Little Prince, and this great soul has caught the secret of the Inuet, the power of pure intent.

The odd thing is that, at the time he wrote this book, it was not the one that sold. His novels were in demand, and he was recognised as a great warrior by the Arabs for his deeds in the French Foreign Legion. He was recognised as a hero by the people of France because he flew his plane through a hurricane to deliver the mail. But his greatest gift was that small, almost silly book he wrote in two weeks while sheltering under the wind of his crashed plane in North Africa. It lay for years gathering dust before people recognised this true example of genius.

And what is more, Saint Exupery predicted this in the front of the book. He spoke plainly of how people are UNABLE to see the obvious until one with pure intention points it out to them, and even then they usually miss it. It is in the introduction.

What we are doing with pure intention is REMOVING filters. When you have no agendas, no expectations, no preconceptions running your emotions or thoughts it is utterly remarkable how much clearer and simple everything appears. At this point, your natural perception can see through a maze of problems like they are glass.

The thing is, you cannot "get" to this point. It is like Jonathon Livingston Seagull, where to achieve perfect speed, he has to STOP and JUST BE. There is no achieving pure intention; it is a state of being where you dwell in it, or not at all. It is a matter of removing the dross from the diamond in the raw, so that the real, and natural, state of the diamond can be seen and experienced.

The young child has Pure Intention. And this is the REAL meaning behind the words "Ye must become as little children". It does not mean "Be Perfect" because a child will always want the cookie in the cookie jar, but the INTENTION is simple and clear: He or she just WANTS it because it is nice, and there is no agenda hiding this fact. It doesn't bring the cookie jar any closer, however.

Are we connecting the dots yet? The section on Free Will points out that we do not want what we do, we are doing what we want. We only THINK we are choosing, but our wants are the real driving force. Become as a little child means to get closer to our natural impulses, our needs and wants. But this is done without any sense of agenda or judgement to act as a filter to blind you to your immediate reality.

Getting the filters OFF is so important. These are the real cause of your pain and suffering, the real cause of your desire to join a bubble group, the real cause behind your generating of bubble, the reason why you lie and distort truth to get your own way. So let's talk a little about Filters.

FILTERS:

Dale Carnegie had an interesting experiment. He gave people sunglasses with Red lenses and Green lenses and he asked them to put these on, then choose others at random in the group (of mostly strangers) to stand beside. So they did.

All the people wearing green filter glasses chose the people with green filters on, and all the red filter pe3ople went to others who wore red filters. What is more, every time this experiment was repeated, the same result occurred. Why? Because these colours oppose each other in the colour spectrum, so to the person wearing a green filter, anyone wearing a red filter will appear to have blacked out eyes. It is vice versa with the Red Filter People. They see the green lenses as black.

If you cannot see another person's eyes, you will not trust them. You, literally, will not be able to see eye to eye with them. You can trust another if you can see their eyes. When people take off the glasses, they often cannot believe what people they chose to associate with, and who they distrusted.

It is a perfect example of old saying: "Do we see eye to eye on this?" And it extends further. When you see people who appear to be hiding their eyes (Mirror Glasses, etc.) it is a signal of potential disagreement. You will instinctively take up a war position within yourself in preparation for an argument. You will prepare for a fight, and even your glandular system will start producing war steroids, while the cortisol-adrenal response will start to kick in. This is an AUTOMATIC response when you meet someone and cannot see their eyes.

Remember the cruel guard in "Cool Hand Luke"? He wore mirror sunglasses and you could never see his eyes. You automatically and easily believed he was a cruel bastard. Why? Because he was HIDDEN.

Thieves and liars hide. I recall clearly walking along, talking on this subject many years ago. I was in Sydney, waking with an old friend and a woman who was a singer in his band. I was saying how you often cannot trust people who wear mirror glasses, and curiously when they wear BOOTS as well, it is a signal that they crave power. People who crave power will often do you wrong if it suits them.

The girl kept asking more and more about the subject, and finally I looked up. Guess what? DER! She was wearing Mirror Glasses and Boots. I have to say, we didn't have much to do with each other after that. Oddly, any time I have ended up with Mirror Sunglasses, they always seem to disappear. However, maybe they are related to sock and pens.

Much of what we decide to be right or wrong in life is really a matter of what filters we have over our eyes. There simply IS no absolute right or wrong, and everything is relative. Rearrange your filters and you rearrange your reality. In normal circumstances you would never kill and eat your neighbour, but if you were at war and starving, and they were trying to kill you? Well maybe the notion would no longer seem abhorrent.

After all, in some societies eating someone is a way of honouring them when they die. Filters create the society we live in. Do you recall how the Ancient Greeks had a sense that sexuality and children was a good combination? The way it worked was like this: When you sent your child to be apprenticed to a master craftsman, it was pretty much accepted that he would live in and give the man sexual favours as well. Now, in our society this is shocking and dreadful, but in theirs it was no big deal.

One of the main reasons the Romans had the purges against the Christians is because they practised ritual cannibalism. This was an abhorrent thought to a good Roman. Yes, Christians only ritually ate another person's flesh, but imagine if your church only ritually practised child molestation? You can see why it was VERY easy for Roman soldiers to put these strange, cannibal worshipping people to death.

Hitler convinced people that Jews were evil. Mao convinced people that intellectuals were evil. Your present government has convinced you that terrorists are evil. I had a neighbour, once, who had lived alone for far too long. The man lived entirely inside his own head, and was basically mad. You never knew if some thing you would do or say would set him off. He would then be either very pleasant to you, or extremely vindictive, depending on what he imagined you did or said.

Well, it turns out that I bought a property he had wanted for himself, and this was enough to make him believe I was bad. But then his mother died soon after I bought the place, this then PROVED I was evil. You cannot argue with logic like this. You cannot reasonably argue with someone who has ANY blind conviction. It will not matter what you say, or how obvious it is that you are right, you are wrong.

His mind had been made up. Anything I did was further proof to him that I was evil. Nothing could be said or done to convince him otherwise. I was the Jew to his Nazi, and extermination was the only viable option. After a few years of spiked water hoses, cutting of power lines, and legal harassment of the most ridiculous sort, I decided I was better off elsewhere, and moved.

I got out of the firing line. Of course, the fellow simply moved his argument to the next person near to him, and started a huge fight inside his own family.

I realised he was mad, but that did not help resolve impossible arguments. It is simply not fun to deal with people like this. However, I have to say, he was a marvellous teacher, and in the course of our battles he helped me activate my RAT.

This goes to show that nothing need be wasted. I learned a lot from him, because he was CLEAR in his intention, and focussed in his goal. OK, we can admit that he was an Obsessive Compulsive Pathological Liar, but regardless, it taught me a lot of hidden aspects of the Human Psyche. He wanted me gone, and eventually it was easier to comply than argue.

There is no way to remove the filter from another's eyes. You either choose to:

1. *Battle it out,*
2. *Change your own ways, and agree, or*
3. *LEAVE.*

In this case, leaving was the best solution, and I moved on to find a better environment for my growth and prosperity.

Here's the rub. By doing so, by letting GO of the situation, I removed MY filters. I no longer needed a defence against his madness. Now I could stand back and see how the man had argued with so many people, for so long, that argument was his whole life. By removing myself from his point of argument, I was curiously enough causing him more grief than he caused me. Why? Because I robbed him of his purpose. The reason he was getting up each morning was to fight the good fight against the evil neighbour, but now that bastard had up and LEFT!

Revenge, as they say, is best served cold. Someone asked me if I wanted him "sorted out", as in, dead. My reply was very simple: "Not at all, I wish him a very long life." (That way he can come to grasp the consequences of his actions.) To which the person said, "You are either a Saint, or incredibly evil."

Saint? I used up my halo as a Colgate Ring of Confidence.

Yes, I generally seek to keep my intention pure, and aim for things that are in the best interests of all. This is really common sense, and not some goody two shoes mentality. Things that are good for all make everyone around you happier. Yet we can all look back and see areas where we could have handled things better. It never pays to get above ourselves, but it pays even less to have people feel you are above them. The person with pure intention knows they are right, but they are humbly superior.

And here is where an extraordinary character we shall call "the Mad Monk" taught me the secret of success with people who you are in disagreement with: *Keep your friends close, and your enemies even closer.*

Only now do I grasp the simple truth: The very fact that I had a problem with the neighbour was reason enough to go out of my way to get him on side. This meant the telling of bald faced lies.

What the Mad Monk explained to me was that he was going to make friends with the problem, and this would entail convincing the fellow that he hated me. Which is what he did. He went and said "Do you still use the mill your father had built?" The mad neighbour said he did. "Do you think I could pay you to mill me up some timber?" The neighbour then says, "But I thought you were friends with Wallace?"

Here the card is played. "I can't believe that bastard over there would cheat me! I wanted to live on his land, but he kicked me off. Can you imagine? Would you mind if I moved onto the public land by the river? I need a little wood to build a lean to, which is why I am here."

My neighbour could not go further out of his way to help the Monk after that. He literally delivered fruit and other things to him, and had cups of tea at his caravan, and thought he was the most marvellous fellow ever. Why? Because the Monk saw what an evil bastard I was. We eventually sorted out the access issues and subdivision of my block was able to get underway, in part because the Mad Monk chose to make the obstacle a friend, instead of an enemy.

There are times when there is a perfectly valid excuse to lie through your teeth. There are times when lying is the best policy, and it is generally when you are dealing with liars. There is nothing wrong with a necessary lie when your survival is at stake. As an example: If someone from the Spanish Inquisition had come up to me and said that I either confessed to being a witch or end up burning on a pile of faggots, I would instantly see the error of my ways, confess, apologise for the inconvenience, and generally suck up to the jailers who held the power of life or death over me.

It's the smart thing to do. After all, I can always backslide, and if I do, what of it? It's the Catholic church and I can then confess! So either way I win more time, AND I get to live long enough to get some more experience of life. Yes, I would lie: But no need to get hot under the collar about it. What I really did was let go of my personal filters, and put on the glasses they wore. Seeing eye to eye makes a difference.

There is the curious thing about filters and communication. If you are in disagreement with someone who has absolute power over you, with enough time and pressure, a remarkable thing will occur: One day you will put on the sunglasses they are wearing and see things their way. You WILL have an experience that will convince you that your captors are RIGHT. Unless you have a very focussed mind, you WILL become subject to their projections, and you WILL crumble under their pressure. Jesus will become your saviour. Praise the Lord!

The paradox is that for the inquisitor, this proves they are right! So be smart: Bow down before the pressure defeats you. Employ the SAS to defend yourself: *Sincerely Act Sincere.* The willow bends in the wind, and does not resist. Bend with the forces that surround you, because if you don't your RAT will concoct some sort of story in your head that makes you believe it is OK to crumble. It will invent a rational for you to give in. Why? Because it wants to get OFF the sinking ship.

This is your RAT saving your bacon. Your RAT will get woken up through torture, and look for ANY WAY to stop it. It will look for a way to come into agreement with its captors, and appease them. If this means creating a vision of the Virgin Mary (Cough Cough: Sure she was a virgin) that forces your outer mind to accept the enforcers demands. Then so be it.

You WILL get the vision or experience that changes your filter of perception, and as a result your experience with the captors will become one of agreement. This is one of the major reasons women fall in love with their kidnappers. It's a protection device that their RAT employs to save their life.

And the weird thing is, as soon as you see something from your opponents point of view, it becomes understandable and reasonable. It does not make it RIGHT, but it does take away our personal conviction that WE are.

Of course, the person already in contact with their RAT will have "given way" far earlier than this, and let the captors win the round. The clever Rat will have already convinced his captors that while they are right. 100% right, and that his story makes him the no exception to the rule, but that maybe they should listen anyway? Soon his/her former captors will be buying him/her drinks down the Bar.

Bring your friends close, and keep your enemies even closer. This is how your RAT will most effectively protect you. Work with it and it will even help you find the words to make a person feel as if you like them, despite the fact that you detest them. In the course of your befriending the enemy, you will invariably discover a way to make your life proceed far more easily.

The Mystic Rat Says: ***Take off your filters, walk a mile in another person's moccasins, and find a way to get AGREEMENT.***

Diplomacy is the technique used to disarm filters and preconceptions. And in this word is the clue: The art of Dipping Low is Dip-Low-macy. Be humble, bow low, act small and be insignificant. Leave the other person with the sense that THEY are right and you will find they will do whatever you ask of them. In short, you will discover how easy it is to win someone to YOUR standard by simply admiring THEIRS.

The Mystic Rat Says: *Rather than BURST someone's bubble, blow it gently to a place where it is no longer in your road.*

It is not always possible to shift someone to a point of agreement with yourself, however. You can remove filters, shift your sense of right and wrong to one side, and bend over backwards to make an enemy your friend, but sometimes it just doesn't work. You may have battled it out, tried to change your filters and accept them, but nothing works. Accept it, and leave.

We don't win every round.

ARE YOU EXPERIENCED?

Let's stop and do a stock take, not on what we have, but on how much experience we feel in ourselves. Businesses do a stock take to see what is in their inventory, and so top shall we stop and see what we have as our experience at/in this moment.

Well, you may own a house, or be paying one off. You may have a partner and a few kids. You may have a degree, a good job, a nice car. It's all good, but none of these things are an experience of Now. What we experience NOW are three things.

1. *Place - Where you are*
2. *Quantity - How much self you feel*
3. *Quality – The clarity of Self you recognise*

What we possess is not what we experience, even though the fruits of our experience is the one thing you can truly possess. And the one thing you can truly experience is a sensation of where you are in this moment. How MUCH of NOW are you experiencing, and how GOOD is the NOW you are experiencing, is the question.

And the NOW is really the sum of the HERENESS, ISNESS and BEINGNESS that you experience. *Place = Hereness, Quality = Isness, Quality = Beingness*

For most people on Planet Earth the sum total of their experience will not be particularly deep in any of these aspects of being. However, I think it fair to say that we all would prefer the highest quality experience we can achieve, with the greatest sense of being present in order to experience it. But what the experience of life actually IS doesn't have an answer other than it IS what it IS. The one thing that is certain is the extraordinary paradox: *You possess life most fully by letting it go.*

I am speaking of a generously of Spirit, that part of your nature that allows life freedom to roam and experience what it will. We cannot own life, but we can let life own us. Ownership is an odd idea. In many ways, to own is to isolate, whereas when you accept that all is a gift of life, you own everything, and nothing. The tricky part is, we can only own the moment when we grasp it is free to leave us as it chooses.

This thought became crystal clear to me one night when having dinner with some friends in Byron Bay. (Australia's Hippie wonderland) In the middle of eating some Thai food, my friend dropped a clanger. I asked something about how they saw relationships, and what he said seemed very odd. "Well, I own my wife, and she loves this. She is MINE. This is our mutual security."

I looked over towards the very independant woman he married.

His wife nodded in agreement, and said, "Yes, he owns me and I own him." Even though I knew she was having an affair with a Doctor at that point, common sense told me not to argue the point regarding ownership. Clearly the woman was happy to have her husband believe what he would. But the comment stayed with me.

People seem to think they can collect, gather and possess so many things, but surely we must know they can all be gone tomorrow? As it stood. My friend had passed away within a couple of years of that meeting. Could he take his still living wife to heaven with him? Of course not. What you truly OWN is that which you can take beyond the grave. So tell me this: what we can truly own? Intelligence, purpose, gratitude, these innate qualities travel with you, the house stays at home.

Let me put to you a different view on wealth. Our personal wealth can generally be added up as assets versus liabilities. But I say that, while an accountant can produce a document telling you what you own, your TRUE wealth is only to be found in the depth by which you can EXERIENCE this very moment.

What use is money if you cannot plunge into this moment and relish it? What good is health if you are blind to the joy of living? What good is owning a wife if you die tomorrow? But LIFE is something else. Presuming that we grasp the fact that LIFE, or at least consciousness, continues after the physical body ends, we can take a broad scope view of some simple metaphysical basics.

Let me ask you this: ***How much LIFE can you handle?*** This first begs the question: *What is Life?* Well really, Life is what IS. Life is a trilogy of ISNESS, HERENESS and NOWNESS. As an obvious example: The greater you can dwell in the ISNESS of Life, the more you feel HERE and NOW. The more you dive into any one of these three aspects causes you to experience more of each These three aspects all work together, and while it is slightly different for every single person, one thing is certain: If you miss any one of these three, you are not truly living.

When we have a depth and breadth of experience then we can say we have savoured Life, in all its colours and shades. And it is only when we learn to savour the bitter-sweet nature of the moment that we grow with, and discover, the ISNESS, HERENESS and NOWNESS that this moment of Life possesses. Then it becomes a hall of mirrors: Once we open our eyes, no matter where we look, we find infinite depth. Yet we can never reach out and touch it all.

It is not really possible to achieve the focus of the infinite depth in each and every moment, but just touching it sets off a peculiar sense of

Self Awareness. At this moment, an extraordinary thing occurs: We remember that we have felt this before. We simply KNOW this is something we already KNOW. It is the ultimate Déjà Vu.

Remember when we spoke of the Baby State, the original state from whence we all spring? It is a depth of Love, and a total sense of knowing, trusting and being. This is the ultimate NOW. That's it, the moment of KNOWING (Now-ing) is really the recognition of self. Does this amaze and astound you, or it is all just words on a page that passes like the wind?

I know this is sounding a little New Age Spiritual-ish, but really it is common sense based on an experience we all share: The Baby State. Babies are always here, now and have nothing between them and their innate trust of life. Could you imagine a baby worrying about the mortgage? It's laughable. But, as we grow, we have more on our plate to deal with, and it gets serious. This is why we need our Rat.

When you are connected to your Inner Rat, you find a balance between this point of Here/Now and your experience of this world. It is like what we used in Book One: NOWHERE becomes NOW HERE when we get to place our Rat in the middle of our experience. Our present moment, and our world experience, rarely flow easily together. But when we align to NOW all moves harmoniously. Like a great river within its banks, flowing to the sea, we are contained yet flowing, and all in accord with life. We feel the permanence of Being (The NOW) and enjoy the passing Moments of Life (The KNOWING)

It is only when you grasp this truth that you realise you have been embraced by life ALL your life. You start to understand that it is a wonderful thing just being, just flowing, just experiencing the sun and the rain and the clouds and the boats and the bridges and the fishermen and the waves. It is all HERE NOW.

You fall into the depths of your being and find only yourself waiting for you. Your RAT is the tour guide who will help you find this perfect place, the zone where you come to understand that you are complete, that you are the ONE.

Your RAT is a beacon installed at your birth. It is a spiritual compass that points unerringly towards the depth of each moment. All you have to do is FIND your RAT and you will be able to find yourself. How do we do this? All we need common sense and a little BAIT.

Your Rat has been hidden for so long, that you probably would not recognise it if it came up and bit you, so you need to trick yourself and get your Rat out into the open. We do this using a curious, and ancient Law: *The Law of Reversed Effort.*

The Law of Reversed Effort

If you put a plank on the ground and ask someone to walk on it, they have no problem at all in doing this. Unless you are dead drunk, it's easy. But take this same plank, and put it between two pylons that are 300 feet up in the air, and suddenly it becomes a very difficult thing to do. This, in a nutshell, if the Law of Reversed Effort at work.

It can work against you, as fear leading to failure, or you can make it work FOR you, as a bait for your Rat. The principle of the law is simple: Whatever you fear will be drawn to you. If you are afraid of falling, then the Law of Reversed Effort will lead you to a position where you MIGHT fall. Here you come to the real choice. If the fear grows stronger it can completely overtake your nervous system, leaving you paralysed: thus you fall. Or you get over it, and you become free to move.

An odd example happened to me over a small issue I had with fridges. I had this weird little quirk where I just hated a fridge door being left open. I walked around all day, like a fridge door vigilante, shutting any fridge door left open. It did not matter where I was, an open refrigerator door just gave me the willies.

Finally a friend of mine took me aside, and opened his fridge door. He demanded I stand there, watching it stay open. I said "Your butter will melt" He said "I don't care. "I said, "You will go through a lot of extra power" He said "Fine" I said "The light might burn out" and so he asked, "And then?"

I am not sure when the corner was turned in the conversation, but all of a sudden worrying about a fridge door seemed an entirely trite and meaningless thing to concern yourself about. And it stopped. I was taken to the edge of the fear, made to look it in the face, and then it just left. That is the Law of Reversed Effort at Work.

Every strong emotion you hold magnetises the world around you and draws out from the ether exactly what it is that you are emoting over. How do you make this work FOR you? Simple: If you want money, HATE it. Detest it, despise it, decry it loudly as a poison and toxin in society. If you do this with every fibre of your being, money will fly towards you.

The obvious problem is, of course, that as you have to really believe this, when you get the money you will not enjoy it. So here is another trick, when you are pulling a stunt like this make sure you give yourself a point that sets an OUT clause. A suggestion might be to tell yourself that you will detest money with a passion for three months, then you will let it all go and accept what comes.

Can you use this "hate" technique to find your Inner Rat? Absolutely. The simple truth is, I cannot stand the miserable low life sarcastic bastard that is my Rat. He is not nice, not pleasant, not even kind in any human sense. He is a rude upstart that cares nothing for how people feel, and does not care if you live or die. I respect him, because he is good at surviving, but I do not like him.

For some reason, however, he likes me. I suspect because I am completely honest about not liking my RAT that he finds this appealing to his rather warped sense of humour. I admire him, I respect him, but I just do not LIKE him. In fact I prefer if he went away, but at the same time I grudgingly admit that I am far better off with him hanging about.

This is a little like using a magnet on a nail. You turn a nail into a magnet by rubbing the magnet on it, in one direction, until the nail takes on some of the magnetic force. Then when you leave it be, it will still attract what it is designed to attract. I accept my Rat, and a little Rattyness rubs off in every area of my life.

Here is something that will shatter the positive mental attitude people when they realise it is true. Being disinterested, but vaguely curious, in a goal works better than the gung-ho "let's go do it" mentality. Why? If you have to motivate yourself with powerful positives, all it means is that down the track you will meet powerful negatives. One will cancel out the other.

A perfect example was a factory being build by the Japanese and the Americans. It was a replica factory built in each others respective countries. The US had the footings in, and stuff being erected inside of weeks. The Japanese were still doing the logistics, yet though the Americans had a THREE MONTH head start from when the first cement got laid, the Japanese had the factory up and running before them. How?

They stood back, and remained detached. This allowed them to work out the options better, and the likely problems, before they got underway.

Hubee was a friend of mine, who, for a time, had this professional Hitman that decided he liked Hubee's company. Of course, if a Hitman likes your company, you really do not have too much choice in the matter. One day when walking in broad daylight through a park, my friend said something out of turn. Casually, in reference to what the man did for a living, he asked. "Do you enjoy killing people?" The Hitman immediately grabbed him by the neck, and plunged his head under the water of a nearby fountain until he passed out.

This was in a public square, and the truly remarkable thing, as my friend explained to me later, was that no one cried out. No one looked. No one even glanced in their direction. They all just walked away.

As our Hitman slapped my friend back to consciousness, he said "Look, you have to be careful what you say around me, because this is what I do. Understand?" I gather the message was understood, as my friend is still alive.

There is a very curious thing about most professional killers. (and other extreme personalities) They are very polarised, and they have the effect of polarising everything around them. What is more, they are very sensitive to lies, and know when people are telling them porkies. Often it is this very sensitivity that drove them to their brutal profession, but that is an entirely different story. The point is that the survival instincts in a polarised person are generally very heightened.

Likewise: When you visit your RAT it will wake you up. It will set your radar to see the false, deceitful and meaningless nature of most people's lives.

When someone with a lack of self-worth is telling me a story, what I hear are the lies and rhubarb that drive the individual. It used to be very distressing. I would see people with two faces, the one talking was simply pretending to be nice, while the other face was a selfish cow that didn't care whether you lived of died. And why should they? Then one day I realised that I, too, had this two faced nature. When I accepted this, guess what happened? The spilt-self united. I became one with my Rat, and I became far more accepting of others and their foibles.

This is what your RAT will do to your sense of perception. It sharpens it until you see the obvious, and then you go a little further, and realise everything you see is really an aspect of our own self.

It happened for me one day many years ago. I as walking down Venice Beach in LA, contemplating, as I usually did, while I walked. I had just had a powerful experience with a wild woman. She was completely raw and had been bruised and hurt by the callous nature of the world, yet she still fought back with tooth and nail.

She was a friend who I did not understand, and I think it fair to say she did not understand myself, but we liked each other. (in part because we didn't understand each other) As I was thinking about the quite powerful resonance between us, a curious curtain was lifted. Everything around me became utterly clear, and suddenly I saw every person walking down the street as pure, naked SOUL.

I could see their pulsating spiritual centre, and all around it were images, and beliefs, and dreams, and hopes, and hurts, and wishes, and lies, and fears, and just EVERYTHING. It was all there like a book, waiting to be read.

What I also saw in every single person who walked past was the stark and remarkable fact that every one of them had only *one or two things* to sort out in this lifetime. If they could but see the OBVIOUS in their life, they could correct the simple things that were out of balance and achieve incredible freedom and happiness.

What is more, it was SO clear that I could have gone up to each and every person and told them exactly what it was that they needed to know. But then another image came over me. I saw what would happen if I did this. I saw clearly that instead of being grateful, I would be seen as an intrusive monster bent on invading their world.

My approach, offering open-hearted freedom, would polarise the surrounding energy and be seen as an attack. This would awaken the beasts within. Those who live in the bubble see everything that approaches as a distorted monster, due to the lens they live inside. Their view of me, as I would come to them through the filter of the beliefs they carried, would be of a twisted, horrible monster. I would be a devil come to taunt them, a creature to be hated because I had the power to take away what they cherished most: Their problems and concerns.

I stopped, and as I did so, I could feel waves of energy pulsating through me. People started to look up, and stare at me for no apparent reason. What is more, I could see hate in their eyes. Now, I have experienced drug paranoia, and know well the illusions that life can throw up. Was it me, was it them? In this instance I considered it wise not to try and understand any more. I turned down the wick of awareness, said "thank you" for the experience, and went back to my rental car.

As I considered things, and allowed the incredible energy I felt to discharge, I started to realise that the whole episode was set up for ME to understand something. It had nothing to do with the other people at all, but was a stage set for me to understand my OWN triggers that needed looking at.

One thing that came through clearly: **We are all SOUL. We are all a spark of divinity, clothed in the rags of beggars. Our false beliefs, our fears, our prejudices, these are what stop us from seeing and being the truth of what we are. Yet they are necessary blockages, required to hold us in check until we are ready to take them down, one at a time, and discover freedom for ourselves.**

I flew back to Australia that night, and soon after landing went to a gathering at a friend's house. In the course of the evening, I got talking to a person who seemed interested in spiritual subjects, and I started to express a little of the experience I had on Venice Beach. I could still feel the energy flowing, though it was far less.

Suddenly the person jumped up and started saying "I cannot believe how ANGRY you are. I have never met anyone so vicious in all my life!" and they stormed out of the room, and left the party.

I had never experienced anything quite like this before. There was no anger or viciousness at all in what I was saying, and certainly I was feeling nothing of the sort. But the person saw this in me, and ran away in fear from the party. Now, it is likely that they were seeing their OWN condition, but I had to give credence to the notion that a part of "it" was also inside myself. And indeed, this is where I first started to come face to face with my RAT.

It took me many years to comprehend exactly what had happened. My Inner RAT awoke while I was walking on Venice Beach. IT was looking directly into the passing people, seeing their weak points and checking out the lay of the land. It happened at the party as well. Over time I came to understand that this is simply what our RAT will do. It will observe the minutest details in what is in front of it. As a result, it will cause a reaction. It doesn't have to say anything. The effect radiates outwards just by being a witness to falsehood. I learned that it is wise not to accent this RAT EFFECT, and stopped staring into passers by.

It all brought to memory a time, many years earlier, when some vicious street people were coming up to mug me. Suddenly they stopped in their tracks, as if they hit a wall. All I did was look at them, see what they were, and I saw it clearly.

There was no time for concern or fear, and all I had was a sense of observation. I was also curious what it was life was bringing to me, so I just looked at them as they came up to me. The effect this had was extraordinary. These hardened criminals became scared, I could see the fear in their eyes. They turned away, and as they did one said, "You are an evil man! I thought I was bad, but I have never seen such evil."

This is the point where I started to realise how my RAT had protected me all along, and that it had already been doing so for many years. I recalled the time when I was sliding towards a row of cars when the front forks failed on a motor bike I was riding. I felt no fear. No fear: Just the urge to avoid dying at that moment.

The Doctors who treated me could not believe I was still alive. Head on into a car at high speed on a motor bike means one thing, certain death. Yet they patched me up and a week later I was up and at a party.

Or the time on the Sydney Harbour Bridge when I FELT a car coming at high speed behind me. It was in the middle of the night in pouring rain and on some instinct I pulled the bike to one side, and as I did so, saw a car travelling at an extremely high speed going right through the place where I had just been.

I can recount at least eight times when death was a certainty, yet something pulled me through. It was the NINTH time death came knocking that I decided I needed to write this book. Maybe my CAT only had nine lives, and my RAT was set free? I wish, it is still there, wanting to interfere, but slowly everything lines up.

Your Rat will help you survive impossible odds. It is the good luck in your Feng Shui, the Aces in your Poker hand, the winning ticket in your raffle. If you can grasp a little of what I have written in this book you will have the tools to start practising how to connect to your RAT, and as a result, become incredibly LUCKY.

But I cannot tell you exactly how to do it, because despite what I say, your RAT has its OWN mind. It will have its OWN way of waking you up.

Yet I do know a secret: If you really do not like that part of yourself that sees the negatives , and understands the low motivations that drive most people, stop and accept it. If you cannot stand that callous side to your nature that looks at children dying in the Unicef ads and think "Oh well", or if you really hate that part of you that reads the newspaper or sees people on the news and says, "Liars". Stop and accept it.

I promise you, you are getting ready to meet your RAT. Accepting and dealing with your negatives is how you grow past your Dark Side of the Force and this allows you to embrace your Light side, without fear of the shadow hiding behind it.

The Mystic Rat Says: *In a world of light, anything you create casts a shadow.*

And here is a little secret: Your RAT (Reality Attention Trigger) is set mostly to recognising the negatives, because this IS a negative world.

This Reality Trigger is set to go off whenever a negative approaches you. What is more, it sparks it up with a clear sense of recognition, so the negative energy that approaches you realises it is SEEN. It will either attack, or invert onto itself, in direct accordance to your innate sense of self-worth.

I had one occasion when I was talking to a fellow about a new job. He really liked me, and wanted me on board. We discussed when and where I would start, and when the interview was finished he reached over to shake on it. A remarkable thing happened. The man was thrown across the room! I mean, it was as if a lightning strike had hit him, and he was thrown, bodily, some 10 feet across the room.

He hit the wall, fell to the ground, then suddenly picked himself up like he was a puppet, and smiled as if nothing had happened. What is more, when I left and went to another country he kept ringing me up, wanting me to come back and work with him. Does this make any sense at all to you? It didn't to me at the time, but I knew enough to realise that this was a little weird, and to stay far, far away.

Twenty years later, I realised that my RAT had something to do with this, that I was being protected. Our Inner Rat has tremendous power, and possibly because of this I am very careful with it. While I DO trust that it will work in my best interest, I still find its whole way of life a little uncomfortable.

I know I write about trusting your inner RAT. It is a part of us, after all. And really, it is just the Trigger that points our Attention towards Reality, isn't it?

It is also the part of you that truly knows and recognises LOVE. The problem can be that the one you Love will feel your Rat Whiskers. Now, if they have embraced their RAT, it is wonderful. If not, they may well grow to hate you. That's the nature of your RAT. It will ferret out the depths of every experience, looking for the cheese of eternal life. In doing so, it upsets a few apple carts.

Perhaps my RAT is now sufficiently integrated so as to not offend others as much as it used to, or maybe I have just learned to duck conflicts before they arise. Certainly, things have changed in my life and I found different ways to do things. For one, I no longer try to make a friend when I feel that the person is not connected to themselves. I know, from experience, that it is just too hard on both of us. But I also know, while I can't trust my RAT not to offend, I truly enjoy it when it gets out of its cage, and happily points out its truth to all and sundry. It's a liberating experience.

The simple truth is that just about everyone you meet is drowning in their own circumstances. Precious few have their head above water, either emotionally, mentally or physically. Even fewer have learned how to sail the seas of truth. You can throw these people a lifeline, and offer them a greater freedom, but rarely will they recognise it. Which is not unexpected, as usually our wake up calls involve whipping, beating and suffering enough for us to want to get out of wherever we are.

So, you see, I am doing people a favour when I whip them with wit and whittle down their waffle with waspish wisdom.

Not many appreciate a Rat walking amongst them, but amongst those who love you, they will REALLY love you. Sadly, it is also vice versa.

Our Life is the Lesson

When I was just 4 years old, I was swimming in the ocean and got caught in a rip. The current was taking me towards some bridge pylons that were encrusted with oyster shells. They were hard and jagged, and I could see myself getting very badly hurt if the waves threw me onto them, and what's more, this looked to be a certainty.

Then I heard a familiar and calming voice. I looked up to see my Uncle Kevin rowing out to save me. I watched with fascination as he dipped the oars, and pulling gracefully he drew the boat through the waves like a pen over paper. Here was an old seaman doing what he did best: Sailing the open sea.

He hauled me on board with a laugh, and his confidence completely removed the fear I had been experiencing, but far more than this, he replaced this fear with something else. I got a new message to run my life with: *Know what you do, and do what you know well.*

The simple act of watching him row his boat, watching him move through the water with such confidence, this mastery of the rowing arts broke the spell of fear. His calm certainty reached out to touch me, and in that moment this planted a seed in my heart. From that point on I always strived to care enough, to know enough, to do my very best. If I could live my life in the same way Uncle Kevin rowed his boat, then I would be alright.

Only a week later, at another beach near where the Oyster shells on the pylons had been, I was walking through the sand dunes. I realised I was completely surrounded by large, very large, ants. They were all over an inch long, and I knew that these suckers could really BITE. I froze with fear in the middle of them, unable to move.

My father must have seen me, because he called me over. But I could not move. If I tried to go past those ant, it was a certainty that they would bite. After a few moments that seemed like hours, Dad came over, picked me up, and just walked through the "ant wall" as if it wasn't there.

I called out "Watch out for the ANTS!" but he just laughed. I could see his bare feet stepping past them and I swear he even stood on some. But it seems they did not bother him. This new message was simple: *Deal with your fears or else they magnify the problems and immobilise you.*

Years later I came to understand how fear will polarise our thoughts, and change the way we see things, and even what we see. A fearful person sees threat where the confident one sees only promise. Fear shifts the perception to the negative, and fear can even change the PHSYSICAL appearance of things. Our pupils dilate, and then the eyes absorb so much light that things can appear to grow and become much larger right before our eyes. It looks so real, therefore it is REAL.

For myself, because of my fear these were HUGE ants. Really, they were probably just green ants, not deadly man eating monsters, but they looked so much larger. It paralysed me. When fear takes charge and starts driving your bus, it will control your thinking. It will lock you up in a hundred different ways, and convince you that things are very, very serious.

There are a lot of people dying from a serious illness. The illness is being too serious, too fearful, and thus completely repressed.

But when you put FUN as a priority in your life, it is much harder for fear to take charge. Things cannot get very, very serious, because when you are laughing, everything stays in proportion. I can't explain why, but the truth and purpose of the court jester bringing a clearer perspective to the court is a very old one.

While we keep our sense of humour, life cannot beat us down. This is possibly one of the greatest lessons we can learn. Keep smiling, it will all work out. If you are smiling, you are not collapsing into fear. When you keep smiling it stops you from locking up, and you remain able to duck and dive around life's arrows of misfortune.

It is all about staying out of the fear bandwidth as much as possible. Yet, let us also remember that fear has a purpose. A little concern in the back of our thoughts can cause us to look more closely at some issue, as an example. We are not trying to extinguish fear, just seeking to increase fun.

But we do need to understand what it is that triggers fear in our hearts.

Understand the Meme, Reduce the Fear

What is the worst thing that can happen? Death? The first thing the Tibetan Buddhists tell new students is to contemplate their own death. The reasoning is simple, if you confront this, your greatest fear, everything else will come into a better, and clearer perspective. Clear perspective means a more focussed imagination.

When you can focus the imagination, you can put a lid of it when fear creeps in. You maintain a better perspective when you don't get caught up in the process of negative possibilities. And here is the secret: Understand the MEME (the image that stirs up the fear) and you reduce the fear

I was extremely fortunate by being able to confront my fear of dying at an early age. What is more, by having a strong energy around to show me the path OUT of that fear, this game me a roadmap for my future. I now understand that my RAT was active way back then, showing reality through the worst of my fears.

YOUR life will have also been presented with certain truths in the form of difficulties at an early age, but here I discovered an extraordinary thing. When asking people what their earliest memory might be, most people could not remember much earlier that seven years of age. I found this truly remarkable. I had a clear memory back to age two, and odd snippets of recollection from earlier than this. I wondered how people survived without the incredibly powerful memories of early childhood.

This was when I realised that people usually throw a blanket of forgetting over their inner child. If you recall early childhood, then you will also recall experiences that you need to resolve. Many just do not want to. It is almost an unconscious decision, but deep down most people just prefer not to know.

Obviously, if you have had incredible stress, such as incest, abuse, etc. this can trigger off the "curtain drawing" over your past. But this was not the case for most of the people I interviewed. What had happened in their case was that at age seven they discovered they wanted to be part of a group. It was this simple, they wanted to have friends, so they COMPROMISED their basic and natural state of being.

As a result: *THEY BECAME WHAT THEY BELIEVED OTHER'S WANTED THEM TO BE.* This is not a healthy way of life.

More to the point, the child forgot it's own past trying to remodel themselves in the image of what they thought other people would accept or want. People let the Curtain of Forgetting fall on their own past in order to fit in to their social structure.

If this happened to you, you are not fully yourself. This is your first Humpty Dumpty falling from the wall moment, where suddenly you are split in two. There is an inner you (hidden) and an outer you (the social face). The ability to perceive your correct path is diminished because your attention has been pulled into two worlds.

You cannot blind yourself in one area and expect to see clearly in another. No, blind yourself and you are blind. That's it. If you cannot remember at least to age four you have a major concern with some of your most basic life elements.

If this is you, you have crippled yourself. It happened to me in a different way. At age 13 I was a table tennis player that no one in my boarding school could beat. I won every game. I was a GOD on the table tennis table, and almost every shot I hit went in, and every shot you sent to me I got back. There was a problem with this, because soon enough no one would play me. What was the point? They knew they would lose.

SO, in order to have friends, I learned to lose. Soon enough, others started winning the odd game, and I had people to play with again. Only I never again played as well as I once did. By minimising myself in order to have friends, I had compromised my ability to perform.

Of course, perhaps I could have taken on older kids with more experience, but in the strict world of Catholic boarding schools and you just didn't associate with older kids. SO, I went backwards and FORGOT the secret of being a God of table tennis. Despite what you presently believe, you have done this as well, somewhere, somehow in your past. If you want to rediscover your true power, and find your RAT, because if you wish to be free, this curtain of forgetting has to be addressed.

One very powerful technique you might like to try is extremely simple. Just imagine what it was like one year earlier than your earliest memory. Ask parents or siblings for clues. Try and get a PICTURE of an event, and allow your imagination to grow around it. In time, your true recollection will start to emerge, and with it your reconnection to a very essential part of your journey to becoming a proper RAT.

Mickey Mouse started out as a RAT, but Disney recognised the mood of the people, and minimised them. All the negative elements of Mickey were transferred to OTHER characters in the Disney stable: Donald Duck, Scrooge, the mischievous Mouse Kids, even Goofy are personality slices of "Steamboat Willy". (One of the very first Mickey Mouse cartoons)

Yet the enthusiastic, can-do Mickey remained. How did he manage to become SO "Can-Do"? It is the RAT inside the Mouse that knows it can achieve and succeed that propels Mickey and gives him his natural power. Plus he is drawn that way.

Remember how, even today, people speak of Disney, and say *"Don't muck with the Mouse!"* Why? Because a powerful RAT drives the organisation, developed and fostered by Walt Disney, and his brother, from its earliest stages. And how did the RAT grow strong? Walt Disney had really tough times, but he always looked with a RAT EYE for every opportunity, and had a nose for every bit of cheese that came his way. And at the same time, he trusted that the Gods would provide.

Walt spent some 17 Million Dollars building Disneyland. An absolute fortune at the time, on a concept no one had even imagined, let alone try to make work. A permanent carnival ride, in essence. The naysayers were everywhere, convinced this would ruin Disney. Yet in the first year of operation he turned over more than the entire build cost of his amusement park.

What drove him on? He remembered what it was like to be a child, and focussed on the FUN. If it was FUN, the people would come, and they did, and they still do.

Focus on remembering your childhood for now, and you will find this a great asset in your growing understanding of your Inner Rat and where to find it.

Your THIRD BRAIN

The Sympathetic Nervous System, the nerve ganglion in the Solar Plexus is your THIRD brain. You have your actual brain, and as discussed your heart that can take over the physical brain in times of stress, and act as a control centre for the body. You also have the Reptilian Brain, which is your spinal cord. This is a brain of sorts, but it really controls the automatic functions and is subject to the brain itself. Your fully independent THIRD brain is the Sympathetic Nervous System.

And, recent research has shown that IT is governed to a degree by the bacteria in your gut. Oddly enough, the natural bacteria in your gut weighs approximately the same amount as your actual brain. Only now are the scientists realising how important the gut, the bacteria inside it, combined with the sympathetic nervous system, is. There is clear evidence to demonstrate that your emotions can be controlled by this area of the body. Depression, mood swings, all this often this tracks back to imbalance in the gut flora. This can be due to illness, fungal infection and/or antibiotics. Regardless, the healthy body needs a healthy gut.

There is a deeper reality at work here. I have not really touched on this to date, but we need give passing mention to a simple reality, we are a multi-dimensional being. Our thoughts have an existence, our emotions have an existence. As an example of this: When we are asleep and dreaming, we can have a dream where we are "really there". So, where were we?

We wake, and the memory of the experience is clear. It is called lucid dreaming, but no one in the scientific community can really explain this, particularly when people can describe places they have never seen or been to in the physical with absolute accuracy. Jung called it the Collective Unconscious, but in truth, we are simply able to leave the physical body and travel to other places in full consciousness. It's in the bible! Saint Paul said:*"I went with a man unto the third heaven, whether in the body or out of it, I know not."*

Whether you accept this, or not, will not change reality. But the point for mentioning this is because the sympathetic nervous system is at the juncture where the physical and emotional bodies of man cross over. It is a nexus point.

This area is the gateway for your emotional elements to connect with the body. It is the meeting point between what is known as your LUNAR body and the physical body. You have probably heard of things like an Astral Body? Well, the LUNAR body is a little like this, but different.

This is a Zone or frequency that circulates through your aura in a figure eight shape. It is a spiral of energy that is attuned to the emotional frequencies around you.

More importantly, it "powers up" your own emotions via your Sympathetic Nervous System (SNS). This connection can be paralysed in times of stress, and the two way "feed" of emotions between the Astral (Feeling) Body and the Physical (via the Lunar Body) can be interrupted. This is when you get "frozen". When a woman is classed as "frigid" what generally has happened is that the connection between her inner bodies has been damaged at the Solar Plexus, and her Lunar Body has locked up as a result. It is another reason why sexual and emotional respect are so important in our relationships.

Now this will seem like New Age mumbo Jumbo to some, but I cannot be held responsible for your personal blindness. This stuff is very real, and very obvious if you have the eyes to see. And sorry (not) but it gets worse for the cynics! (And please, while I do not mind if you wish to be cynical, I would remind you that this is NOT your job. You are stealing this role away from your RAT, and it will demand payment later on for this theft.)

On the various planes of existence, there are entities that literally feed off the emotions of human beings. However, when we are secure and confident there is no opening in our aura for these creatures to get their emotion sucking tendrils into us. But when we get fearful, and particularly when we get PARALYSED with fear, then this is like an open invitation to any entity in your area.

You are literally turning on a flashing neon light on the Lower Astral Plane that reads "Eat Me". And they will eat you, if they get half a chance. Tendrils are sent in via the holes created by fear in your aura, and the entities feast on your suffering. It is a tasty barbecue for them. What's more, these creatures will seek to set up situations where you feel fearful, because they like the TASTE of your fear.

This is often why otherwise very decent people seem to keep ending up in abusive relationships, chronically poor marriages, and/or going out with gambling addicts, alcoholics and all the crap of the planet. They have a doorway open to fear.

One of the first things to learn as a good RAT is how to overcome the effect of fear. How to keep functioning in the midst of fear is a powerful lesson indeed. The way it works is that you get taken back again and again to the State of Fear, until you wear out the conditions that create this road block for your heart, or beat them. It is "Ground Hog Day" in real life.

Your Rat is the teacher. This is the hard part for people to grasp: It will USE these entities to educate you about your fear (and all your negative emotions) but this is all it does. It is your responsibility to clear them out of your aura. Your RAT will send out the signal where they are, but YOU have to remove them.

This means a period of time needs to be set aside each day for "cleaning" yourself spiritually. Every day, you need to set aside time for contemplation, consideration and consolidation. When you experience a FEAR of any sort, this is a bell calling your attention to an issue that has gotten under you skin. In time, you will learn to accept these "air raid warnings" for what they are, and you will slowly become immune to the negative effects of Fear.

But always remember: Fear is a survival mechanism of the body, so it is NOT wrong to feel fear. It is simply not healthy to have it control you. *Understand the Meme behind it, however, and fear automatically lessens.*

How do we repair your Lunar Body and the connection at the Solar Plexus? It is not so difficult. You simply open your heart to to a deeper and deeper appreciation of this moment. This sensation is the best way to repair the links broken through fear and self-loathing. It is just means holding a sense of Love towards yourself, really. Love is a sensation that negative entities truly find unpleasant to taste.

They would prefer a feast of negative emotions, and so they simply leave the area where a person is full of good vibes. They prefer to find an easier, tastier target. Happy thoughts, clear thinking, wisdom, altruism: These higher notions are anathema to your fear-based realities.

As an important side note, you can also get unwarranted sensations of fear and panic from such things as wrongly prescribed medication or from parasites in your liver and gut. If you feel you have fears that seem to have no basis in your life, I recommend finding up a good homoeopath or herbalist and seeing if there is a physical basis for this. Which brings to mind a statistic I find extraordinary: In just about every mass killing / suicide instance (not related to terrorism) in recent years, nitrogen salt based anti-depressant medication have been part of the equation.

What is important to remember is that FEAR is a reality. Fear has enormous power over the body. It can break down your cells, destroy your liver, and slowly erode your sense of fun. If it carries on long enough, you fall into a shell, just dreaming of what your potential might have been. Yet when we look INSIDE fear, there is a reality that should not be ignored. Every fear is a signal that there is something within us we need to observe, and be careful of.

However, what happens is more like an air raid siren going off. Peasants are working in the fields, growing things, making things, and the air raid siren goes off. So they stop what they are doing, and go underground. They wait for the "all clear" signal before they emerge to continue their daily affairs.

This is what your cells do when faced with stress. They go into defence mode. When you send them a FEAR signal, they go into protection mode and stop producing nutrient for your body. You metabolism starts making WAR steroids, not building ones. You get pumped with adrenalin, ready for an emergency that never comes. The problem is that after the Fear signal came up, no "All Clear" signal got sounded. So you stay there, in your cellar, locked in the Fear pattern.

Your RAT will ring the "all clear" bell for you, but you have to ALLOW into the room. You must breath deep, acknowledge the problem, and look at getting going. That part of you that looks at the world, and says "That's no big deal" and has the courage to start over, this is your ALL CLEAR signal. You have to tell yourself every day that it is a NEW DAY, that you are STARTING AFRESH.

The Reality Attention Trigger is that part of you that looks out of the Rathole (Yes, that's what they used to call air raid shelters) to see if there are any planes buzzing about. When it sees the sky is clear, it signals for everyone to come back out.

Once more time: Your RAT sees the OBVIOUS and does not live its life playing out the patterns of taught and projected beliefs, as if they are a permanent truth. These are our Memes, if you will, and it treats these myths as myths, not reality.

Your RAT resides in the Sympathetic Nervous System. It resides in your GUT Instinct and you must learn to trust if you are to do well in life. This is, in effect, is a FORTH BRAIN, one that resides in your awareness. When under threat your body automatically seeks to wake it up.

Fear and living life by rote are the enemies of your RAT. Laughing and loving life are it's friends. But everything we have to rise above, surmount, conquer, etc. always comes down to a very simple truth: Fear based realities that drive your bus.

The Mystic Rat Says: *Your Fear is the Child of the Fear you Fear*

ROUNDUP

This next section is by far the hardest to write. Not because the discussion itself is harder to write about, but because WHAT we are talking about is going to be an aspect of yourself that you will not want to see. We are going to speak directly on the topic of the internal controller, the thing itself that shapes and rearranges what you see and hear, otherwise called the Censor. This is the thing that reforms and alters every sensory input you receive into a message that is deemed acceptable.

I have spoken of the Censor as that part of yourself that gets build to repair the cracks in the early psyche, the splitting that happens when we first Humpty Dumpty ourselves. The Censor is created by the mind in order to bridge the cracks that appear as the child moves through the fracturing experiences of growing up.

If you accept that you have an agent inside you, one that alters every single thing you observe, and changes everything you think into something acceptable to your present set of conditions, then the discussion will be easy. But no-one does. This is why we have to focus so much on just seeing the obvious, for this is almost the only thing that will break the spell cast by your Censor over your emotions and mind.

The path to discovering you Inner RAT is quite simple for the most part. See the obvious, accept the issues and let them go. Breath in the moment, see what comes, go with the flow. The problem, and it is always a problem, is that the process is always a little different for each person, because of our internal filters, and our auto-pilot.

However, the constants are:
1. *Learn to see the OBVIOUS*
2. *Take nothing personally*
3. *Forget the notions handed down on how you SHOULD behave*
4. *Understand and practise the Rules for RATTYNESS*

Everything else is a detail. Yet the devil, as they so rightly say, is in the detail. Add to this the fact that, if it was easy, everyone would be doing it. What happens is that when you start to free yourself of the emotional and mental baggage, almost automatically, something quite extraordinary and difficult happens. As soon as your Inner Rat starts waking up, it triggers a terrible response from your Auto-Pilot.

And we ARE all flying on auto-pilot. Thank goodness for that! Our heart beat is on auto-pilot, we breathe at night on auto-pilot, so much of what we do that is life preserving is automatic, and so auto-pilot is a good thing, yes?

Well, yes BUT! The problem is that we have allowed the Auto-Pilot a little more power over us than we generally realise. The first glimpse I had into this controller behind the scenes was when I was coming back from the trip where I faced the oyster encrusted pylons and the huge ants.

At age four, I was on a train journey with the family. It was a long 1000 mile journey, so I had a lot of time to myself and wandered about up and down the train looking for things of interest. I looked out the window, and to my delight, and also a strange horror, I saw what seemed to be NAKED people swimming in a pond. I felt my head being turned away, yet I wanted to watch! I was fully aware of some force, like a hand on top of my head, turning it away from the swimmers. What could be causing this? I realised that while "I" wanted to watch, something else was forcing me to act differently.

My rational brain kicked in, and reasoned there was nothing wrong with people swimming without clothes, and this forced my eyes to go back to the pond, where I discovered the people were wearing skin coloured swimming costumes. The result of my discovery was both a disappointment and a relief. An argument had been averted inside me, but it stirred up a far greater question.

The OTHER side of my thinking said "I have a problem, there seems to be TWO of me acting independently here." I looked inside and instinctively understood that the part that wanted me to pull away was the Catholic Meme, which my mother had inserted. Yet the thing that actually CAUSED me to look away was something else. There seemed to be the "real" me, and someone/something else. The real me was the one that was curious, interested, and wanting to know things. But what was this OTHER part of myself that was trying to control the real me?

I had no idea, but I knew it was not my friend. In fact, it was my sparring partner for many years, and sadly, it was clearly tougher, meaner and stronger than myself. As many times as I felt I would win a round, it would win the war. I kept losing to this controller in a thousand little ways, and it felt as if it was eating up my freedom, piece by piece.

It would be YEARS before I understood anything about the Censor, that aspect of the mind that takes control of the recognition and action vehicle in the mind. Fortunately Jung had understood so many things and written about them that when I grew up, I had a reference point t start from. But no one was teaching Jung and the Collective Unconscious at the convent school where I was educated.

You have a CENSOR. It sits in the forefront of your mind, and it inspects every image and every thought that passes through you. It AUTOMATICALLY judges whether this is right or wrong, good or bad, up or down, forward or backward, and it sends signals to the rest of your body in accordance to ITS decision.

This is part of the reason why, when you meet someone, you can automatically distrust them, or dislike them, or love them. The problem is, this would be fine if YOU were making the choices, but often you are not.

No one is completely certain what the Censor comes from. It is an aspect of you, that is certain, but it seems to be a gestalt of FEELINGS and BELIEFS from your earliest experiences of life. It seems to take on the imprint of your mother, in particular, and this seems to be pressed into your Psyche in the first 2 years of your life. Like a coin pressed into clay, your mother's beliefs and actions are stamped into your young mind and emotions, and the shape these beliefs take root in your mind become the nature of your Censor.

Susan Blackmore in her book "The Meme Machine" states that these are MEMES. Or, as we call them, "hand-me-down" tags of consciousness that are put over you like clothes, and which osmose into you until you believe what you have been GIVEN by parents and society are your OWN thoughts and feelings. They are not.

The Censor that grows from these MEMES is like a self-regulating bureaucracy, with a thousand rules and regulations of how things SHOULD be. If you do not question it, your life will usually carry on in uneventful and mostly peaceful ways. But if you start looking at the Censor, if you start to CHALLENGE it, you are in for one hell of a ride.

Apart from the fact that it is the ultimate Shape Shifter, combined with Gateway Guardian, (Mythical Stereotypes denoted by Professor Joseph Campbell) your Censor is usually quite ruthless. Its view is simply, "My way or NO way".

When I saw the people on Venice Beach, I was looking at their MEMES. I was looking at the hand-me-down tags that have become the controllers of their life. Many years prior to this event the image of my OWN Censor had come into view, and I have to tell you, he was a nasty, arrogant piece of work. He didn't care if I saw him, in fact, he was HAPPY I could. I suspect it made the game of controlling my thoughts and emotions more fun, like you could finally see the bat that was hitting the balls in the table tennis game of your life. This all started after a period in my early 20's where I was not able to eat for almost two years.

Starvation and fasting, whether voluntary or forced, break down preconceptions and your attachment to the things of this world. At this point it was incredibly easy for me to look into the inner planes and see what was there, and in many ways, I was not far from going there on a permanent basis, anyway.

I survived. And this was when Life's game of ping pong really got underway. I lost round after round after round. Whenever I got used to one shot, a curve ball would come, and when I learned to get that one back, a slam would hit me between the eyes. But then a remarkable and totally unexpected thing happened. I fell in love.

An extraordinary Angel walked into my life, and everything stopped. All I could think of was her! If she walked in the room, I could not breath. If I had a dream, she was in it. When she looked at me, time stopped. She had complete power over me, and I adored it. It was the most wonderful state to live within, and being with her was a walk through heaven itself.

I did mention to you that the Censor is a callous, ruthless bastard, yes? What I never guessed at was how he would go behind my back. It took me years to discover this, but a whole process began to happen from unexpected quarters. People I barely knew were apparently writing to the mother of my Angel, saying the most ugly things about myself.

Now these were people the Mother knew quite well, and as no one was EVER good enough for her daughter, she made sure the girl read every letter. I had no idea what was happening, other than I could feel the dream slipping away. The Ping Pong match was starting up again in my mind. I was losing my grip on love as the tensions around, and inside me, grew.

Finally the girl asked me to leave, and her mother quietly confirmed to me that her daughter HAD made this decision, and that I had better go. So in emotional pieces, completely shattered, this is what I did. Many years later friends said to me that they didn't know if I would survive, because apparently I was pretty nuts. I didn't realise it at the time, I didn't know anything other than this huge gaping hole that I stared into every night, and with nothing to fill it, I started falling inwards.

After 13 long years of loss, I finally was able to contact my great love from that time, and I discovered the view from her side of the fence. It was her honest belief that I had abandoned her. I scratched my head, and wondered: How on earth could anyone possibly imagine such a thing? Leaving her was like having my teeth pulled, but I did as I was asked.

Surely she HAD asked me to leave, but then it dawned on me, maybe I understood her words wrong. Had she had only been asking me to leave her mother's house? (where we were staying) Maybe what she WANTED was for me to take her with me? Perhaps she was looking for someone stronger than her Mother Image to take charge?

But when you are young, lost in love, and feeling helpless, you get confused. However, for her sake, and mine, I felt it was important to somehow clear this up. But how? She didn't believe anything I said, because I had gone and left her high and dry.

Then a truly remarkable thing occurred. As I was clearing out a shed on the farm, asking myself how this had all come about the way it did, I found a LETTER. It had been written in the months just after the breakup, and it contained every thought I had of losing my Angel, and how completely helpless I felt at being asked to leave. Can you believe I still had this? And after 13 years, can you believe I had somehow FOUND it?

You see, my RAT had done it. Without me even realising it, that part of me shoved this document away in a place where it would be saved, who knows why, but instinct is important. It is our natural intuition. The letter had never been posted, so I scanned it, and sent it via Email. This one thing turned around the terrible hurt my loved one had suffered, and far more than this, she finally began to realise how controlled she had been by her mother.

No, it was not a happy ending, other than our daughter found her way to come over and get to know her estranged father. But my loved one was gone. She has her life and I am no longer a part of it, but at least we had both been given an opportunity to see how our Censor will twist up the events of our life, and paint memories that never happened. It does this trick so perfectly that we will believe the images it places before our eyes are 100% real. The truth, and nothing but the truth.

So! Help me, God. Have you ever considered how important a role punctuation plays in our thoughts and dealings with others? When the prosecuting attorney asks: "Do you swear to tell the whole truth, and nothing but the truth, so help me God?" you can say to yourself the following.

"I swear to tell the truth? The WHOLE truth? And nothing BUT the truth? So! Help me, God." Read it this way, and you are admitting to yourself and the court that it is well nigh impossible for you to tell the absolute truth. And THIS is the real truth.

The truth seems like a moveable feast, yet in this case there was a sort of diary note, something concrete from the period of time in question allowed us both to discover greater understanding. In my former love's case, she realised that her mother had controlled the situation and painted pictures on her heart, and that it was her mother then had turned around and told me I should leave because her daughter really wanted me to. We both had little chance against these odds.

That said, I still get on very well with the mother. She is a wonderful woman. How can I say this? HER Censor was at work as well. My Censor, Angel's Censor, the mother's Censor, these were all striving to find their own voice and create their own story, and the love between people was the collective enemy of them ALL.

Likewise, you, on your own, have no chance against your Censor. When it looked as if I had become deaf to it, as I was too in love to hear anything but love, then this creature reached out and touched the Censors of OTHER people and painted pictures before their eyes, and drew them out to act in ways they normally would not.

I cannot express to you the extraordinary POWER this creature has. It has an awareness, an intelligence, and a life unto itself. Many people would call this the Devil, and in a sense this is correct, but really it is just the collected parts of YOU that have given up their autonomy and freedom, and formed into this Jig Saw monster.

And you have MANY parts. You have MANY children of Light and Dark playing on the plate of your being. They are the chorus of opinions, beliefs and notions that have been controlled and governed by the Censor. In a sense of irony, your Censor has been democratically VOTED to its position by the many pieces of YOU that live inside your being. But, is it is also letting you read this book? No, this is your Rat at work. Your inner Rat has called out to you, and told you to pick this up.

Only your RAT has the power to gnaw away at this controller, and piece by piece, it slowly takes the illusion apart until you see the jigsaw before you.

Now, you may well BELIEVE you have the jigsaw sorted. You may truly believe the picture before your eyes is true, because you can see it. But I promise you, spend a day with a Scientology Auditor and you will discover how fractured you, and your reality, really are. (Not recommending it, just pointing it out)

The way the Censor works is fairly simple: It paradoxically uses your BLIND SPOT to help things make sense to you. We all have our Blind Spot, all of us, and the Censor makes sure it puts this over the holes and cracks in the logic of our being. Thus, you see no cracks! THIS is where your battleground begins. Learn to see the OBVIOUS and the Blind Spot evaporates. Do this and you will save yourself years playing a losing streak in the infamous Censor Games.

This "Game" can be explained easily. Take any number of Censor/Controllers in any number of people. Give every person the SAME pieces in a complex Jigsaw puzzle. Come back in a day or so and you will see everyone has arranged the pieces to suit whatever their prejudice might be, and they will ALL see this particular version of perception as the correct solution to the puzzle.

But to the few who see the OBVIOUS, they will see how most of the pieces simply do no fit. You will see where one piece has been shoe-horned into another, where there is a gap and where the colours really do not match up. However, to the person, who is experiencing the GAP in REALITY, their CENSOR will place their BLIND SPOT over this area, so that all the person sees is continuity. As far as YOU are concerned, all the pieces will fit perfectly,.

This is where Socrates came in with his deductive reasoning and Socratic Argument. He would ask a question, and a person would answer. He asks the SAME question a few minutes later, yet the person would give an opposing answer. Why? Because he asked it with a different slant. Yet so often the person being questioned will simply not see a problem with this, two different answers to the same question. To everyone else, the Blind Spot is revealed, but to the person being questioned, they simply cannot see why everyone is laughing at them.

Of course, the Censor is not so easily defeated, and in Socrates case it cost him his life. Because he embarrassed so many powerful men, in the end he was ordered to take his own life with Hemlock. What most people do not understand is that in Athens at that time, this was effectively a choice between suicide or leaving the city. Once you left the city, the order no longer applied, but you were no longer a citizen. His students wanted to help him escape, and had indeed organised this.

Yet Socrates said "No". His entire life had been a teaching that death was not the end, but that it was the beginning. He also realised that the CENSOR of Athens (Yes: Cities, Suburbs, Streets, they also have a mind and a Censor. It is the Collective Unconscious that makes "rules" for the inhabitants.) would be reinforced and never be broken if he escaped and left them to it.

There is a great deal to learn from this story. Socrates had been one of the venerated few who had survived a blockade of Athens where everyone had virtually staved to the point of death, but NONE had given in. This action had given great strength to the inhabitants of the city and indeed ushered in its Golden Age, an action which is STILL with us today in our own art and architecture.

Socrates knew that a stand for truth HAD to be made. The Blind Spot HAD to be revealed. And, on the flip side, he was over 70 and not likely to live much longer anyway. So he sacrificed himself rather than compromise his principles. More to the point, he would NOT rationalise his escape as reasonable, because it went against everything he had taught.

His action shocked and altered the fabric of Athenian Society, and from this point a greater more compassionate grasp of Law and Social Justice was used. This has echoed down to the present day. One man made a difference, because he highlighted the Blind Spot. However, if his RAT had been stronger he would have avoided the Hemlock. How? Well, in his trial he would have made better work of his defence.

Yet we must allow for the fact that he WAS over 70, and in truth I suspect he was so mortally hurt by the accusations by his fellow countrymen that he almost wanted to die. His brothers, his own family, had turned against him. His RAT was not strong enough to deflect their attacks, and so eventually the mob ruled, and he lost his life.

The message is STAY LOW. You might think this really means be humble, but really, I am saying duck the arrows and slings of outrageous fortune by simply not being a target for them. If you do not want to get shot at, then don't stand up and say "Shoot me Please!"

This is one of the unwritten laws of Ratology, and if you obey it this will save you no end of trouble. In fact, I am VERY concerned because I am currently breaking this Law by writing this very book that you read. When all the arrows and slings from outraged people come falling onto my head, I will only have myself to blame.

However, if you always remember and keep uppermost in you mind this simple truth you will survive better in life. The rule: *It doesn't matter what you SAY, it is what people HEAR that counts.*

Given what I have told you about the controller that runs the mind of virtually everyone, can you guess what your chances of someone hearing exactly what you say might be? Zero. Accept it, people will not HEAR what you say. Yet when your RAT is strong, they will FEEL it. "Feel the Force, Luke". *(Unasked for Advice: Be wary of palms at your feet, however. Within a few days you may be handed a cross.)*

The Censor can take charge of a person if it feels threatened, and it can be a very dangerous creature. Yet there is one way to move around the Censor, both in yourself and in others. It is to develop focus through a passion for excellence.

Indeed, all strong passionate energy puts the Censor to one side. SO! *Generate strong feelings for the goals and aspirations you have. Let a passion for your work, and your desire to really experience life, do the talking for you.*

The time I first became free of my Censor was when I was in love, but this is not something that happens everyday. Do you want to be free? We need to be IN LOVE with our direction in life. We need to have a deep abiding desire to experience the day in front of us. Only then will our Censor relax, because it will believe there is nothing that needs protecting. All is well with the world, it believes it does not have to save your sorry ass, and it (censor) is feeling good because YOU are feeling good.

This brings me to the second rule: *It doesn't matter what OTHER people say, it is what they MEAN that counts.*

People are largely talking through the filter of their Censor. If you pay close attention to their words, you will find the cracks in reality peering out. Point these out, and you get attacked, but understand where the person is REALLY coming from, and you will be loved for it.

And this is incredibly important. Life is for living, not weeping, or being bitter about. It's all about getting out there and finding the cheese that satisfies your hunger, because this makes you happy. But if you are all alone, if there is no one around you to share the joy, it is a very empty experience. If you want friends, if you want to have love in your life, listen and understand what people MEAN when they talk to you.

We need to grasp this notion of a Greater Joy. If we are to succeed in life, and in RAT terms this means to survive well, we need to connect with a sense of love in some way. We need to feel motivated, to have a WANT to experience the day in front of us, and surprisingly, we need to start being GRATEFUL for that bastard Censor. Why? Because it has kept us alive to now, and from here our real self can take over.

What would your life be like WITHOUT your Censor? Well, the question is rhetorical because you don't know, and never will. You have your Censor for LIFE, it is a part of you as much as your fingers and toes. Yet WITHOUT a Censor you would have no sense of identity as you know it. Why? This is a strange one.

You have an identity BECAUSE your Censor tells you lies, BECAUSE it uses your Blind Spot to cover up the cracks in your reality. BECAUSE of this you are able to function. We need our illusions, until we don't.

How so? No sane person would get up every day and work a nine to five job with the notion of doing this for forty years and retiring. So without your Censor pulling you into line, getting you out the door, and making you more functional, you would starve. No one would be bothered to do what they should, and society as we know it would break down.

In all honesty, if you saw your mind, emotions and beliefs for what they really were you would be like an orphan in a den full of wolves: Totally vulnerable to the vagaries of life. Your Censor is protecting you from yourself.

Everyone is different. Some people have very mild controllers, others have right pratts in charge of their thoughts and emotions. The various Censors each person will possess are always a gestalt of your inner nature, your upbringing, and your society, mixed with a few ambient beliefs and experiences.

My Censor allows me to write this, and now-a-days it helps me, but only because my RAT gave it a savage bite and it finally started to get the message about who was boss in my head. In fact, without my Censor I would not be ABLE to write this. It does the job of organising the phrases, the structure of vocabulary, and all the necessary elements that form the mechanical process of writing.

It also likes the idea of beating YOUR Censor in the Game of Logical Thinking. My Censor now works for me because I have shown it a way to WIN, and for the moment it seems to be giving me some lee-way. Things might be different tomorrow, so I will enjoy the sunshine while I can.

Really, we have many selves inside us. It is very much like we are sharing a house with many different Souls. We do this in order to lessen the cost of living, and now we must find a way for everyone to get on.

And so the message is this: *There is nothing inside you that is your enemy. Even your worst habits and most miserable belief patterns have a useful purpose some where in your life.* Your job is to find a place where they can be put to work, and I will tell you a secret: You never entirely get rid of a habit or fault. You CAN arrange things so that your habits or faults want to either leave or work for you, however.

I am working around the edges of things here, and really there is no way I know to say this directly in a way that you will understand. But if a single word could summarise the solution to your life concerns, and all your most serious issues, it would be "PLAY". Learn to PLAY with life, and you will find solutions to every concern that arises far more easily.

Life is a game. So begin to play it, and things will improve enormously.

...our tests indicate that your little Robert is a vain, ruthless and devious opportunist without empathy or imagination and we suggest that he pursue a career serving his country as a politician.

ANCILLARY NOTES

These ancillary notes are to help you focus on the true nature of the Rat Within. It may take some time to grasp the whole significance of these, but when you do it will be self-evident.

WHISPERS OR ASPIRATIONS?

Symbolically speaking, there are Two Vases at the Portal of our Conscious Awareness. These are the Vases of Aspiration and Whispers. One is full of our deepest dreams and wishes, the other is full of our fears and unexpressed feelings of failure, repression, and lost love. Every day, each moment, and often unknowingly, we sip a dram from either one, or both, of these Vases. Every moment of every day we dip our cup in one of them, and sip on the dreams or the whispers we extract.

These dreams and whispers are very powerful. They arrive as secret, silent advice on how to act or behave in any given moment. They lead our imagination, and this paints pictures before us that determine "how" we see things. Not "what" we see, but HOW we see. What we receive from either Vase effectively determines how we will act and feel for the next cycle, however long.

In both Vases, the messages are not so much written on paper, as distilled to a sweet or sour wine. Each drop of this wine carries the flavour of a thousand secret promises. One is bitter to taste, yet, like coffee it can be addictive. The other may be too sweet and unrealistic for the reasoning mind, yet we may have a sweet tooth that desperately needs this nectar.

The question for us here is very simple: *Do we choose to take from our Vase of Whispers, or our Vase of Aspiration?*

The Vase of Whispers contains all the hidden secrets within our fears, all the tags of those who have told we are no good, and all the combined dramas that have caused us to develop the fears we hold dear are present. This Vase hides within the dark angry places of our hearts.

This Vase of Whispers contains the sum total of our thoughts of control and domination over others, and it is the place we tend to go when we believe we are in opposition to the world about us. Your Whispers will always encourage you to TAKE and DOMINATE.

The Vase of Inspiration is where we have stored all our finest thoughts. The hopes, dreams and wishes for a greater future which we put there (or were placed there) in our childhood are distilled as an essence of kindness. Your mother's love, your trust in family, your close-knit sense of affection, your ability for intimacy, they are all stored here. This is where Superman is you, and the hero always wins. It holds messages that tell us how we can grow and develop, and become great. Inspiration seeks to make ourselves, and the world, a better place. Your Inspiration always encourages you to GIVE and SERVE

How do we know what is feeding us? When we feel free and independent within ourselves, we are supping from the Vase of Inspiration. When we are insecure, and needing, we are supping from the Vase of Whispers..

Every day in a thousand ways we choose which Vase we will draw from, and often we are pulled in two trying to decide. Do we need the sour taste of hard experience or the sweet aroma of dreams in this moment?

Many know what they must do, but they doubt themselves so much they cannot act rightly. This creates a split inside them, which causes them to lead double lives: *One face to society, one face within.* A passive, kind person without, a hungry panther within. Shine a friendly smile, while looking to get a dollar from another's pocket.

If you see this inside yourself, do not despair. The answer is to be found in just choosing. Start to choose what you want, who you speak to, where you work. And if things cannot change, choose to accept it. Simple choice removes the inner turmoil.

And here is the simple truth: We need BOTH Vases if we are to survive in this world. They are BOTH a gift, and it is how we USE these gifts that will either help, or hinder, our spiritual and emotional growth.

The greatest secret of all is found when we learn to match the sweet with the sour, the high with the low, the small with the grand. These Vases represent the polarities within our own being. We have in our hearts a map. It guides the left to the darkness, and the right to the light. Or it may be vice versa for you, but we innately know right from wrong for ourselves. This means that, despite upbringing, social influences, or what happened to us in the past, that personal CHOICE is still there.

As long as we start accepting ourselves, as long as we accept that we have both good and evil within, we can find a way to freedom that leads us away from the patterns of the past. But people generally don't believe they are good enough. True freedom is for someone else. The whispers rule the day.

Perception will free you. In an extraordinary change in the Justice system in New Zealand, the prosecution of indigenous people charged with violent crime was moved from a traditional court to one closer to the tribal court. Here, offenders were brought face to face with victims and their families, and they were required to sit through and hear the ramifications of their actions.

In this instance, two Maori men had beaten up an entire bar full of people, and it took a squad of police to stop them. They denied everything, and accused the police of assaulting THEM. But when confronted with person after person telling them their story, of what they did, the two men eventually broke down. They truly did not remember beating up all these people, and truly believed that they had merely defended themselves against the police.

And they STILL did not remember beating up the people, but they came to ACCEPT that all these people, their OWN people amongst the witnesses, were not all lying. They were genuinely shocked at their own behaviour, and puzzled at how they could not remember any of it. As a result of this acceptance, they started to change.

Without accepting ourselves, as we are, our so-called CHOICE is really like Eve in the Garden of Eden. She was always going to eat the apple, it was just a question of when. The truth is, what we will choose has usually been cast like dice at an early age. A pattern was set up in formative years. We have the number of our fate written, and we are playing out it's chance. As a result, we are generally choosing through REFLEX to sup on the negatives or positive in any given situation.

Until we have a change of heart, or a breaking through to a greater love, we will simply follow the set course that the inertia of our upbringing has chosen for us.

So the question remains: What are we CHOOSING right now?

FINDING a STATE of TRUE CHOICE

Most people are running on automatic. In the aforementioned case of the Maori men, their Censor drew a curtain of forgetting over their actions. It is an automatic survival response, very common in men who have seen intense physical fighting, where the inner warrior is unleashed and the conscious awareness takes a back seat.

There is only "survive" left as an option, nothing else. I have witnessed this in my own son, where what I call "The Bear" is released. Someone throws a punch, and my son leaves, and only this bear remains. It does not feel pain, lives by reflex, and is incredibly strong. But when my son returns, he remembers nothing of what the bear did. He realised one day, because he used to keep a collection of the weapons, shoes and wallets, of those who assaulted him, that this bear would eventually cause him to go to prison.

It started when his girlfriend was calling out his name, and he "came to" while beating a guy over the head with the gun that the man he was beating had, a few moment earlier, pulled on him, while demanding money. The "Bear" was saying "How does THIS feel! How does THIS feel!" and when he came back to himself, this was when he realised he may well have killed the fellow. If this had happened, his army record as a paratrooper who was an unarmed combat instructor, all this would go AGAINST him in a civilian court. So he took the gun, the man's wallet and his shoes, and went back home. He decided that things needed to change.

Realising that things need to change is the first step on removing yourself from automatic, and moving towards a true sense of choosing. But few of us see anything so dramatic and obvious as my son saw in himself. For the vast majority of us, the inner choices we are making are far more subtle. But we do share cores issues.

As an example: *Are we listening and deciding, or deciding then listening?* Think about this in particular, if you will. Most DECIDE with a secret prejudice, then pretend to listen. This is HABITUAL with humans, we have the good grace to be one of the few species that can listen and understand language, yet we are like the Maori in the court. We have made our mind up as to the reality, and have already decided what has happened before we hear anything.

There is NO CHOICE in prejudice. As we listen to the inner whispers, we shut down all possibility of change, and remove any chance of new choices being made.

The core issue is one of selfishness. Our mothers tried to teach us not to be selfish, to share, but to what purpose? Life experience teaches most that by BEING selfish, they get what they want. So self-interest rules, for the most part. Look out, and see everything that is built! It is built by self interest. It is just a short step to see that selfishness works. But self-hood, self-sufficiency and plain old selfish are different things. Self-hood keeps an openness and trust towards life. Selfishness shuts it down.

We know life supports us, we trust it, but we also have our own goals. This is self-hood. Selfish happens when we shut down and internalise. It is a distrust in life that creates it, and a lack of faith in the power of growth that cements it.

So we are really talking about a baseline attitude, one of TRUST.

Trust gives us a generosity of spirit, and this opens us up to listening to what the world is telling us. Kindness and consideration leave us open to real choices, because we HEAR what is going on around us. Selfishness shuts us up in our own mind, and stops the process of listening to anything but our own whispers.

These basic, fundamental choices are things we are choosing every day: *Eat, Sleep Love.* But it is the subtle inner patterns, the feelings of kindness, the sense of selfishness, that really control our choices. THESE are the voices that tell our hand to select from the Vase of Whispers, or the Vase of Aspirations.

It's not a question of right or wrong, but a matter of balance. Everyone has a Positive and a Negative potential, and depending on the nature of our being, we draw a little from both aspects. When we discover inner balance, our neutral state, we learn to refine and take what we need from each moment, and use what we have within to match the situation we face. This is your only true "Response-Ability".

And this is something that could well appeal to you. So much of our world is about being "cool". We have entire generations since the "Fonz" in Happy Days that has focussed on the essence of cool. So what IS cool? It is the neutral state within.

As we find balance in ourselves, which is found inside the neutral state, we learn to resolve and COMPLETE each moment in our outer world. As we learn to be neither for nor against anything, to "resist not evil" as the Bible says, we find the neutral state.

As we discover this point, we find this is where all our personal moments start and end. Now it is more a question of how we might fully experience this moment.

How do we live completely within a moment? Just look at any young child, and re-discover what the art of immersion feels like. Then you will soon understand what it is like to completely live in your given moment.

In time we all will learn to draw from each passing NOW whatever it may be that we need, and this will create a future that will be the best for all. How well we do this is based on: Where we place our attention, and: How pure our intention is. These two things of themselves are the cornerstones of our truest belief and faith. This area is a book all on its own, but suffice to say, all acts based on harm to self or others will not resolve to a good outcome. You may get money, etc. but you will lose far more.

In truth, we dip the cup of our present awareness a little into both Vases, mixing them up and seeking to find the right balance with which we can deal with our environment. But we tend to do so unknowingly.

Fact One: The hand compulsively reaches for the Vase that our habits have been trained to reach for. Like any habit, it must be broken, substituted or left behind before we can rise above it.

Know this: In this process of "habit removal" we will discover there are deeper secrets in our hearts, and that a good deal of the "thought" that we believed was our own is really "hand-me-down" clothes from parents or society. These "Hand me Downs", or MEMES, form a collective energy that reinforces the CENSOR. To find inner contentment, we need to get past our Censor, and our habits, to find the natural path that leads us to an increase in freedom and harmony.

The Study of Truth, wherever you may find it, and whatever it is to you, is one way to help break the "reflex" habits we have collected in our upbringing. As you go through this process of self growth and inner understanding, you will find more and more that you are moving into a position of choice and understanding.

Fact Two: In the end, we must learn to Master ourselves to the degree where we CHOOSE our action or reaction to any given moment. At this time, we learn to choose not so much from either our fearful Whispers or our Aspirations, but from the well of our true inner being. And how do you find this? Maybe your RAT has something to do with it. It will show you the way.

In time, we go past ALL of that which is the past within us. We break the back of the karma that has entrained us to act like the mouse on a wheel and finally we establish a fountain of new awareness within ourselves. This is the only true Initiation. Only then in this "reborn" state do all the aspects of the past and the potential futures become less important to us than the process of our present.

Here is where we get a little esoteric. You can HEAR the energy flowing through, sometimes you even see it. This is the Fountain of

Youth, and we already have it. This ever present flow of energy gives a clear message of the way to go in every moment of every day. THIS is the core nature of your RAT, it is the awareness of this energy communicating itself to your outer awareness. You just have to rediscover it.

How do we re-discover this eternal stream of life? Take the time to listen to life, and then decide how best to go in any given moment. Sadly, most will continue to decide, then listen.

Pythagoras taught that we must listen to the Inner Music, the Music of the Spheres, every day. This IS the fountain of Youth. He also taught that we needed to discipline the imagination, in order that the choices we make do not ruin our connection with this moment. His greatest disciplines were in training the mind with science, and the heart with music.

We all have an Inner Song that our heart wants to sing. You know this, you know there is a deep aspiration within you to be special. We ARE beings of wonder, and we need to tune into this, to listen to the quiet, inner direction. And here your RAT makes the difference. It tempers aspirations, and it has no fear of your inner whispers. It is the balancing act between your Yin and your Yang.

Life here is all about polarity: Positive versus negative, high versus low. Yet your RAT is egalitarian. It sees everything as equal, and only the goal as important. Your Rat is harmony in action, and silence in noise. Spend time each day, put the mind in park, and look within to find this harmony. With patience and focus we will grow beyond the confines of our past conditioning, and arrive at the reality of our present.

Fact Three: We must EXERCISE our right to choose if our ability to choose is to grow strong. The question is: *How best to do this?*

Easy: Spend 20 to 30 minutes each day in quiet contemplation. Look for the Light, which can come as a blue of white star or moon, and listen for the sound, which often comes as a high pitched tone in or around our ears.

In a short space of time, you may find yourself drawn deeply into this simple gift of the Divinities. If this is so, you will find your conscious awareness lifted out of the Physical Body, and you will (in the words of Socrates) "Be lifted unto the Ethers, and shall thyself become as the Gods"

We, as Soul, are the mirror of a divine nature. Our choices either polish, or distort, the reflection. Our job is like Alice's, gaze in wonder, and fall through the looking glass. Now we must make sense of the new world we encounter.

Right now you are at the doorway. This is the place which IS the new horizon, the new experience, the greater state of BEING. Walk through this very moment, and you will find yourself waiting for you. You can explore it all RIGHT NOW. When you do, the new paths, the new choices will open to you. Like a flower opening to the sun, so too will your heart open naturally to the new day as it dawns.

How do we allow the Sun into the heart, and find this new dawn?

By letting go of our hold on our dark night, where all the whispers and fears come to haunt us. Slowly, we will transfer our trust to the Vase of Aspiration, yet at the same time pay heed to the doubts and warnings of our whispers. We need them both.

Fulfilment and Aspiration are waiting for you to drink your fill, but without the Whispers, you will too soon be drunk upon your own divinity, and fall like Iccarus.

And through it all, through all the dark nights, the lonely afternoons, the ups and downs, through all the clouds and rain and sunshine, there is a letter from the divine that has our name on it. Yet it will always arrive on our doorstep as a paradox.

The paradox is ever this: *Without the night, we cannot recognise the day.* Until the Day is Night and the Night is Day, we will know nothing of either, and we will remain chained to the skeletons of the past.

Your RAT will not whisper to you, it will BITE your ear to get your attention. It may not be inspirational, but it will remind you when you are going down the wrong path, and it will also remind your dreamer-self not to go too far. Inspiration can be the poison of sugar if allowed to rule you completely.

Your RAT sits in the middle, like Blind Judgement weighing up the scales of Justice. It will nip you into place, and into balance, and in this way it becomes your defacto conscience.

It may seem that in all the changes that you are being ripped apart by circumstance, but in the push pull of life you will one day discover that in nature is like a muscle: It will only ever PULL.

Nature itself is the Law of Attraction working at a high level.

Push or Pull?

Most people have heard the terms, "He's pulling my strings" or "She's pushing my buttons". We believe the Push-Pull of life is part of what is normal, and in the Social Consciousness it is. However, in Life there are many levels, and as many truths to match the levels.

Da Vinci discovered many things, but the area that revolutionised and radicalised his world view was something we all take completely for granted. Da Vinci was the first person to grasp the simple concept that Muscles only PULL. This is the highest truth of anatomy, and it answers WHY all the muscles are arranged as they are.

Prior to this, people generally believed muscles pushed and pulled, and this was how action came about. Da Vinci proved this to be wrong.

At the time, anatomy and the study of dead bodies was a black art. Da Vinci was considered a necrophiliac with his new discovery, and some postulate that his was the lever that caused him to give in to the church's demand for a holy relic. Thus he created the Shroud of Turin. This is mere speculation, but what IS known is that his discovery turned the world of science and religion upside down.

His anatomy drawings were banned, he was ordered into silence, and the church sought to have this radical notion stuffed back in the box. How his science was interpreted meant there was no "Push-Pull" from the heavens, only Pull. You no longer fought the Devil, and just trusted in God. God would pull you up into Heaven if you were good. The Devil would pull you into hell if you were bad. This made the need for a priest somewhat redundant. If the public don't need a priest, they don't go to church, and no church attendance means a lot of money is never collected.

Like the false beliefs of the Middle Ages, often we believe we are being pushed and pulled along by life, but life of itself only PULLS. Call it the Power of Attraction, and it is a form of Love in its simplest form. What is pushing is our will, and usually in the opposite direction to our love.

The church and the society we live in IS push-pull, and is like a spinning wheel. To remain in place you needed to find a balance between the centrifugal and centripetal forces. One pulls to the axis of the wheel, the other throws to the edge of it.

In our social world, do wrong and you are punished (push) and do right and you are rewarded (pull), The trick is to put yourself in a position without too much of either. People have struck a balance of where they are placed in this wheel. Via agreements they make with employers, peers, and social circles, individuals seek to work with the social forces, and make some sort of gain where possible. Do it right and you rise to the "centre of influence", do it wrong and you are cast out to the periphery.

It is so Roman! Do it right, you rise to "Head Man of Rome". Do it wrong and you are ostracised from society and have to go live with the barbarians. Most plod along in the middle, trying to get by in the push-pull of their existence.

There are many small rules in every society that determine where you are placed, and your own experience will tell you enough about this. But they are no measure of you, the individual. They are just a measure of how well you play the game.

Shakespeare says in one of his sonnets, speaking about the love in the heart of man, "Whose worth's unknown even though his height be taken". He is talking about the inner man, who is outwardly measured by society, but his inherent worth can only be found in the heart.

The depth to which you rise or fall in the tides that exist within yourself have nothing at all to do with society. These are completely ruled only by one truth. Love. Lovingness pulls you to a high view, a better place within. Or you have issues with angst and grit your teeth, and suffer a loveless life. Life just leaves you be, and the natural weight of your circumstances pulls you into to the base desires within.

Consider the motor cyclist racing along the highway, all it required to change direction is to shift the weight a small fraction and you will go around the upcoming corners. It seems effortless. However, most people do the opposite. They tense up, frown, complain, and try to drive their life. They try to MAKE it happen in a particular way, and the tension that comes of this causes the natural balance to disappear. You start to feel you are in Push/Pull again.

The natural energy of life only FLOWS, like water, and it flows along the easiest route available. Life never argues with blockages, never gets angry with delay: it simply moves around things as it seeks the point of balance in the ocean. Just relax, and let gravity pull to you the ocean.

But people just don't. They get tense, frustrated and want to make things happen. This is the energy of Push/Pull. It is the effect of fear. This is the internal dialogue that causes friction in your external world. The problem is that it's a one legged race of you hopping along, arguing with yourself. Life does not argue, it simply moves on and around. Fear is what ties us to the Social Wheel, the reward and punishment wheel, and to the friction this generates.

Stop being a mouse on the wheel!

The secret is that you can change this. You can change your

relationship with any part of your existence simply by learning to shift where you place the weight of your attention. And the deepest secret I discovered when learning to ride a motorcycle.

If you are on a bike, and you see a pothole you want to avoid, the hardest thing to do is NOT to look at it. If you look at it, you will hit it. You need to train your attention to look where you WANT to go, not at what you want to avoid.

You can change anything, any condition or belief inside you, at any time you choose, but the flip side to this truth is that your fears (and the fears of those around you) will seek to stop you from doing so. Your fears will cause you to focus on what you do not want, and you will most surely head straight into it. This is the core conflict. On the road of Life this is the one thing that stops us all in our tracks.

The Mystic Rat says *"We either move forward in Love, or retreat in Fear"*

Let's look at the dull, scientific side to things. Those who prefer nice sweet elevator music consciousness now need to turn off their brains. Just go over the words until you get to the next not-so-technical bit. However, if you really do want to reconstruct your life, you need to understand each brick, and where it belongs in the house of your being. The basic bricks are our NATURAL WANTS.

Natural Wants: These are the ATTRACTORS. These are the muscles that pull us towards or goals. We want affection, we want human warmth. We want food, health, fitness, etc. We want freedom, happiness, and justice, etc. But no society we live in truly provides these things for us. All societies are wheels based on Push-Pull.

Social pressures work on reward and punishment, right and wrong. Attainment works only on expectation, anticipation, and the sense of being worthy. We get what we expect, we go in the direction we place our attention, and our natural wants give us the guiding lights that show the way.

Our natural wants have generally been frozen into two areas:
1. *Patterns of Need* and
2. *Patterns of Convention*

In seeking an answer to the want that has turned into a need of some sort (such as the natural want for affection becoming a need for sex) individuals tend to "substitute" their natural want with an artificial need. You may want freedom, but feel trapped, so you turn to video games and other ways that avoid society. You may want adventure, but cannot leave your circumstances, so you turn to books to substitute adventure for you. There is nothing "wrong" with this if you understand your process. The issues come when your entire attention gets twisted up, and your focus shifts to false needs. As an example:

- *Instead of wanting affection, the person may crave sugar.*
- *Instead of wanting acceptance, the person may crave Authority.*

In each case this starts a spiral where we end up spinning around some point of substituted desire. This is where a free flowing "Want" becomes a "Need Signature".

This "need signature" then becomes incorporated into the natural "Want Arch" of energy that is what the Tibetans call the Mudra, or opening. The combination of wants and needs actually forms doorways in the inner worlds, and directs where our feet will step on the external journey. And often it directs us to a confused place.

The soft and gentle "We beseech thee oh Lord" turns into "God, I need a new car". And when it doesn't arrive we can no longer trust that God will provide, so we become aggressive in our money seeking. We start realising that things are not working out regarding our wishes for more, so we need to go from the attitude of "Survive" to "Strive" if we want to change things.

We enter a life of PUSH, rather than a Life of PULL. The rule here is: Man pushes, life pulls. Remember that Leonardo Da Vinci made the startling discovery that Muscles only PULL. The nature of life is to "pull" what we want towards us.

We need certain things to survive, and this gives us a sense of imperative, a sense of urgency to make it happen. But as we strengthen our connection with Life we discover a strikingly simply truth: Life works best with Harmony. In fact, Life only works with harmony, and retreats from dissonance.

The great composers understood this truth, and in many compositions they use dissonance that resolves to harmony. This creates the tension and beauty of the music. Look at the opening of Beethoven's Fifth: Ta da da DA. It is harmonious, yet verging on dissonance. It strikes up a tension that involves you from the get go, and through out the piece it never loses for a moment it's perfect balance..

In order to find the point of balance within ourselves you only have to understand this: *Life adores harmony.* Once you have learned this you have all you need to survive. Harmony resolves all things. Fear disrupts and dissipates harmony, while love and freedom create and then flourish in a field of harmonic resonance.

Our FEARS are like magnets, and they pull to us what we fear. Our HATES pull what we hate towards us. Every thing we experience is something we have PULLED towards us in some way. So why do we push so much?

This is what we call Karma. It is not necessarily a bad thing. The Push and Pull of life is like exercise in one sense. Our experiences strengthen and improve our connection with life, and like a stockbroker playing the market, good or bad is not important. It is the way the game is played that creates a profit or loss of experience. Anything that improves vision and understanding is a profit.

But there are some situations where the mind or emotions will just not let go. Like the dog with the bone, the problem is held onto with fierce determination, and life really needs to shake you up in order to get you to loosen your grip. Your Rat will call up powerful forces to shake your world, to tumble dry your stupidity out of your brain. And when it finally shakes you out of the Mind Lock, that's when you feel the incredible new rush of energy that sets the heart free.

This is the "Ah Ha" moment, the opening.

A man meets twelve great spiritual leaders

MUDRA (The Opening)

Now, what is the opposite of a Mind Lock? A Mind OPENING, of course. In RATOLOGY we understand that these two apparent opposites are indeed entwined like the opposing poles of a magnet. This opening we speak of is a sincere and deep awareness the Tibetans call Mudra.

We all know that when we approach the end of any given task, incredible obstacles seem to get in the way. Napoleon Hill talked about the "one more inch" principle, where some fellows missed a huge gold vein because they gave up their mining just one inch short of the prize. The miles travelled in a marathon count for nothing if the line is not crossed at the last inch.

Yet today we want to believe otherwise. So many often believe they should be paid for their efforts simply because they put in an effort. This is a false belief. If a cheetah chases some prey that gets away, is there some sort of self-service counter he can go to where he gets fed? After all, he put in the effort, yes? In the jungle, just because you TRIED to spear the prey does not mean you will eat that night. You either do it, or go for some smaller, more easily achieved goal. RESULTS count in the jungle, not effort. Remove the lie that life owes you because you put in some effort, and the Mudra will come more easily for you.

The other lie we live is the belief that results only come through effort. This is not absolutely true either. A smart hunter earns his keep, but he lessens the effort required because he learns to sit in the right spot, and waits for the game to come to him. He still has to throw the spear, of course, and still needs the killer instinct, but he doesn't really have to WORK for the prize because he has learned from experience the economical way to do things. That is: Sit by the waterhole come sunset. In fact, the person who survives best and longest is the one who has learned to do the LEAST amount possible in order to achieve the necessary goal.

This is the Wu Wei Wu, or effortless effort you hear about.

Have you seen crows in the country? They hang out on roadsides waiting for a car to kill their food for them. So easy! Just position yourself and wait for life to do the work. You don't have to do anything but eat what is served up! Of course, if no cars pass that day, you might go hungry.

So to get what you want, you can either
1. *Try to control everything*
2. *Go to the place where you can get it, or*
3. *Sit and wait for life to provide.*

What has this to do with Mind Locks and Openings? Much more than it may first seem, because principally we have to be able to feed ourselves before anything else can be expected to work in our lives. If you are sufficient unto yourself emotionally, mentally and physically you KNOW how to survive. It sounds good, but really how many people do you know who have all their ducks lined up?

Most people respect organised achievers. These are the people who have not only worked out where their best openings are in all the areas of their interest, they have learned to place themselves where opportunities will most likely arise. In this way they can walk a straight line through life and feel in charge of their environment. We believe these people have truly mastered their life, but really, what they have mastered is organisation.

This doesn't mean they are free, however. It simply means they are organised. It does not mean that life will open for them, and often it can mean the reverse. Because they are always engineering openings for themselves, they are actually shutting down certain natural flows, and paradoxically locking themselves up with their success.

We need some organisation if our life is to function, we need a little luck, and we need a helping hand every now and then. But most of all, we need ourselves to carry a sense of being FREE. Freedom! This is the cheese that attracts the Rat. Rather than try to force or find openings out of your present situations, learn to bring your RAT to the fore, and then allow IT to find the solution for you.

How do we do this? We generate a feeling of freedom in the heart. Appreciate the moment, feel the joy of living, be grateful for whatever comes, and learn to cherish the fact that you are alive. Do this and your Rat will always be your friend.

Let's look at little at the process of openings and locks and how they work in the individual's life. Did you know that immediately prior to EVERY major symphony that Beethoven wrote, he experienced an extraordinary period of difficulty? That's often just how things are, the storm before the calm. Things do not HAVE to be this way, but so often this is how it pans out.

SO, am I saying *"if you want to succeed expect difficulty"?* Is this the message? No. The message is that if you expect difficulty you will rarely be disappointed, but also you will, usually, be better prepared to succeed and to accept your success.

In fact, if you LOOK for the difficulties before you even start the journey, you will succeed incredibly well. What is more you will never suffer the "anti-climax" so many get at the end of a big project. *Expect difficulty and you will never be disappointed.* It is a very true cliché.

Why is this? Why does using the negative mean that we can turn our life to a positive? Doesn't this contradict everything the Positive Thinking people say it true? What all the positive thinking crowd forget is that the mind is not stupid. If you have to affirm to yourself that you are wealthy, healthy and wise, then obviously some part of you knows you are telling a lie. Your own mind cannot be fooled if underneath you are really miserable, poor and stupid. Why would you otherwise try to convince your self you weren't?

We need to understand that LIFE IS CONSCIOUS. Whenever you set out on a journey, it is like casting dice into the wind where a super computer calculates every parameter and works out the odds for every scene that will unfold. It doesn't matter if you believe it, this is what happens. Your choices affect the roll of the dice, but they do not affect the shape of the table. What is more, we have no chance of figuring it all out. So to succeed you are better off just telling life where you want to go, and why this is a good idea.

If you had a child who came up to you and said, "I want to go to this school because they teach this subject, which will mean I will get this qualification, which means that I can then help these people have a better life, as well as give myself a good life" then you would go out of your way to help that child, wouldn't you? You would be amazed how effective common sense and just asking for assistance can be when dealing with life

To succeed in any given venture, we need to trust life. Life of itself can work things out far better than you can, and it has been doing this for far longer.

LIFE is what prepares the road, the potholes, the hills, the corners. Everything is made ready for your journey. Now this is not just New Age Sewage being thrown to the wind! It's a very real and tangible thing.

A curious confirmation of this is a thing that happens in advertising. When an advertising company plans a big campaign, they advise clients to get the goods being advertised into the stores at least three weeks EARLIER than the campaign start.

Why? Because THAT is when the sales rush will start to happen. What is more, when Ad Companies have tried to FAKE this, telling people a large campaign is happening, doing the ads, preparing the staff, making everyone believe it is all go, but they do NOT run the ads: Well, they get absolutely no improvement in sales three weeks prior to the fictional advertising campaign launch.

You have to send SIGNALS OF INTENTION to Life if you are to activate the process of manifestation, because LIFE IS INTELLIGENT. If you trust it, if you ask nicely and with good intention, you will be amazed at how miracles seem to happen in your life. This will cause sceptics to laugh, but the facts as presented above are common knowledge in the advertising community. For some reason, sceptics who love reason fail to see the obvious when this contradicts their pet beliefs. But who really cares? What matters is your survival, and your success is part of this.

Now does this mean if you want something you do nothing but ask? Not at all. By planning, working out the difficulties, ironing out the possible concerns BEFORE they arrive, you are mapping the road and consciously signalling your clear intention to Life's Super Computer. Whatever this may be, whatever goal you seek to achieve, life is there with you. But you need to work in order to keep up with IT. Your clear intention is like a go ahead for IT to get to work and help your plans unfold. Trust it and you will see how well it works.

We give this Life Intelligence thousands of names. Shelldrake calls it Morphic Resonance, Christians call it the Holy Spirit, Chinese call it the Tao, The Ancient Greeks called is the "E" or "Ekstasis" (Where the verb Ecstasy comes from, not the drug). Take any a culture and you will find a name given for Life's Intelligence.

Now think about this, if you will. Every single culture has a NAME for the Intelligence of Life, but we in the Western World seem to think we know better than everyone, and say this is all hogwash. As the wise man said, "Right. Ok Then."

When you make a decision, any decision, you trip the Super Computer and it sets wheels in motion. It creates a path by which you get from this NOW, to the future point of whatever NOW you wish to achieve. The remarkable thing is that when you let life figure out the road, what you find is that the path it picks for you just happens to include all the materials you will need to build the opening to your new state of consciousness. Did I mention that any goal worth achieving comes ready made with a new State of Consciousness? Well, it does.

It is this change of consciousness that allows you to figure out how to re-stack the rocks of your experience and rearrange them into the doorway that gives you access to the "new you".

"In my Father's House there are Many Mansions" said the Bible. Well, maybe he meant rooms, but the fact remains you need a DOORWAY to get into a new room. All the steps leading to the right place mean nothing if you cannot get in the door, and guess what? The door to a new room is always locked until to find the conscious awareness that is your key. Consciousness is the key to life.

Life is incredible. In the process of you FINDING this door, life scatters things you might call problems and obstacles in font of you. When you collect and pieces together, the jigsaw puzzle of what all these delays, frustrations and concerns means to you, you get a picture of what is REALLY up. This image is an impression that the stuff of life pours understanding into, and when it sets VOILA! Your awareness has grown, and here is your KEY to open your door.

What is more, the OBSTACLES that you meet on the road form the material you need to build the doorway to your new world. Think of the rocks strewn in your path as the building materials of your future.

Life wants you to discover new ground, and open the door to a new world. Why? Because obviously life lives THROUGH you. As YOU experience LIFE, it experiences YOU. It wants you to have the greatest experience possible because IT gets this as well. Believe me, no-one in Theology College will be teaching you THIS.

There are just SO MANY examples of how the Intelligence of Life opens doors of all sorts. One remarkable example comes with the importation of camels into Australia. The Acacia tree in Australia learned to excrete TANNIN into its leaves when camels were introduced here. The tree in Africa exudes tannin to stop the camel eating its leaves, because they now taste bad, but get this! The Acacia only excretes the tannin when it SMELLS a camel. So camels in Africa now approach the trees from downwind.

The Acacia tree in countries where it has natural predators has done this for centuries, but in Australia where it had no natural predators and did not exude tannin. This was until the camel turned up. Somehow Australian trees learned to do what their overseas cousins have been doing for ages.

How could this be? Life is intelligent, and it pulled from its basic genetic material the information it needed to help the plant survive. Jung called it the Cosmic Unconscious, but I just call it the intelligence of life.

If a TREE can find a better pathway by trusting life, how much more can YOU do? The opening, the solution, the doorway to a new world: It is there waiting for you. But here is the secret: You must first to frame the right questions, which prepares you for the answers, that bring you to the place where you can begin the journey.

Your RAT is the ideal candidate for this question creation. Why? It is designed to work through the NEGATIVES in order to achieve a POSITIVE. This character inside you is the perfect person for dealing with, and expecting, difficulty. This is why approaching something negatively works, it means you are preparing the right questions BEFORE you look for answers.

Even if you cannot trust life, even if you don't seem to be able to learn the best place to set yourself up to achieve things with the effortless effort, (The Wu Wei Wu) you CAN trust your Rat to train you in this ability. Why? Your RAT is naturally LAZY and the sooner it gets you to the point where you get more self-sufficient, the easier ITS job becomes.

As we started this chapter, we close it. The Tibetans coined the word "Mudra". It is an archaic term that means opening, but it also means the journey, the difficulty and the solution that go into creating it. Remember this in times of difficulty, and it will help you to refocus your efforts to attain a good result.

ENEMY LEAFLETS FALL FROM ABOVE...

" give up... you are beaten.... you will never make sense of it alone ... stop trying now."

"accept it ... you are outnumbered.... overwhelmed... surrounded come and join us."

" you are not a hero... there is no glory in your cause... your fight is worthless.."

" stop your pathetic, lonely struggle..: join us NOW

" turn to page 6 for our great television guide... sport, page 32 politics. page 10 modern living. page 14 "

Leunig

Short Note: Hope versus Intention:

One of the great door closers in life is an attitude of Hope. Does this surprise you? After all, we have all been taught that HOPE is the great saviour of mankind. Well, in many ways, it is our greatest curse. Hope is a last resort used by an immobilised person. You are stuck in situ, tense, frozen, hoping things will change. You are no longer DOING, you are PRAYING.

We need to develop Pure Intention rather than Hope if we are to succeed. Here we learning to train and educate the mind and heart in what we EXPECT, rather than what we hope for.

The best example I gave earlier, when I was learning to ride a motor bike. I discovered fairly quickly that the bike went wherever I was looking. If I saw a pothole, and wanted to avoid it, I always hit it. Why? Because I was LOOKING at the damn thing.

When I trained my mind to look where I wanted to go, and not at where I didn't want to go, suddenly everything started to work. What I was working with, deep inside, is the EXPECTATION I would be fine. I stopped getting locked in the hope I would miss the pothole. I moved forward with the confidence of going where I chose.

And here is the truth: *We never get what we hope for, we get what we expect.*

EXPECT to find an opening, and it appears almost miraculously. Merely wishing for it, hoping it will come, these are all ways of telling life you don't expect to get it. Thus it will take a longer, be harder to achieve, and consume more energy to get there. But think about this: When you start out on a journey expecting difficulty, this means you expect a solution to be found. Why else would have bothered starting?

The mind is a complex, subtle instrument, yet on the other hand it is really quite simple. If you can grasp that the mind is really a series of oppositions in balance (Or not in balance, in some cases) you will understand that all you need to do is to shift things just a little in your favour and let the weight of the scales work out the rest.

EXPECTING a good result is far and away the greatest lever you can use to move the obstacles to one side, and shift the balance in your favour .

Relationships:

Everyone loves to talk about relationships. How to find the perfect marriage, what is the best way for sorting out differences, are there new ways for making better business connections, or bright ideas for developing a network of friends: It is all about relationships. But the ONLY one that really counts is how you relate to LIFE. Tell me, are you looking at your life as if it were your girlfriend, a De Facto, or your Wife? (Please convert to boyfriend, etc. as is suitable)

I have to tell you something, and make it clear so there is no confusion: If life is not your most intimate friend, you are not really living. If you are doing nothing to have FUN, you are not living. If you are trying to be better every day, but not enjoying the moment, you are not living. You are just a puppet doing whatever the internal controller inside you decides you will do.

If we are to find true happiness, we must stop being puppets. This means learning to choose how we feel, what we think, where we go, and who we associate with.

Any choice you make is fine, but you DO need to understand that you need to choose what it will be. And whatever you choose cannot be 'wrong" if you remain flexible. If, during the course of the natural state of growth, things change and you need to make another, different choice, so be it. Accept it, and this is also fine.

Now, I already know most will have automatically assumed that it is "better" to have "life as a wife". After all, it rhymes better. But why? So you can more quickly take her for granted? Don't be stupid. Start living your life as if it is your girlfriend! Flick her around, go to parties, drive wild and fast, be careless and laugh! As you do so, life will learn to love you all the more for it.

Then maybe settle down to a more intimate connection, and finally, as you realise that this is what you really want, you discover the deeper connection. This is to have your life with you at all times rather than passing by as a visitor.

Some covert other people's lives. They wish they were more successful, richer, more famous, etc. Tell me, what does this mean to your inner mind? Simple, you are saying to yourself that that your own life is worthless. Worshipping and adoring other people's lives is the ultimate in unfaithfulness to your own true self.

Your greatest relationship needs to be with yourself, and only when you choose to marry yourself will you understand the intimacy of

KNOWING that certain sense of the Omphalos, the still certain point, within. Your surety of being, your clarity of purpose, all this will increase, and finally the natural result of your union with yourself will come about in the Children of Consciousness being born.

These children will look like the best you can imagine yourself to be.

New Inspiration, bright shiny new concepts and directions will be born within you and, as you tend to their growth, your whole life will shape around their needs. In living and breathing this new ideal, you yourself will become transformed.

Outer relationships will then reflect the inner changes, so do not be too concerned if these come and go. Be warned: The process of true growth can burn those around you if you are not careful, but even so, let it happen as it will. Children always find new friends when they go to a new school. Remember this, because life IS change, and the only permanent mark that exists is the true, and natural, love you develop for your own life.

The Mystic Rat Says: *Unto thy own self be true.*

Of course, you would have to know who you are if you are to be true to whatever this might be, yes? Here we have the PURPOSE of external relationships. This is to help us see ourselves more clearly through the eyes of another person, situation or circumstance.

But if you need to know more about this sort of stuff, turn on Doctor Phil. I am talking about embracing Rats and don't have time for the cute and cuddly or deep and meaningful right now.

our way of life is being threatened by a dark force.

we must defend our way of life.

WHAT IS THIS DARK FORCE WHICH THREATENS OUR WAY OF LIFE?

it's our way of life...

Leunig

PYTHAGORAS: All is Number

Going back to our roots we find that the first person in Western Culture to ever formulate a study of the mind was the Greek Master, Pythagoras. He invented the concept of Philosophy as a Science, and indeed pretty much invented the entire concept of science of itself, being that he introduced a system of proof, test and measure.

Pythagoras was one of the first people in what was destined to become our Western Culture to identify and quantify the Sciences as we know them today. He is a pivotal figure that marks the change over from the old world to the new.

He introduced geometry, trigonometry, mathematics and created the first university. He revolutionised the process of education by taking training and apprenticeship away from the guilds, and instituting a simplified form of language across all the sciences and arts. He introduced the decimal system, the Harmonic Scale of Music, the basis of Logarithm and Ratio equations, but above all, he founded the concept that a notion or a belief must be TESTED before it is accepted as true.

He was the first true scientist, a great gatherer of truth, and a marvellous assembler and translator of the arcane teachings into the common language of the day. One of the great truths he organised was the notion that "All is Number". He spoke of a Divine Order, and how we are all a part of this, whether we know and accept it or not.

He proved that HARMONY is the core of not just mathematics, but for music and social interaction. He described harmony as a sign of ORDER at work. More than this, he proved how harmony follows rules, and, as a result of his research, created (or should I say proved) that which we now call the twelve tone musical scale.

It all started when Pythagoras passed by a blacksmith shop, and heard the ringing of the hammers. They all sounded wonderful, but one of the five hammers sounded wrong. This of itself fascinated the young man. Why did one thing sound WRONG while other things sound RIGHT? He knew the term harmony, but what was it? What was harmony? Where did it come from? Can it be repeated in other areas?

He purchased the hammers and started playing around with them. His curiosity was sparked by his inner RAT, and this started his journey.

Then he did the research. He weighed each hammer, and long before Archimedes shouted "Eureka!" (and invented the basis for weighing loads in the shipping industry) Pythagoras has already looked at the water the blacksmiths hammers displaced in a marked tub, and used it to compare the relative volume of each hammer. Thus he figured the MASS by volume, and the WEIGHT by using scales.

He then had the hammers beaten out to form tongues of metal, and he struck these against the same anvil, which he had also bought from the blacksmith shop. Lo and behold, the same four remained harmonious, while the fifth remained dissonant. No matter what he did, each hammer retained the properties of harmony or dissonance, and this remained until he took away a specific measure of MASS from the dissonant one. Here he found a point of harmony between all five.

This is where he started to work out the science of Ratio, the harmonic scale of music, and so much that is still the basis of mathematics and physics today. But what really interests me is the fact that there are twelve specific harmonic points in any given length of string, weight of metal, or mass of material.

Take any stringed instrument and look at the frets. You will see between the open string and the first octave (The half way point on any string) that there are twelve frets. Now, the RATIO of these frets is interesting, because it reflects the SAME ratio of ripples expanding on a pond, which is the same as the ratio of sound expanding, or of any given light frequency modulating. The ratio is but one aspect, however you need this specific ratio to create harmony. This is the division by eighteen on a diminishing return.

Take any string length on any instrument, and divide it by eighteen. Subtract this from the string length, and mark it. This is the first fret. Then take the sting length from the bridge to the first fret, divide be eighteen, and subtract this, and mark it. Here is the second fret, and so on.

On a fretboard, if you keep the proportinal ratio but squash it down to get 13 frets you will get 13 perfect notes OR you can expand it to get 11 Frets, and 11 perfect notes. The only problem is that not one note will HARMONIZE with the other ones.

This means no chords, no duets, no symphonies, no MUSIC as we know it. But keep everything to the Pythagorean ratios, the ones the ratio of mathematics decided worked, and everything we know of as music today comes about.

BMW uses this science today in their cars. Each panel they make is designed to have a specific frequency, and at the end of each assembly line for parts, there is a man with a tuning fork who puts it on the panel or part to check its HARMONIC response. If it is in tune, it sings, and the man knows that specific part is made in the right proportion and is sound. Literally.

Did you ever wonder we describe something that it right and in good order as being SOUND?

YOU are Sound. At the core of yourself is this high frequency that you are probably already hearing, and which your doctor calls Tinnitus. This is your Life Force you are hearing. It is what the Pythagoreans called, "The Music of the Spheres". *In the beginning there was the WORD.* That's you, that's your divine spark, your true, eternally mobile, centre of being.

And like twelve dominant notes, Pythagoras taught that there are twelve main archetypes or categories that humans, and life in general, is created within. The Greeks explained it as a series of various TYPES, starting with the "Ec-Typal" (Universal) moving to the "Arch-Typal" (The Divine Pattern) then to the Typal (The Human State). You have heard of an Archetype, yes? That's the middle area, so let's look briefly at these three concepts.

The EC-Typal is the great unformed "stuff" of the undirected pure life energy we tend to call "God" or similar. This primary state is the ONE, or "EC". *From the One to the Many to refold back to the One.* From this point the ONE, the harmonic central energy of life, breaks up to the various threads of existence. This is where the divine current splits into the twelve main sub-groups, described by the twelve notes in music.

The Archetypal is when these twelve subgroups first form and take specific shape. When a person is "archetypal" it means they have a characteristic that is typical of that type. Homeopathy deals extensively with this area, and treats people in accordance with the archetypal energy of their body.

Finally we get to the last division, the Typal. This is you and me, and just as a person born in January all share a specific Sun Sign, we all fall into groups according to the natural energy that we possess. We all follow a line from the Ec-typal pure state of being, to the archetypal form, which then becomes personalised as the TYPE.

Despite what we imagine to be a random walk, our life, and this universe, is remarkably ordered. Please do not get me started on the Big Bang theory, which is the principle of the random event creating the random sequence. So much mathematical and scientific evidence points to the entire notion being completely wrong that adherents simply cannot believe they could be SO wrong. Thus they keep inventing holes to plug up the gaping pieces of evidence that prove it wrong

Let's be archaic and suggest that the Pythagorean concept of the universe and the person was indeed roughly correct. In this way of seeing things there are twelve basic options, or doorways, for energy to come into the physical universe. Now whether you believe the Gods sit behind the doorways is not relevant, the point is that the whole show IS ordered, and following the patterns of order. YOU come into the physical universe through one of these mystical mathematical matrices called a HARMONIC DOOR, or Mudra.

Now whether you believe any of this is irrelevant. The point is that you are a TYPE, and that there are natural doorways for you to walk through in this lifetime. Your RAT knows these doors instinctively. It knows YOU better than you know yourself. Trust it to find the way.

It is your mirror, your guide and your battery pack. All you have to do is FIND IT. For this, you need some cheese.

BAITING CONSCIOUSNESS

You have heard the term, "Waiting with Baited Breath"? Well apart from the fact that I would prefer not to wait with you, and your smelly breath, the point is simple. It is about living inside a level of expectancy. Expectancy creates a door in the psyche that draws the object of desire, like cheese draws a mouse.

It goes back to primal stuff. Women bait men using the powers of attraction, we believe, but the CORE to this is the female curiosity and expectancy. What will he be like? Will he be good in bed? All these questions form a gestalt of expectancy, and this creates a powerful sense of attraction. The man looks over, sees the interested eyes, and thinks, "Hey, nice!". The general inclination is to go and talk with this soul.

Now, of course we have to work past the filters. The guy might be a hung up religious nut, and interpret the arousal signs as threats to his divinity by the devil, etc. Everyone has different filters to work through, and we cannot go through them all. However, truth is true on all levels, and YOU can lay this same sort of bait to attract consciousness.

Everything we have talked about in this book is about BECOMING CONSCIOUS. It is all about listening to that aspect within you that knows how to survive, your RAT. The net result of this listening is greater awareness of your surroundings. But this alone will not bring joy into your heart. We must also have to have the conscious awareness of what we are, if we wish to fully enjoy life.

Carly Simon sang a song called "Anticipation". A good song. It is about a lover waiting for the beloved. Well, this anticipation is what we need if we are to fully experience consciousness. Anticipation is the flame that draws the moth. If we have have an expectancy, an anticipation, of the experience we are already building a doorway to find it Curiosity: This is what draws your Rat to the surface of your awareness.

And here is the Secret: The Rat desires consciousness, needs consciousness. It lives in anticipation of becoming the very awareness that tickles it into life. Not to eat it, as you may expect, but to protect it. The RAT, your Reality Awareness Trigger, has the term "awareness" right in the middle, remember.

That little spark of knowing, this is the RAT within. Tender it, respect it, and let it grow to a flame. Soon enough there will be a fire of clarity burning through the obstacles and collected pieces of rubbish we have gathered during our upbringing. So let your self burn, first with anticipation, then with the light of a new day dawning.

Consciousness, while it exists in all things, is like a flower. It will only bloom in its season. Yet the season for consciousness is NOT time based, it is attitude based. It needs a culture of kindness, consideration and confidence before its seeds will germinate. And to GROW it needs Truth, real Truth. But between this point you are aiming for, and where you are now, there are usually a whole lot of lies and false beliefs to conquer.

This is where your Rat is all important. It is the only part within you that can discern the steps needed to get you from the wilderness of social acceptance and programmed responses to stimuli, and keep you on track.

Your Rat is also your vigilant protector, but it only works when you are willing to both protect yourself, and invest time in understanding your own process. Let's cut to the chase. We live on a Planet of War. Surely some say, this is a Western Civilisation thing. Not really. We in the West may well have perfected war, but we did not invent it. Those nice American Indians were out there killing each other long before the white men got there to speed it up for them. Aboriginal societies in Australia were regularly killing each other for land rights and women. Imagine how it could have been if they had the weapons of war we had today?

The Maoris in New Zealand were expelled from Hawaii because of their Black Magic and the tendency they had to eat their enemies. When they got to New Zealand, they hunted down and ATE the Mori Ori's. (The natural indigenous race.) Apparently they tasted pretty good.

Does it shock you that native cultures were so brutal? Here I may surprise you, but the truth is that War of itself is not a bad thing. Your RAT is that part of you that is willing to go to war. Now obviously this can be abused, but equally, the Rat's warlike nature can be put to a useful purpose. The suggestions within this book are all aimed at you doing something useful with this part of your inner ID. (Or your inner ISness)

But it is your choice as to what you do with it. You can use your RAT to sniff out trouble, and seek to create peace, or you can look for peace and create trouble.

Your Rat won't care. It loves the PROCESS of war, not the war itself. It loves figuring out what people will do next. It loves calculating its odds in a given situation. It is fascinated with balancing things, finding the point where least resistance occurs.

Your Rat worships no God but the collected Gods of Chance, Opportunity and Luck. Surprised? While your Rat knows there is no such thing as happen-stance without history, or that there are no coincidences without karma, it also understands that LUCK is real. Opportunity is the door opening from the Gods, and it is your luck to be at the right place at the right time.

Yet as much as your Rat is attracted to War, Gambling and Free Booting around the globe, it has a weakness, a catnip it cannot refuse. The most attractive thing of all to a Rat is the smell of purity. This may sound like the strangest thing, but the Inner RAT adores the smell of purity. Perhaps the natural bitterness of the Rat needs the balance of sweet nectar. I do not ask WHY this is so, just as I do not ask why a light turns on when I flick the switch. All I do is look at how best to utilise this odd aspect. And this is, oddly, where Virtue comes in.

Here we come to the real reason for Virtue, which is not what people imagine it to be. The Pythagoreans held that Virtue was a striving for the perfection of what IS. True Virtue is Reason, Power and Choice combined in a State of Being.

Thus the Virtue of the Eye is to see clearly. The Virtue of the Arm is to be strong. The virtue of the Hand is to be Dexterous. It has nothing what-so-ever to do with countering passions. other than the fact that indulgence can make us weak. True Virtue is simply voiced as: *Caring enough to Know Enough, to Do your very best.* Caring, Knowing and Doing: It is being the best that you can be, living as fully as you can, and choosing wisely the things of your life. Practice this, and all things will become more obvious.

The Virtue of the MIND is to be clear and focussed. The Virtue of Soul is to allow the greater good of divinity to flow through you. The Virtue of the Heart is to be true to your self. With Reason you inspect, with Power you remove obstacles, and with Choice you remain true to your path. True Virtue is the perfect unison between Mind, Soul and Heart. Are we understanding what Virtue really is, and what it is your Rat finds attractive about it? It is like admiring the perfect athlete.

By YOU being the best you can be in any given circumstance, you activate your RAT. Beyond a level of anticipation, you BAIT your RAT by your actions, and your attempts, to wake up and smell the cheese

So, paradoxically, your RAT, the lowest, most socially law breaking aspect of your being, the part that loves to ignore correctness and decorum, that part of you that snortles at the lies politicians say, which detests the strutting peacock of the stupid media, which distrusts every word spoken by the pompous Bishop: This is what adores purity. This aspect of such apparent negative energy within yourself is the same aspect that encourages you to come to the place of your highest good, your place of purity.

Amazing isn't it? Your anticipation, your purity of intention and clarity of action are the Bait that draws your Rat out of its hole. When you "dress up" to attract your Rat, it cares nothing for money, prestige and external influence, it wants clarity, kindness and confidence. Once brought forth using these seed thoughts as bait, IT will hone your skills, sharpen your mind, and improve the health of your emotions in order to get more of what IT wants: Which is, simply:

A/ **Purity of Action**, and

B/ **Purity of Focus.**

This, in turn, attracts greater levels of consciousness, more opportunity, and greater breadth of choice. Thus the circle is joined. These qualities are the natural rewards from the process of waking up, and utilising, your Rat.

The Reality Awareness Trigger is exactly what the words say: That part of you that encourages you to pay attention to REALITY as it presents itself to you. It is also that which also understands where Reality is polluted with false belief.

Here is something worthy of a book all on its own: *It is much harder to spot a half truth than a lie.* Your Rat, because it understands the black and the white and the shades in between, helps you to determine the correct steps through the chess board of choices we all face.

So, we spoke of the Virtue of the Arm is that it becomes as strong as it can be, the Virtue of the Eye is seeing clearly: What then is the Virtue of your Rat? What is ITS perfected state? It's very simple. Freedom, that's it. That is all it is. True freedom, and the clarity to choose wisely.

The Mystic Rat Says: *The inalienable right to BE what we are can only be found within the freedom to express our being.*

But these are just words. What is the EXPRESSION of the Awakened Being? What are the hallmarks of an Awakened Soul? They are specific and clear:

1. *An Appreciation of this Moment.*
2. *A Gratitude for Moments that have been*
3. *An Anticipation of Moments to Come*
4. *A Sense of Surprise as these Arrive*
5. *A Stillness, an Ability to PAUSE, and Rest in the Now*
6. *An Understanding that there is only One Certainty, One Truth: This is that our present reality will always change.*
7. *And finally: How it changes is defined by the choices we make.*

These marks are the indicators that you possess the Universal Passport. A person who clearly possesses the above will not be shaken by circumstance, because they appreciate it is simply another moment of experience. This person will not suffer immobility with significant loss, because they know such moments will come. Such a person is vulnerable to experience, yet invulnerable to the circumstance around it. This Soul seems to be able to achieve without struggle. Yes, there is effort but a pure and naturally focussed effort always seems effortless.

Such a Soul is an expression how the many can add to the one, while the one adds up to the many. Because we are all many, we are all scattered pieces of a jigsaw puzzle tossed together. We become ONE through the path to a whole self image, and holding a pure picture of ourself is the path to happiness. The above attributes show the world that you have created yourself into a single state of being. And this is a powerful thing, a thing that cannot be shaken by changing events.

And when you achieve this state of self-hood, you finally realise the truth. Your Rat is not something you have, it is not something you are, it is not even a piece of the puzzle that is you: It is a place within you that is a doorway to consciousness.

And here is one of the most extraordinary things of all to understand: That you have been GIFTED with this knowing, this internal compass. The general geography of your life has already been mapped out, and you are in the process of exploring what is already here inside you. Life loves to meet life, and in all you do, in all the choices you make, in all the thoughts you think, in all the emotions you feel: You are meeting yourself before anything else.

T S Eliot said, *"We shall not cease from exploration, and the end of all our exploring will be to arrive where we started, and know the place for the first time"*. To get back to the origin of YOU the journey must cross many boundaries. You must meet many conflicts, and in rising above them, you break your Shoulds in two, set yourself free from Cannots, and utterly destroy your Lack.

Your Sword is your Perception. Your Shield is your Intuition. Your Heart is your Guide. But at every major change point in your life there is a border patrol, and you need a ticket to go through the gate. This is where you need your RAT.

Your Rat is a Passkey installed at your birth by an invisible friend. Imagine, if you will, a passport that serves as an "open sesame" to all areas. Imagine that you have a badge that reads "Access all Areas" and it allows you to go wherever your heart desires. This "Badge" is the shimmering quality of consciousness, of KNOWING, and THIS is your RAT. Your Reality Attention Trigger.

Look at Bob Dylan as a young man. He sang songs that seemed to simply flow from his being. He didn't even realise what he was writing, only that it flowed well, and worked. How it worked was not important. He trusted his RAT to guide him. He broke all conventions, ignored the regulations of what he "should" do. Just when he was successful in folk, he went electric. He created the first "Rap" song and though drawn from the influence of the Black Poets in New York, and Woody Guthrie, and a thousand sources, he continually transformed whatever influence that came his way. He allowed it to pass through his consciousness and become new again. He stamped everything with his perception, and he demonstrated with word, song and action that he was AWAKE.

There is a part of you that never went to sleep and which is trying to wake up the rest of yourself. The alarm bell is already ringing, you know it, you hear it. So! The questions is: *What to do?* You have heard all the reasoning, you have been given a power of words, and you have been offered many options and choices. What to do now? Do you roll over and go back to dream land?

Most will try to ignore this wake up call. Most will pad their sleepy eyes with notions of "Well, that was interesting, now let me read about the Presidential Race." or employ other techniques of distraction. Most will know that there is SOME truth in this book, but they will not want to do anything about it. After this they will minimise the truth, usually by comparing it to other forms of psychology or philosophy, or by simply saying that there are better authors who write better words.

And they are correct. The the paradox is that ALL of this is truth. There are better books, other versions of truth that exist, and who the next President is does count for something. It is all pieces of truth, yet inside you already know it is not the whole of things. You know you have not reached that point of wholeness, of complete and clear beingness. Whether you like it or not, this little book has scratched the surface and exposed a little of a soft underbelly by revealing, to some degree, the LIES which all of us live with, both intentionally (for convenience) and unintentionally.

The cold, hard fact is, I didn't write this book for you. I wrote it because time and place fell my way to do so. If I wrote it last year, it would be very different, and tomorrow who knows how it would have emerged from the dust of consciousness that is scattered in my head. The fact that it took twelve years from the original two week stream of consciousness to get to what you now hold is possibly worth something, however, it is not necessarily so.

The Mystic Rat says: *Do with IT what you will, and seek to harm no one (This includes yourself)*

However there is something I know. Now you have read "my" truth there will be a problem. Now, no matter what you do, something inside you will always be gnawing away, wanting to get out.

The Logical Fallacies:

How Your Rat sees the World:

In some ways Ratology is an inconvenient truth. Because really, it is just a matter of time before you come to realise your Rat is in control, despite all your best efforts to avoid it.

The greatest enemy of inner freedom come in the form of the false truths that drive our actions. They are dangerous because they force us to act wrongly. We laugh now at the irrational burning of witches in the middle ages, yet inside 50 years the next generation will be laughing at the absurdity of trying to kill cancer with a radiation that almost kills the person.

This chapter looks at the LOGICAL falshoods, or the Logical Fallacies as they are known. These are the Lies of Logic, and you see them in every news broadcast, in every school room, and at every university, in some shape or form. So don't laugh too much at the stupidity of the past. We all have an absurdity of some sort inside us that we believe to be true.

If you wish to be free from being trapped by any one, or all, of the below noted fallacies, you will need to commit them to memory. More importantly, learn to spot them. Newspapers and media commentaries are chock-a-block full of them.

The Pythagorean Fallacies of Logic are ancient and simple, and, in all, these represent the bedrock of all wrong thinking. When the ancient Pythagoreans first coined this notion, they noted that faulty logic equated to poor decisions and trouble in life.

In truth, wrong thinking is the cause of more than 90% of the issues on this planet. If we adjust our thinking to be more correct, which means making our thinking simpler and clearer, it follows that out lives will become simpler and clearer. "I think therefore I am" is a fallacy of inversion. I am, therefore I think, is significantly more correct. "I sink, therefore I swim" is FAR more correct.

If what you believe you are is proven to be inherently wrong, as in, what you were trained to be is wrong, then logically, all logic that follows from this will be flawed. Yet when your "I am" is rooted deeply in a sense of being that is bound to your natural self, the thinking that follows will be more correct.

If you know the enemy, you can conquer it. The examples given are snipped pretty much verbatim from the web. What is NOT supplied is the way to grasp and understand where, when and how they are being used.

Fallacies that result from errors in induction:

Dicto Simpliciter or Overstatement: An unqualified generalisation. "My English teacher never gives A's." "Almonds are good for the heart; everyone should eat two handfuls of almonds every day."

Hasty Generalization: Stating a conclusion based on too little evidence or based on ignoring some evidence. "Running must be bad for your heart. Look what happened to Florence Joiner." "My little Yamaha motorcycle never gave me problems. Yamaha motorcycles are the best."

Stereotyping: Giving the same characteristics to everyone in a group (related to overstatement and hasty generalization). "Used-car salesmen can't be trusted." " Utah State graduates are all nerdy." " Mormons all have several wives." " Southern Utahans are all right-wing conservative fanatics who refuse to pay taxes and want to destroy the environment." "California blondes are all as wild as they can be."

Forced hypothesis: Reaching a conclusion that is not supported by the evidence or a conclusion that is more complicated than necessary. "Jerry and Kim live next door to each other, so they must be really good friends."

Non sequitur: From Latin, meaning "it does not follow"; this refers specifically to conclusions which are not logically derived from the reasoning that precedes them. " Al Gore is a wonderful father, so he would have made a great president." "President George W. Bush admitted to getting a DUI ticket when he was younger, so we can be sure the booze flows freely at White House Parties." "We don't see as many women in calculus classes as we do men, so clearly their brains are not capable of handling difficult math concepts."

Slippery slope: An argument in which we assert that X should not happen because it will inevitably be followed by consequences Y and Z, which are terrible. "Utah should not legalize parimutuel betting on horse races because that will only lead to gambling on other sporting events and finally to casino gambling." "We should never allow families to have doctors disconnect the respirators and feeding tubes of brain dead patients. If we do, pretty soon we will be asking doctors to kill people with Alzheimer's disease and children with Down's syndrome."

False dilemma: An argument asserting that only two (or a limited number of) options exist when there are actually more. "We must either ban Hustler and Penthouse or our children will never learn respect for women." "You either support the war in Iraq or you are a traitor to your country and an enemy to freedom."

False analogy: An argument based on a comparison of two things when the differences between the two are too great. "There are 10,000 deaths from alcohol poisoning to 1 from mad-dog bites in this country. In spite of this, we license liquor but shoot the dogs." "It is true that an embryo can grow into a person, but an acorn can grow into an oak. We don't criticize people who step on an acorn just because the acorn could become an oak, so we shouldn't think it is a big deal if someone decides to abort an embryo." "In a pack of wolves, there is always an alpha male, the powerful male who makes the decisions and makes sure the whole system runs well. Likewise, a man should be firm and forceful in his dealings with his wife and children; then, the whole family will run more smoothly."

Post hoc: From the Latin "after this, therefore because of it," this means simply assigning a cause-effect relationship where none exists or where it is difficult to prove there is a cause-effect relation. "A black cat ran across my path on the way to work this morning, and sure enough, I got a flat tire on the way home." "The president had been in office just a few months before the stock market went into the toilet and unemployment soared. People in the market just lost confidence because he was elected." "Ever since my teacher saw that I had my tongue pierced, my grades on tests have gone down. I think he just doesn't like body piercings."

Collected Fallacy: What about a Slippery Slope Forced Hypothesis? Feathers are light, light comes from the Sun, therefore the Sun is made of feathers. We saw a lot of this in the Middle Ages.

There are also many COLLECTED Fallacies, or wrong logical frameworks, that have linked together to form a Mother of a Fallacy. It is difficult to give examples, but when a non-sequitur marries a forced hypothesis, you get absurdist thinking like, "We don't see as many women in calculus classes as we do men, so clearly their brains are not capable of handling difficult math concepts. So clearly, as Hillary Clinton is a woman, she will make a terrible President."

Fallacies that result from ignoring the issue:

Begging the question: To assume that part or all of your argument will be accepted as true without support. "The federal government should not subsidize development of alternative-fuel automobiles because gasoline is the cheapest and cleanest fuel." "We should give every American the right to have assault weapons in his or her home because we know that a nation in which its citizens have assault weapons will be safer that one without."

"We know that our police are never involved in bribery, dishonesty, or abuse of the law because the police report issued in January of 2004 said so."

Red herring: To introduce an irrelevant side-issue and divert attention from the topic at hand. "Mary Gordon shouldn't be elected to the school board because she doesn't have any children in public schools."

"The officer said I was going 50 miles an hour in a school zone. Can you believe that? There are rapes and bank robberies going unsolved in our city, and she has time to worry about people's driving habits!"

Straw man: To accuse your opponents of holding erroneous or ridiculous view or attitudes and attacking those instead of attacking their arguments. "Environmentalists are trying to save the spotted owl because they want to run American loggers out of business." "Some conservatives are angry that the Supreme Court recently banned the death penalty for kids who commit crimes under the age of 18. Let's face it; conservatives hate kids. They want as many of them to die as possible." "Feminists are upset with all the laws passed prohibiting same-sex marriages. They want to live in a world in which no woman ever uses her womb for something as subservient to a man as bearing his child."

Ad hominem: From the Latin meaning "to or towards the person." "This is the strategy of attacking the proponent of an argument rather than the argument itself. "Of course you believe that--you're a woman." Or "I'd expect something like that from a socialist like you!" "You students are always trying to cheat and get free money from the government; of course you are going to be in favor of Social Security." (A special form of Ad Hominem arguments occur when someone attacks an argument by attacking the speaker before he or she speaks. It is called "Poisoning the Well." "Jane Fonda is going to speak tonight about how we ought to give more to help Tsunami victims. Don't forget; this is the same Jane Fonda that visited Hanoi and criticized the war when our G.I's. were dying in Vietnam. We should not listen to her.")

Argument ad Miseriocordiam: "Argument to Pity": An emotional appeal to a logical issue. While pathos generally works to reinforce a reader's moral sense, if a writer relies on an appeal to emotion only to accept a conclusion, it is a fallacy. " I know my paper is late, but I have had the worst pimple on my nose for a week, so I was too miserable to bring it to class. Please don't mark it late." "Or "Janice, you have to marry me! If you don't, I will be the most miserable person alive. Who knows, I may even turn to drugs and alcohol."

Common practice: Sometimes called "bandwagon" fallacy. This is to argue that an action should be taken or an idea accepted because everyone is doing it. "Don't worry about using your older brother's research paper. It's only a general education requirement, and half the kids in the class are doing the same thing." "Dad, I can't live without a cell phone and a laptop. All the kids have them now."

Argument ad populum: from the Latin "to the people"; appealing to the beliefs of the multitudes. "Republican candidates are the choice of red-blooded Americans who believe in the traditional American values of liberty and prosperity and America first." "Everybody knows that women care more deeply about their children than men do." (A form of this called "snob appeal" is often used in advertising: "Buick is the choice of intelligent discerning Americans."; "Caring mothers choose Pampers.")

Argumentum ad Baculum: Appeal to Force, bullying, or the "Might-Makes-Right" Fallacy. This argument uses force, the threat of force, or some other unpleasant backlash to make the audience accept a conclusion. It commonly appears as a last resort when evidence or rational arguments fail to convince (Most of us have mothers and fathers who used it with us.) Some years ago, a student newspaper at Dixie wanted to publish a story that was controversial. The administration opposed publishing the article. When the editor brought up the first amendment and the rights of free speech and a free press, the administrator replied, "Oh, of course you have a right to publish whatever you wish. But we also have a right not to fund the newspaper. If you publish this, there will be no newspaper here at Dixie." The argument was very effective.

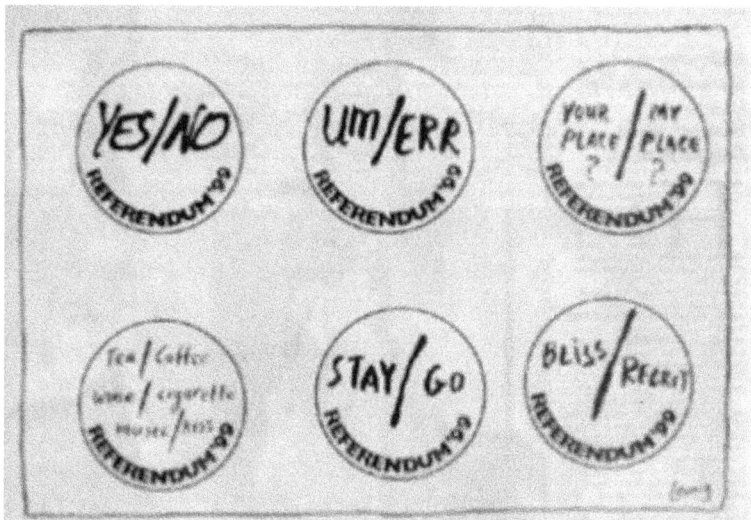

SUMMARY

This last argument in particular cannot be proven wrong, as it is the basic Law of the Jungle: Might makes Right. However the argument is essentially that correctness equals strength, because you use strength to create what is believed to be correct. The two are simply not connected in a way that includes the two elements to make a logical third. The Communist trials in the US under McCarthy is the perfect example.

This notion that two things must add up to a logical third is the core to what is possibly the most important message I have for you in this book. This is the concept of maintaining and directing our lives according to what is obvious.

ALL the above fallacies are incorrect not because some God of Logic has decreed it. They are incorrect because they do not invoke correct mathematics. One Plus One must equal Two. Take any of the faulty arguments presented above, and you will find that, when separated into the core components, they simply do not add up to the result presented by the argument. The Red Herring argument is possibly the most common in our society. (and ALL of the Logical Fallacies appear regularly on TV)

Example: "The officer said I was going 50 miles an hour in a school zone. Can you believe that? There are rapes and bank robberies going unsolved in our city, and she has time to worry about people's driving habits!"

The person is triangulating their present moment with unrelated matters (bank robbery, rape, etc.) and bringing this to an existing situation. The actual "triangle" here is: Speed Limit, Driver, Official. If the driver does not exceed the speed limit, there is no fine. That is IT, there is no other related argument. If there is a mitigating argument, it would need to be based on the reason the person was speeding.

There are many arguments that fail the test of logic, but the understanding of exactly where it fails is invariably found in how the argument internally triangulates facts to obtain a conclusion. You can go to a complete list of Logical Fallacies at: en.wikipedia.org/wiki/List_of_fallacies

TRIANGULATION:

Here is where the fun begins. Let's say you want to get married to someone. Are you thinking about what they are right now, or are you thinking about what will come of the union? Most would say that courting is "right now" but that marriage means we are thinking of what will come when we add one plus one. Obviously, we get three.

Yes, it is a pun on children, but the reality is that One Plus One always adds to a THIRD ELEMENT. Triangulation is the process of how the third element is created, and what it is likely to be.

And here all we need do is observe the obvious. Obviously, if you are having a great time with a playboy/girl/person millionaire, you would be foolish to think they will suddenly become wonderful home bodies helping to raise the kids in domestic bliss. Yes? Here you are using Triangulation. You are adding one plus one to get to a logical conclusion.

There is no mystery to how surveying works, you get a series of measurements, and by triangulating the results you can define boundaries. There is no difference in human relationships or business. When you learn to triangulate a situation correctly, when you measure the facts properly, you can come up with a fairly logical and obvious result that is likely to come from most situations.

Logically, you Triangulate the drunk in the street with the "End is Nigh" sign around his neck, and you can see (one) his present circumstance, (two) his likely attitude, and from there calculate with reasonable certainty (three) a sense of direction. Conclusion: It is very unlikely this person will become the President of the United States. It is also unlikely he will attract a gorgeous wife.

The MAIN REASON he is unattractive to women is because they take one look, triangulate his trajectory, and stay well away. It is just common sense, but what I am asking you do is understand the principles outlined in this book are ALL common sense. I want you to extend seeing the obvious like this into all areas of your life.

The reason for including the Logical Fallacies is specifically because they are examples of how to triangulate facts incorrectly. So first we need to grasp the process of correct logic, and this requires more than understanding where faulty logic lies. We need to understand and apply HOW it works, as much as grasp WHY it works.

Clear thinking is obvious. If we think clearly we can act clearly, but here is the difficult part for most people. Acting clearly is often difficult because they have too many strings and attachments pulling at them. The solution to this is to snip the ties that bind, but just finding them is the hard part. That is, until you learn the art of correct triangulation.

In keeping with the Pythagorean notion of harmonics the principle is this: *Whenever we come across two distinct energies, they will intermingle and create a third.* This goes all the way back to Paracelcus in the 15th Century and his Spiritual Law of Three: *From One to the Second whereupon the Third must then appear.*

As an example, I had an ongoing problem with a person who was a controller. They didn't like me, they didn't trust me, and I had the general notion they would far prefer I wasn't around. But it was as it was, and every time we had dealings with each other you could feel the tension. I was getting pretty much over this, when my RAT clicked into gear.

I saw with absolute clarity what the issue was. And to my surprise "I" was the problem. Not directly, but inwardly I was expecting more of this person than they were capable of, and was getting annoyed when they failed to live up to my standards. I had become a reflector of the Controller that this person was.

That was when I saw the solution. It was simple: Apply the Law of Three. I am One, she is the Second: What will the Third be that is generated? By stopping my reaction to this person, I was able to start creating a better "third option". In this case, just stopping my mental resistance seemed to change the person's attitude. It was a remarkable turn-a-round, and we started to get on with each other. Get it? I was part of the process of creation, but not taking responsibility for my part of it. Sure, they were a controller, and maybe not the ideal I expected, but so what?

Whenever I thought of this individual, I started seeing the Third Option was a bridge. That is all. I started looking for a positive to be created from the friction between our two natures. And you know what happened? Nothing.

Absolutely NOTHING. No more angst, no more sense of back-biting, no more sense of backstabbing. It all just STOPPED. I admit, I was surprised, because not one word was said, not one action externalised. The problem just vanished.

Correct Triangulation means YOU are the one who sets up the parameters for the created options between two opposites. Let me give you some hypotheticals: A man has a great time in bed with his wife, the wife tells her friends about it, they get curious. He is now unfaithful because her friends throw themselves at him.

It's not HIS fault, his wife created the triangle, and he just followed his nature. Obviously he was good in bed, that's why she bragged, but in doing so she took him, herself, and then created a triangle with her friends. If she had said NOTHING, just allowed the love that was created to be the SOLE manifestation of their union, all would have been good.

I can hear some people crying out "Misogynist pig!" because it appears I blame the wife. I blame no one, and have no concern at all what people do in their private world. I am simply pointing out that one plus one equals two. Triangulation is the way we put our Spiritual Arithmetic into practice. (Remember that at the start of the book?)

This is both internal and external. Internal Triangulation is part of the "mind chatter". Some examples are:

1. I feel alone, I feel weak, therefore I do not deserve a good relationship.
2. I want something, I am rich, therefore I can take what I want.
3. I am young, I am healthy, therefore I am invulnerable.

External Triangulation involves the relationships around us, and they need not be singular. Groups collide with individuals and triangulate with shared beliefs, companies can triangulate with ideals. There are also the enmeshed social and belief patterns that control most people actions. Some examples are:

1. We believe in Jesus, Jesus saves, therefore I am saving this person by converting them to Jesus.
2. Macedonia is a wonderful place. The United States is suggesting Albania be given control of Macedonia. This means the United States is against Macedonia.
3. I love this woman. But she appears to be in love with this other man. Therefore I must kill that man in order for her to love me.

In all, they are internal/external statements that are accepted as facts, but they simply do not add up in any logical framework.

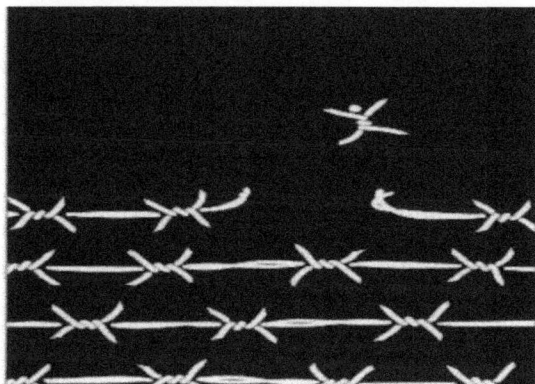

Hypnosis

Have you ever wondered how it is that in Hollywood, dead humans, Zombies can rip apart a persons ribs with their bare hands, but they can't a packet of potato crisps? A Zombie is really unfocused aggression without any sense of "should not", and this is probably part of the subconscious fascination we have with this horror genre.

Zombies love to walk about with their arms outstretched, dealing only with what hunger drives them. We think they are the stuff of horror movies, but they are already here, and they are everywhere. Go to almost any office and look about, and there they will be. Zombie-like people who just sheepishly do what they are told, while inside they are seething with frustration and angst, desperate to have or get something that feeds their hunger for substance and purpose.

Usually it is substance abuse that substitutes for substance, and distraction that substitutes for purpose. Distractions come in many forms and we cannot go through them all in this chapter, but when you hear someone all caught up in some political cause, or committing their life to long discussions about the fate of the forests of Borneo, but not actually DOING anything about it, then you have a Zombie on your hands. A Zombie is a person hypnotised by the beliefs projected upon them by others or by media, and they are noted by their aimless walk towards nowhere in particular, other than that which feeds them.

When I hear "Politically Correct" arguments, all I hear is a wasted life echoing a monologue someone else wrote for them. If you really want to save the whales, get on the boat and go do it. This will be too harsh for the sensitive New Age types and for those that believe the world's problems can be solved with discussion and cappuccinos, so let me place the context of political correctness (or any of the Zombie Habits) into an Analogy.

Most of us have been to the Dentist, yes? You don't know what's going on there inside your mouth, do you? However, you feel like it is something big. There is usually some fear and trepidation because of the likelihood of real pain, and then when the drill starts its work it becomes an all encompassing reality. Your attention is absorbed by the process. It's a total experience and YOU are in the middle of it.

Yet the view from the Dentist is that you are just another customer in a long, long line of customers. What HE is doing is something very small, and inconsequential. It is a tiny little filling in a big mouth. The question here is simple: Who has the right viewpoint?

What you perceive, and what the dentist actually does, rarely matches

up in your imagination. You see and feel a big thing, he sees and experiences a little thing. The Politically Correct Zombie person is like the one in the Dentist Chair. They see and genuinely feel the pain, but few ever understand that what they are experiencing are very small issues from the viewpoint of life. Life, of itself, does not care for your viewpoint, nor need it. It does its job very well, as it will, when it will.

Even so, little things DO count. You are not pointless, and your life can have meaning. However, you have to DO something about it. Going to a rally to protest the scarcity of three eyed toads is not DOING anything for the three eyed toad. But if your voice joins other voices, and in cooperation the three eyed toad is eventually saved, then you may have done something. Mind you, do people ask if the three eyed toad wants to be saved? However, we do what we must do, and the point is that if you are interested in saving whales, discussion alone won't DO anything.

I think it is fair to say that it IS important that SOMEONE takes care of the whales, the three eyed toads and the trees in Borneo. For the whales that someone is currently the Captain and crew of the Sea Shepherd, and if you fund them, or do something else that is directly related to the political and social process (Such as Movie Stars and surfers bringing the slaughter of Dolphins to the attention of the Japanese by placing themselves in harms way by swimming out to the fishing boats) you really are doing something to help. Otherwise you are just pissing in the wind.

Yet people believe that having a discussion on how to right the wrongs of the nation is doing something. And once it mattered. Once people discussed matters in the village square, and the discussions had ramification as to whether they voted for a person, or otherwise. Now real discourse is all but gone, and what we have are opinions by experts on prime time. This is a relatively recent event, and the blame for the destruction of true discourse lies squarely at the door of modern media.

People have been hypnotised to believe that Media is important. Media has become their experience of the world, and it is their ritual diet of information that they feast on every day. It has become a substitute for real dialogue and meaningful discussion. In place of this we now have a universal pin the tail on the donkey show.

Every Current Affairs and News program serves up a diet of the little guy versus the big guy, the good guy versus the bad one, the sad story, the corruption scandal! You name it: Anything but sincere and well structured arguments that assist in training people how to THINK CLEARLY.

People no longer THINK in a way that has beneficial long term effects. Most are merely imitating media and hand-me-down viewpoints with the level of thought more akin to the intelligence of an echo. If you go back to Ancient Greece, the thinker was the respected person in society. Now it is the Footballer, the Pop Star, the Politician, and accordingly the level of thought has devolved to this common level.

I find it difficult to believe that the higher echelons of society, many of whom are extremely well educated, are not aware of this dumbing down effect. It is my view that the current process of media and education is simply a way to oil the cogs of society. Entertainment is now distraction. Education is now socialisation. In all of this dialogue has suffered and media discussions are just confrontations, or affirmations.

Hypnotised people do what they are instructed to do. What do governments want you to do? Simple: *Give unto Caesar what is Caesar's.* Go to work, pay your taxes, buy your stuff, take your pills, watch TV, go to sleep. Do things that make society work, and thus make more money for rich people.

But this is the EASY Hypnotism to cure. All you need is a bankruptcy or a disaster to befall you, and suddenly the floor drops away and you are outside society. In the gutter you discover a whole lot of people who have been de-hypnotised and decentralised. In a month of being outside of the cogs of social order you discover there is an entirely different world where the rules are completely changed.

This is the survival of the fittest jungle society. Go to prison, and see how a "Save the Whales" discussion goes with the inmates. We know what will happen to our high ideals and great notions at that level. Survival of self suddenly leaves the whales to fend for themselves. You quickly learn to do whatever you can to avoid pain.

Rats so often live in the gutters. Why? Oddly enough, because they are safer there. And also, more honest. It is a place where you live or die by how well you can survive the moment, but if you survive you LIVE. You know you are alive.

However, discover your Inner Rat and there will be no need for you to lose the house, wife and furniture in order to find your true self. There is no need to go to the wild jungle to feel alive. You just need to start recognising where you are running your life by rote, by habit, which is to say, the opposite of choice.

Some years ago I had a woman try to tell me that I said something that I simply did not say. She was in a position of authority, and she insisted I had said a particular thing, which I had not. She then cast about the room, and asked "Who else heard this?" and one of her followers said "Well, perhaps I heard something like this." which was proof positive for the woman that she was 100% right and I was lying.

This is why it is wise avoid cliques and groups not in harmony with their nature, where possible.

You know, I just do not have time to correct everyone's wrong thinking, however life does have a way of correcting things over time. Some months later, the woman declared the same "truth" about what I said, but this time she changed what she said I said last time, and now claimed I said something different.

It made no difference to the woman, but it helped me grasp the obvious: Her perception was being shaped by what she wanted to see. However, she was "Shoulding" on me, and so I resisted her suggestions, and simply re-stated my position, that what she imagined I said was simply not true. It really annoyed me.

Then the IRONY struck. While the woman was shoulding on me, I was thinking *"She **shouldn't** be doing this!"* I was shoulding her back!

Once more I was saved by my Jester! The Jester, the Cynic, the Dreamer, they are all archetypes that allow us to become more of ourselves. I started laughing at my stupidity, and THIS cut the hypnotists puppet strings on my emotions. I was the one creating the situation. You may say "No she is at fault" but there is no blame in Ratology, only survival. To survive, we must cut the strings that bind.

Our internal puppet master WILL try to keep the strings attached, to control us, and we all need to figure out how to cut them. *We need to develop, and keep sharp, the tools that help us break up the moments on our life where we get hypnotised by circumstance.* In this instance I was the deer in a spotlight, pinned by the viewpoint of a woman who really had no importance to me.

What tools will help snip the strings? There are three main ones.

1. *Humour*
2. *Patience*
3. *Perception of the Obvious (the big one)*

But more than any of these, surrounding these is the most powerful tool and it may surprise you. It is called Dyhana, or simple, garden variety COMPASSION.

I was trapped in a relationship where I had come to hate the woman I was with. I started to absolutely detest her, because she had consciously done truly vindictive and outright nasty things to me. It never occurred to me that there was another side to the story, but then one day in the shower I decided a very simple thing. It was not worth me suffering this pain any longer, and then compassion spoke. It told me that this pain was the same for her. That's when it hit me! I saw the complete picture.

I was thrown back to a past time and watched first hand. I saw the woman I had married in this life and how I had been married to her a past time. The man she was currently going out with had been in the army and in that life she had fallen in love with him. It was outraged my sense of dignity, so I simply locked her up until the army had moved camp.

This was the source of her hatred for me, she still wanted revenge. She did not know it, but the seed cause from a past time was propelling her

TODAY'S PUZZLE
WHAT IS WRONG WITH THE FOLLOWING WORDS?

COMPASSION
noun

pity, sympathy, empathy, fellow feeling, care, concern, solicitude, sensitivity, warmth, love, tenderness, mercy, leniency, tolerance, kindness, humanity, charity.

ANSWER:

IF YOU LET THEM IN THEY COULD RUIN YOUR WAY OF LIFE.

actions in the present. Now it really doesn't matter if you believe me regarding past lives, the point is that the experience of Compassion opened up the door to greater understanding.

We parted soon after, and I came to understand that my connection to this Soul was now ended. It was finished, and done with. This is the Power of true Compassion: It is a sword that cuts the ties that bind.

Thus you become free to choose a new path. This is the opposite of what HYPNOTISM does. The Hypnotist always seeks to put your attention on matters of THEIR choosing. (You are feeling sleepy, etc.) Once your attention is snared, images are introduced, interest is created, and a desire activated. Soon enough you will act in accordance with the suggestions made that promise to fulfil this desire.

The Hypnotist places an IMAGE before the minds eye. People do this in many ways, but traditionally, by either creating arguments or by creating agreements with you. Overall, a suggestion is made that you are prepared to accept, and this can be done in a thousand ways. A woman might want to influence people to her view after a divorce, yet she may say nothing, do nothing. But people believe she was wronged. How? Natural curiosity means you ask what happened. Then the trap! All she does is to look away, breath deep, sigh, and say it just isn't something she can talk about.

Most people presume the worst, but also, most people will assume she is a saint for not running down her Ex, and therefore he must be a REAL bastard. Now their imagination gets to work, around a central image of the ex-husband being so cruel that she cannot even talk about it. Can you see the subtle hypnotism at work? The woman has carefully placed an image in front of the people without saying a word.

The whole trick to REAL hypnotism is to allow, or create, an opening into which belief can fall. This can be done via stress, with a person insisting they are right in some way, or through cooperation, by getting you to accept that you share the same view. A professional will use both to manipulate you.

Police use the "Good Cop – Bad Cop" routine all the time. One is nice, cooperation, the other is nasty, stress. This is to create an artificial push-pull energy to force you to come to the "good" guy with your story.

The trick to getting around suggestions made by others is to simply to not be for nor against things. Just choose to not have an opinion either way! We do not have to choose ANY of the options served up by others. The salesman who tries to "Early Close" someone by saying "What colour do you prefer in this dress, the blue or the red?" is trying to hypnotise you. Even if you say "Green" you have fallen for the trap. The ONLY solution is to be detached, holding a "neither for nor against" policy with all things. Yet paradoxically, "I like ALL the colours!" also effectively stops the hypnotism. This is saying you have no preference either way, but in a different way.

I was away for several weeks in the bush, and as I had no knowledge of the then current news events. My father said "You know, what if the world ended or we had a nuclear war? You wouldn't even know it!" You know, I think I might not need Media to tell me the world had ended. Practice being disinterested when watching the news or listening to what a politician says, and you will snap out of the belief factor they are projecting, and realise it is all waffle.

Hypnotic suggestions are absolutely everywhere in our society. Zombies are multiplying, and common sense is disappearing. It is one of the greatest dangers you will face in seeking to find and awaken your Inner Rat. How so? You can get drawn into other people's beliefs and opinions, and forget your own.

The ROCK

Peter, the Apostle, was apparently so-named because the word Petra meant "Rock". It is curious to me, because this is one way I look at the most culpable of all spiritual crimes committed by organised religion, the Rock of Judgement.

Imagine if that a person believes that trees are bad. No matter what you say, trees are bad. Most people would agree that the guy has rocks in his head. Solid, non-negotiable pieces of unintelligent fossilisation: Like most clichés, the term exists because it has some truth to it.

Figuratively speaking, most truths we hold dear are really just solidified belief that has become an inner "Rock" upon which we stand. Often these are things we have initially disagreed with, but were tasks we had to do. We had to push a rock uphill. We do so right up to the point where we have decided we have pushed enough. Then we stop, and the rock stops with us. Well, we are now pretty familiar with our Rock. It is almost like an old friend, and a curious thing happens: all those beliefs foisted on us now turn into OUR beliefs, OUR reality.

At this point, a remarkable transformation happens: The Rock is no longer our enemy, it is now proof of how strong we are. It is no longer a struggle we must overcome, we have struggled, and now this rock is proof of our victory.

I had a neighbour who, as a protest over a road I was putting in, placed a large three ton rock just inside the road boundary. It was his symbol of defiance, and a claim to territory. Well, I had an excavator pick it up and put it outside my front door. So he went and dragged and even BIGGER rock from the bush, and this time he put it just outside the road boundary, where I could not legally touch it.

This is what people do with beliefs. Remove one belief, and they will instantly go looking for a bigger one to replace it. Argue with a religious person, and prove your case convincingly and they will answer "Yes, but WE Believe!" What is more, this suffices as a perfectly good and logical reason for a religious person.

People are always pushing some weighty thing into place in their heads. In fact, the mark of a serious, worthwhile person in our society is often related to the size of the rocks in their head. Don't laugh too much: It is true.

Take any person who is established in a position of power, and you will discover they are a gestalt of strong beliefs forged through the fires of experience. Any person who achieves power always does so at the behest and agreement of other involved persons. Usually, they have all shared in a struggle to rise to power, but the one who rises to the top is usually the most pathological of the group. For him/her to maintain a grip on power, there needs to be powerful points of agreement between themselves and their supporters.

And just as Hitler bonded people with a common hatred of Jews, or the Klu Klux Klan binds people with a common hatred for the black race, most power sharing arrangements have some sort of irrational hatred or emotion that is the common ground between all parties. Yes, they have rocks in their heads, but it works.

So much that attains any degree of power here on Earth is bound together by a sort of collective madness. Like a church that speaks of love as the cornerstone of its faith, yet its God destroys whole cities. Even though the citizens were not followers of that religion, its God saw fit to kill them all, because they acted the wrong way.

It is my way or the highway, people! Or I could say, it is my way or off to hell you go. And let me hurry it up a little for you with a little fire and brimstone in your streets. Or maybe I will flood the entire world, and put the future of the human race in the hands of an unschooled labourer with a penchant for collecting pairs of animals.

Here is the paradox: A Lie that is believed by two or more people becomes a "truth". It may not be an eternal truth, but for the believers of that faith, it IS truth, pure and simple. Logic matters for nothing, faith, hope and belief are all that matters. So the real cause of organised religion is to focus a disparate group of people under the umbrella of one system of belief.

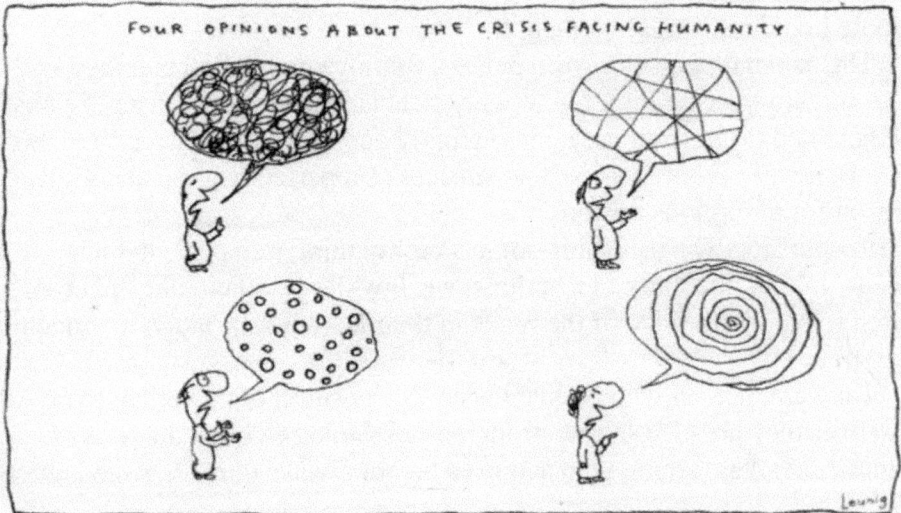

FOUR OPINIONS ABOUT THE CRISIS FACING HUMANITY

This all comes about as a result of hypnotic suggestion, and once accepted, it becomes real. The reflex result of this is that anyone who disagrees and challenges this is AUTOMATICALLY shifted out of any form of agreement, and put into an adversarial role. Like the old Movie line: *You is either for me or agin me!*

Have you wondered why we always have two party system democracies? We may have a hundred parties, but eventually it basically settles down to one lot versus the other lot. This is all because of the Rocks in our heads.

We ALL have fixed beliefs. These are the ROCKS that damn (dam) you, yet they are also the foundation stones for the building of your life. This will sound ridiculously easy, but the trick to discovering real freedom is simple. Accept your rocks, but learn to rearrange them to suit the occasion. Do you need a door where there is a wall? Simple: Make a door by reorganising some rocks.

Of course, you need something to stop the wall collapsing while you do it, and in building this is called a lintel. In practical terms, a lintel is a piece of wood or stone that sits atop the opening of a door. In spiritual terms it is your sense of certainty in your vision. YOU are your own lintel. It is the belief in YOURSELF that opens up the possibilities to create a doorway to somewhere else.

Most people cannot accept this, and this is why we have so many faiths that all say with total certainty that the individual is puny, unimportant, and only acceptable because of Gods good grace. You pacify people by making them insignificant, than you unite them into the group by saying, "We are the one true path!" This gives people a certainty they need, and sense of purpose and focus. The GROUP becomes the lintel, the thing that supports the new doorway. But of course, if your faith shall fail, so too shall the doorways you created fall on your head.

However, when you truly start to feel the pulse and rhythm of true inner belief in YOU, then the group becomes the insignificant party. When you become your OWN lintel, your options increase and you start to see you can go in any direction you choose. The rocks of your experience become the building stones for your future. You can build a wall, a bridge or a doorway with them. It's all simply a matter of choosing what to do. Choice only comes with confidence, and confidence comes with choosing. This is one of the better Catch 22's of life.

So often will laugh about the stupidity of the past. If the witch drowns she is innocent. The world is flat. Bleeding is the solution for illness. Leeches are essential medical tools that every good doctor must have. But soon enough, people will be laughing at us and what we believe.

We ALL have rocks in our head! The question is what are you going to do with them? What CAN you do with it? The Rocks of conditioning, belief and certainty inside us appear to be utterly immovable. Pushing it all uphill will get you fitter, but it won't get you further. You can use all your beliefs and convictions as a way to strengthen and discipline the mind, but really, you still got rocks in the head. But apply imagination, creativity and the pursuit of excellent and we start to soften the rocks inside us, and make our fixed notions more pliable.

The Imagination of Soul is like a wind that passes, yet only this wind brings into you a brilliance and perception of a greater IS, a greater state of being. At this point, as you open your heart to new possibilities, the sense of freedom is enthralling and possesses you completely. You become the open channel through which the universe pours. All opposites seem alike, all things alike seem opposite. You become the Alpha and the Omega! Unfortunately, it will never last.

That's just the way it is, but if you pay attention, the change that comes about inside you when your Rat finally breaks through all the conditioning will be profound. You will start to Love your Moment. You will begin to cherish the eternal change. Rather than fear consequences, you begin to laugh as the pin ball bounces around the loaded spring-walls inside yourself, and finally you learn to master it by relaxing into it.

The Mystic Rat Says: *Truth? Pluck it freely from the Tree of Life, for it is heavy with such fruit. It bears the Knowing of Self, the recognition of that eternal spirit which flows through, and the taste of its juice is a love that enlightens us all.*

Enlightenment. People think of it as something coming from some distant truth to illuminate your mind. But have you ever considered, what really happens is that in the process of rearranging your rocks of fixed belief into a door or window that lets the light in? You stop carrying them as useless weight and put them to work. In this way you let go of them. And when you drop those heavy, serious beliefs, you feel light, like you are walking on the moon.

Your natural self, your Baby State, is an incredibly light being.

Have you ever considered that Lucifer, whos ename means "light" was doing Eve a favour? God had put these dumb-ass humans to wander about in this garden, yet they knew nothing of the real world. So he says "Hey kids, come here. Really, it's time to grow up. Taste this apple from the Tree of Knowledge and you will understand what the real story is.

And what happens? This nasty God creature says "Hey, totally uncool! I only want ignorant people in MY church, thank you. Everyone, out of the pool."

Think of the logic here. God knows all things, yet he places Adam and Eve in a Garden with a snake and he KNOWS they are going to bite the forbidden fruit. So why put it there? An all kind, all loving, all knowing God creates people who he will then force into suffering from the consequences of an action he already knew they would choose? The only sincere conclusion is that God wanted you to do it, but that the religions who wrote the book do not.

Unless God also has Rocks in his head, of course.

As a note, just for the people who will see this paragraph as proof that the whole book is "of the devil" the Snake in the Garden was originally Lilith, the first woman. The Old Testament was taken in part from Babylonian texts, and the Garden Myth starts out as Lilith being Adam's equal. By the time the Semitic religions get it, the matriarchal society had been displaced by a patriarchal one, and now the wife, Eve, is the underdog, and the "real woman" is now Satan. Think about it, if you will.

The Mystic Rat Says: *If you want to be free, allow others to be free*

We all have rocks in our heads. We are all madman walking on a stage of becoming, and other actors around us are doing the same. We are all surrounded by small judgements made by other people about how we dress, act and smell. You have a right to participate in the mutual throwing of roacks at each other (because this is a good part of our social programming) or you can be free of it, and leave the playground.

It's your call.

Hopefully by now you have started to give up on your ideal of perfection. Should I say, the ideal is OK, but can we let go of the belief it will happen? It is an imperfect world and I am an imperfect being. WE are imperfect. What we have been taught is largely a lie, but this does not necessarily make it wrong. Just ill-informed. This book is not to say our culture and society is bad, only that it is imperfect. And here is the simplicity of the message: *This is how it is meant to be.*

If it were perfect, there would be nothing to learn.

A perfect culture is a stagnant one. If everything was in balance, the ball would no longer roll down the hill, the earth would have no seasons, and life would be dull. Thus we come to the paradox: *The very lie that we live, the falsehoods we endure, can be the fuel that drives our growth.*

When we truly accept this, we are made perfectly imperfect.

Go figure.

The END

There comes a moment when all the cables, leads, battery chargers and power adaptors we have ever owned, gather together and assemble themselves around us and ask us the terrible question, "WHAT HAS HAPPENED TO YOUR LIFE?"

Author Outro-troduction

This book is essentially a series of essays linked together. It will take time for you to "connect the dots" of all the thoughts presented here, but if you can, an image will form in front of you that is unmistakable. It is like looking at those 3D images that just look like dots until it "clicks" and you see the picture.

But there are some "absolutes" we need to accept before any of the dots will connect. The first and primary one is: *We are all Liars.* You may earnestly and fervently believe you are honest, upright and truthful, but this only advertises the fact that you do not know yourself.

How do I know we are all liars? I see it with my own eyes everyday. I see how people pretend to be one thing, but they believe deep down that they are something else. What is more, I see myself reflexively (deflexively?) doing this as well, much to my own dismay.

I saw this reality at Age Four when I was first taken to church. At the time it was like a red hot poker in my face, when I saw how people who shared the same religion lied to each other, blatantly. I was scarred forever by this strange, and apparently anti-social understanding, that people are liars. Indeed, we are not just two faced, but many faced. This truth has affected the way I relate to people, what I think, how I act, and who I have become, and this continues inside me in any given moment of living.

Prior to Age Four, all was bliss. It was a Golden Age where I played at my pond and spoke to my "invisible" friends who would visit. At the time it seemed perfectly normal, but now I realise I was listening to something most people have no idea about. But for me, this mystic pulse, this distant drum, was for years my driving force, not just a childhood memory.

At the time it was my entire world. The pond in the backyard was everything, and no one understood how a young child could spend whole days and weeks gazing into the water, playing with ships, and apparently talking to himself. Of course, from my end I was discussing things with people no one else could see. Fortunately no one bothered to stop and listen, because a young child talking about quantum physics before anyone in Australia had realised it was invented, well it may have possibly caused some ripples.

Ripples indeed! This is all most people see in day to day events, the ripples of circumstances. Few see beneath the surface the surface to the forces that are the Cause of things. But the ancients knew. I remind you again of what the Tao says: *Why does the King of the Ocean Rule? Because he rules from below.*

Below appearances is where truth and reality live and breathe. These things are the unseen fish that swims through the events of our life, causing events to unfold as they will.

In your pocket there is a gift, a set of eyeglasses, or an ability to perceive things. This allows you to see these mysterious forces at work, and this gift is called the OBVIOUS. When we learn to look through the eyeglass of the Obvious, all things reveal themselves. But first we have to find the pocket where we put the glasses. Only your Inner Rat knows the way to this secret compartment in your Soul, because this is where it lives.

For myself, as a child sitting at my pond (Which in truth was a mere puddle I had created with a hose in the back yard.) I had stumbled across this secret, inner place. Here different teachers would come and speak with me about matters of the universe, philosophy and science. I had no idea what I was being taught, but I listened because it was interesting, far more interesting than what people in the "real world" had to say. Particularly I listened to the one called Jesus. I found it fascinating that others knew this one, and that it was perfectly OK for me to talk to him, and about him, but it was not OK to talk of my other friends.

I learned to be silent over my day to day activities, speaking only to my much loved Aunty Von. She would ask of my day, and what I had discovered. (Usually such things were discussed as we rocketed through the universe on the old treadle powered Singer sewing machine. I would be pedalling faster to break the light barrier, and she would be watching with a smile, encouraging me to go further.)

I still feel her with me. I feel all those I have loved and who loved me.

My childhood was a Golden Age of Imagination made real. I had no real sense of where the physical universe ended and the other inner universes began, nor did it matter. Watching other young children over the years, I saw this was pretty much the norm for most young Souls, until we are forced to deal with society. That's when the Golden Age ends and harsh gates of judgement start to shut us in.

This is where the primary dividing line of Self occurs, and this is where most of us get lost. The transition point between the inner being and the outer experience is the place where the first lies inside us germinate. It is right where the natural self must meet and deal with the artificial world of "Should" and "Should Not".

The Land of Judgement is that place of compromise between natural freedom and necessary rules. We pitch the tent of our spiritual self in the new social space that has opened up for us, but it comes at a cost. We must use the stakes of Critical Belief, Sceptical Views, Self Doubt and Fear of Consequence, to anchor ourselves.

We are not chained there, but for all the world if you try to move someone entrenched in the land of judgement, you will discover how solidly they are nailed to their beliefs. It seems an impossible thing to move, and yet it is simply a matter of choosing to be free. Just as we pitched the tent, and nailed ourselves to the spot, we can simply unpack it. But, and it is a big but, we can do this only if we really chose to be free. We all, each of us, can up and move to a different space where the Social Lie no longer rules. You just have to want freedom more than the need for security and the lie.

The Social Lie! I look back and think of how much trouble would have been avoided in my life if there had been anyone to explain it to me. No one told me what to expect, and it completely blind-sided me when it first arrived.

It all changed for me the first day I was required to go to church. I remember it with perfect clarity, walking along with the family up to the doors. We went in the side entrance, and the first thing I noted when I stepped inside was that my "invisible" friends stayed outside.

I called to them inwardly, "Come in!" but they answered "We do not belong in there". As one of my invisible friends was Jesus, I immediately recognised that there was something distinctly wrong.

Indeed there was. Everything seemed wrong. Everything seemed madness, people speaking in a foreign language, (Latin) kneeling to some fellow up the front wearing purple and gold robes, and everyone singing dull songs. Specifically, muttering "Mea Culpa". I had never felt so alone in my life, and I just wanted OUT.

Finally it all ended. I escaped out the doors, where all the people were gathering and talking, but this only made things worse. Because everywhere I looked, I saw people with two faces. One face was smiling and speaking "polite" conversation, yet their other face, the ugly one, was twisted and whispering nasty vindictive words, or nervous fearful words, or sad, depressed words, to themselves.

If there were any truth to Hell, I was in it right there and then, and it terrified me.

My dog knew, and she had come all the way from home and walked into the crowd to find me, to be with me. She was a comfort, a rock of certainty in a world of madness. I walked home with her, and her love soothed the pain of reality. But it could not be mistaken, I have been born into a terrible place. I realised, with absolute horror, that I lived in a world of liars.

Then, a few months later, and after I had recovered and adjusted to the new reality, I was walking along and a fellow called me over. He knew my name, and he seemed oddly familiar, but I did not quite place him. Maybe an Uncle? I didn't want to appear forgetful or careless, so I bluffed that I knew him, hoping that I would connect the dots in the course of the conversation.

At the time, I knew I was lying. I was pretending I knew who I was speaking to, when I could have simply asked "Who are you?" But I did not. I felt I "had" to look as if I knew him. Why would a five year old child think like this? Take your pick! There are a thousand possible reasons: I didn't want to look stupid. I didn't want to look as if I didn't care. I didn't want to appear forgetful, etc.

Here is the rub: The question of WHY we act the way we do is far less important than WHAT we do and HOW we are when doing it. If love is a verb, then the social lie within us is ALSO entwined into our personal grammar. But WHERE is it entwined? Is it a Noun, or an Adjective? Past tense, or presently tense? This is the hard part to sort through.

As a clue, in dealing with the fellow I met, I was bluffing my way through (as we all do to a greater or lesser degree) or in other words, hiding. That is where the Social Lie takes root, in that hidden place of doubt and quandary. The Social Lie is buried in the Shadows of You.

It was 20 years before I realised that this had been one of my invisible friends that had come to see me in a physical body. Without words, the message he had for me with his visit was all about understanding WHY we pretend, WHY we lie, by showing me WHAT I was doing. He was just the mirror, and it was up to me to catch the reflection. When we understand WHAT we are doing, we start to uncover WHERE we are caught up in the false images and dreams that possess us.

And this is the purpose of this book. I am handing down to you an ancient truth, one handed to me like a baton in a long, seemingly eternal race: The Human Race. I want you to begin to understand what on Earth you are doing.

The message is simple: *You are free when not trapped in the Lie of Yourself.* **Speak your Truth, not your Echoes, and you will be set Free.**

Our culture, and our life, is based on avoiding truth and embracing a lie. It may offend you, it may insult you, or it may awaken you. It will release you, but only when you realise this simple truth: *Nothing will change the reality of self, other than a higher reality being found inside self.* This is just how it is.

It is caterpillar turning into butterfly stuff.

Not only is OUR culture largely based on a Lie: All cultures are. Equally universal is the fact that those within it are almost never able to recognise this truth. Have you wondered why terrorists want to bomb cities and murder innocent people? Simple. Because of a Lie they believe to be truth.

This is also why the US administration rejected Castro and the entire Cuban people for so long. This is why the Japanese saw no problem murdering and enslaving other races in World War Two, or why Hitler could only see a benefit in getting rid of the Jews and Slavic races. This understanding does not make the Japanese, the Nazis, the Muslims or the Americans bad or evil, but it DOES demonstrate how powerful and all pervasive the Lie can be.

Before we can get to the WHY of this Lie, we need to know: *WHERE is the Lie?* What shape does it take inside you? How can you recognise it, defeat it, and learn to grow past it?

Your Inner RAT will help you sniff out these answers. Your Inner RAT is the only being that can.

May the Great Rat be with you

There is a tide in the affairs of men, which taken at the flood, leads on to fortune. Omitted, all the voyage of their life is bound in shallows and in miseries. On such a full sea are we now afloat. And we must take the current when it serves, or lose our ventures.

Shakespeare

A Final Positive Note

On the wall, hanging up as I write this book, is a very special T-shirt. It is from the Hearts and Tears Motor Cycle Club. I wore it to death, really, but I wanted to preserve it because it meant so much to me. It came to me via the mails, on a promise, and as as a gift, from some very special people I met in Nepal.

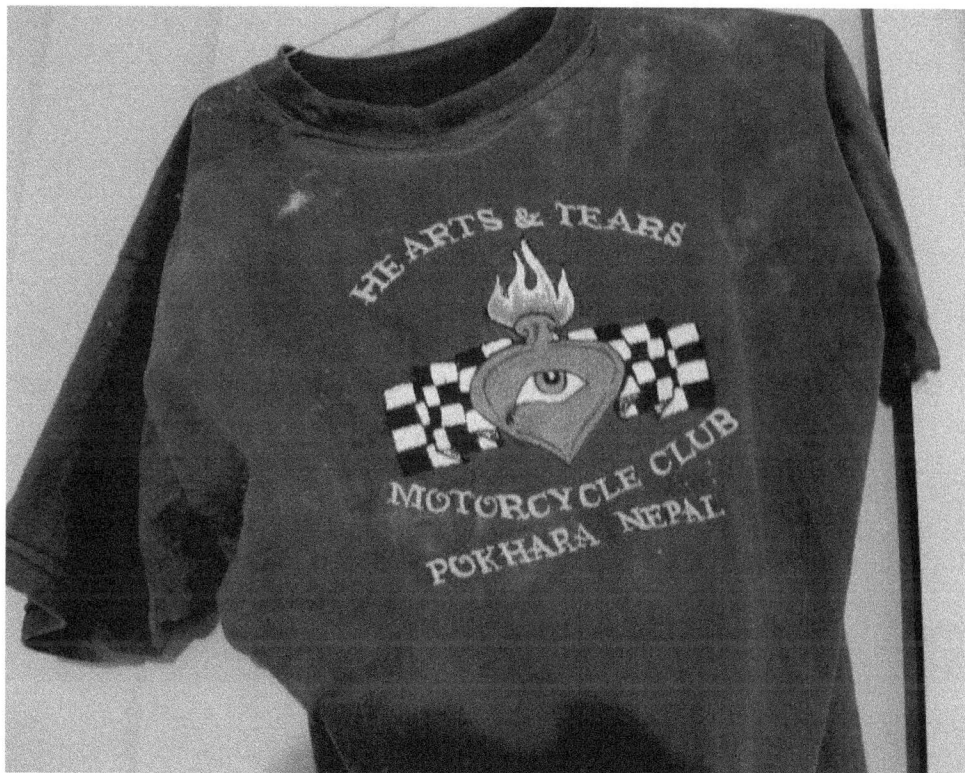

Over a decade ago, shortly before I first sat to write RATOLOGY down, I travelled with my youngest son to India, and through some odd circumstances we ended up at Pokhara, Nepal. On the bus going there, I got talking to a remarkably attractive English girl, one not afraid to talk to a stranger. She was not afraid because she knew she was travelling to meet the love of her life, a man who ran a motor cycle touring business in the town we were both heading towards.

It is odd, in normal circumstances, meeting a beautiful woman on her own who was happy to talk, you would think that maybe it was because she had an interest in you. But she was in a pure state, a state of utter openness and trust. She was in the Baby State, and utterly beautiful because of it. All I felt was a need to cherish and protect her, and make sure she got safely to her man.

After we had settled into a very nice room in Pokhara, and had a wonderful dinner in a place recommended to us by the owners of the hotel, my son and I then went to the motor cycle club to catch up, and to meet this curious man she so adored. Well, to say he was a hard man, a man used to a very tough life, was understating the obvious. He looked at me, clearly extremely defensive lest I be there pursuing his love, but I smiled and asked if I could sit. He handed me a beer, and in the universal language of acceptance, I took it and we started speaking.

The thing that got me, the thing that really set me back into my seat, was that this rough looking character which the amazingly pretty, demure young English girl loved, well, he looked a lot like my own inner Censor. Scarred, dangerous and with a deep sense of latent anger. Yet he and his equally tough partner in the business accepted myself, and my then 15 year old son, with ease. They loved the fact that I travelled the world with my young son in tow. They asked me about this, and I said "Well, I could hardly leave him behind, could I?"

There was something in this that softened the hearts of these hard men. Maybe it was what they wished their fathers had done, but whatever it was, they laughed. When people enjoy a genuine laugh together, all barriers of race, creed and social standing fall to one side.

We spent quite a few evenings after that, talking, hanging out, doing nothing in particular. My son and I looked at the motor cycles they had salvaged and rebuilt. All genuine 1950's and 60's Royal Enfields, not the modern version, but the real deal.

The story was simple: Two Englishmen from the wrong side of the tracks had ended up half a world away from their home, doing what they loved most. Motorcycles: repairing, modifying, making them better. And what's more, they made a very tidy income renting these out, and going along with people as guides on motorcycle tours in the mountains of Nepal. I "kind of" presumed they were there to avoid prison in England, and asked if they were happy away from home.

"This is our home. Our hearts, our tears, our journeys have all end up here, right here." It was an off the cuff comment, but it struck me deeply. We are all strangers in a strange land, and only our hearts and our shared experience can anchor us.

I got this, I got this right in the centre of my being, because I have lived it. I freely accept that I am a stranger in a strange land, and, being totally out of place, I paradoxically find myself perfectly at home wherever I go. I loved these people. I loved what they did, how they lived, and the fact that an ugly son of a bitch like the one before me could pull a stunner like the sweet thing I met on the bus. THIS is something that deserves real respect.

Many adventures ensued from our time in Nepal, but when it came time to move on, I asked if I could buy a T-Shirt, which I saw on the wall. "Hearts and Tears Motorcycle Club", it said. I liked that. They said "No". I wondered if it was some sort of ritual thing, but they assured me it was because they had run out of them, but write down my address, and they will send it on when they get in fresh stocks.

Of course, the very last thing I expected when I gave them my home address was a T-shirt. I presumed it was a nice sort of push-off, but some months after we returned to Australia, a package arrived from Nepal. Inside was my T-shirt, fully embroidered, not printed, with a note from the pretty girl saying, "By putting this T-shirt on, you accept membership with the Hearts and Tears Motorcycle Club"

My heart smiled broadly.

They had sent me their colours. Now, for those who do not grasp what this means, to be sent the colours of a motorcycle gang means you are accepted into the inner circle. Yes, I know, it's not exactly Hell's Angels but the principle remains the same. It means that they "got" that you understood them, and that you were welcome to return.

Forget worldly honours, fame, recognition by the masses, awards, knighthoods and all the paraphernalia of social acceptance. This meant more to me. By sending me this T-shirt, they were saying that, in their own way, that they "got" me.

Tears and Hearts, Hearts and Tears, my dear reader. They go together. A weeping eye, on a red heart, overlaying a banner of GT Stripes. It says "yes" to me.

People are always at a crossroads, at that point of choosing between the life they currently live, and the life they could lead. Your Rat will wake you up to the possibilities within, but only you can make the decision of what direction to walk in.

ISBN: 978-0-9941798-1-4
Copyright 2016 Michael Wallace
Publisher: Ladder to the Moon Productions (T/A Vital Aqua)
PO Box 1355 Kingscliff, NSW 2487 Australia
Email: qrcaustralia@gmail.com
`

Other books by this Author:
Jerimiah Versus the Grabblesnatch (www.grabblesnatch.com)
Divinity Dice Series (www.divinitydice.com.au)
Water: More Precious than Gold (Story of the Timbarra Protest)
The Borringbar War (A Decade living the rural life - written in 3 days)
The Book of Number Trilogy (Pythagorean Number Analysis)
Hello Planet Earth
Fragments of the Mirror
RATOLOGY: Way of the Un-Dammed

Available on Amazon or at www.laddertothemoon.com.au

Are you ready for something different?

From the same writer, we bring you the Divinity Dice Series. This series introduces a series of games that cast dice to give clear answers to questions you ask. It is remarkably accurate, and part of the

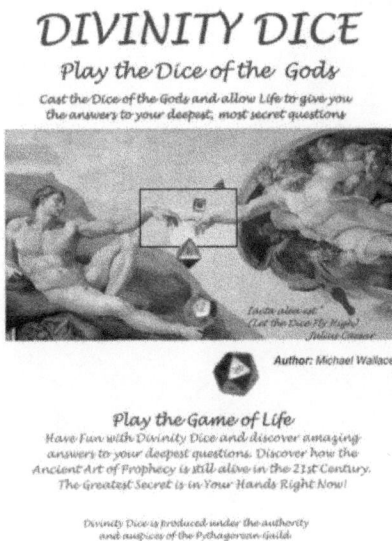

DIVINITY DICE
Play the Dice of the Gods

Cast the Dice of the Gods and allow Life to give you the answers to your deepest, most secret questions

Iacta alea est
(Let the Dice Fly Right)
Julius Caesar

Author: Michael Wallace

Play the Game of Life

Have Fun with Divinity Dice and discover amazing answers to your deepest questions. Discover how the Ancient Art of Prophecy is still alive in the 21st Century. The Greatest Secret is in Your Hands Right Now!

Divinity Dice is produced under the authority and auspices of the Pythagorean Guild.

These books were written to help the individual grasp how number combinations worked. They provide an easy, practical way to give a natural "Oracular" readings, based on the various castings of the polyhedral dice.

Go to divinitydice.com.au for more information and pricing.

There is also a series of fun workshops available, which allow an individual to grasp the power of the Dice in a group atmosphere.

Absolutely ground breaking stuff!

Without doubt, the most comprehensive books on Dice Divination on the planet.
George Cockcroft, writer of "The Diceman"

Hello Planet Earth

This is an utterly delightful tale of a child discovering his truth. Set as a series of short vignettes, this book is simply a joy to read.

Available on Amazon or through laddertothemoon.com.au

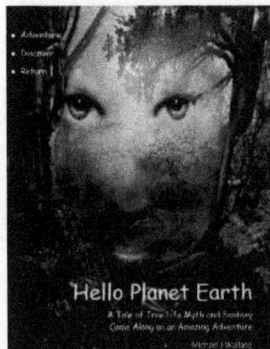

Hello Planet Earth

A Tale of True Life Myth and Fantasy
Come Along on an Amazing Adventure

Michael J Wallace

The Book of Number Series

Available on Amazon

Have you ever felt that there was something more?

The ancient art of Divination by Number is an extraordinary study you may wish to contemplate. The author of this book has written a complete course on "how to do" Pythagorean Numerology. In just WEEKS you can learn to discover and understand all the numerical secrets of the Ancient Greeks.

The Book of Number is a series of four books that cover the whole teaching of Number Divination as taught by the Ancient Pythagoreans. This is, available on Amazon or direct from the author. Details are below if you wish to know more.

www.bookofnumber.com.au

For further enquiries and updates go to the official web page at bookofnumber.com.au.

You may also write to info.numberharmonics@gmail.com.

Here you will find all current information on Pythagorean Numerology, as well as where you can find study groups, on line classes and areas of interest to the subject.

Michael Wallace

Michael Wallace is a remarkable individual. He is a Master Musician, Master Body Worker, Master Numerologist, Dice Master, Recording Artist, Songwriter, and Publisher. On top of all this he is also a prolific writer with over seventeen titles in print.

Aiming for the Stars is much easier if we stop off at the Moon. We are out of the atmosphere of our past, and can see things more clearly. We are lighter, can jump higher and further than ever before, and it takes far less energy to start each journey.

The hard part is climbing that Ladder to the Moon.

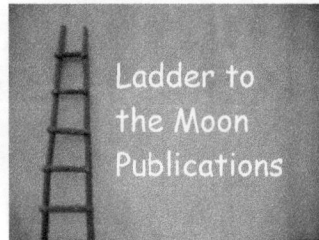

Ladder to the Moon Publications

www.ingramcontent.com/pod-product-compliance
Lightning Source LLC
Chambersburg PA
CBHW031043110426
42740CB00048B/802